# on track ...

# 10cc
## and
# Godley & Creme

every album, every song

Peter Kearns

sonicbondpublishing.com

Sonicbond Publishing Limited
www.sonicbondpublishing.co.uk
Email: info@sonicbondpublishing.co.uk

First Published in the United Kingdom 2020
First Published in the United States 2020
This edition 2024

British Library Cataloguing in Publication Data:
A Catalogue record for this book is available from the British Library

Copyright Peter Kearns 2020

ISBN 978-1-78952-075-0

The right of Peter Kearns to be identified as the author of this work has been asserted by him in accordance with the Copyright, Designs and Patents Act 1988. All rights reserved. No part of this publication may be reproduced, stored in a retrieval system or transmitted in any form or by any means, electronic, mechanical, photocopying, recording or otherwise, without prior permission in writing from Sonicbond Publishing Limited

Typeset in ITC Garamond & ITC Avant Garde
Printed and bound in England

Graphic design and typesetting: Full Moon Media

**Follow us on social media:**
Twitter: https://twitter.com/SonicbondP
Instagram: www.instagram.com/sonicbondpublishing_/
Facebook: www.facebook.com/SonicbondPublishing/

Linktree QR code:

# on track ...
# 10cc and Godley & Creme

## Contents

Introduction: Lights, Action, Sound, Roll 'Em! .................................................. 5
Thinks: School Stinks (1971) – Hotlegs ........................................................... 7
10cc (1973) ..................................................................................................... 15
Sheet Music (1974) ........................................................................................ 26
How Dare You! (1976) .................................................................................. 48
The Split ......................................................................................................... 59
Deceptive Bends (1977) ................................................................................ 60
Consequences (1977) – Godley & Creme .................................................... 71
L (1978) – Godley & Creme .......................................................................... 82
Bloody Tourists (1978) – 10cc ...................................................................... 88
Freeze Frame (1979) – Godley & Creme ..................................................... 95
Look Hear? (1980) – 10cc ........................................................................... 103
Ismism (1981) – Godley & Creme .............................................................. 109
Ten Out Of 10 (1981) – 10cc ....................................................................... 115
Birds of Prey (1983) – Godley & Creme ..................................................... 124
Windows in the Jungle (1983) – 10cc ......................................................... 129
The History Mix Volume 1 (1985) – Godley & Creme ............................... 134
Goodbye Blue Sky (1988) – Godley & Creme ............................................ 139
...Meanwhile (1992) – 10cc ......................................................................... 145
Mirror Mirror (1995) – 10cc ....................................................................... 152
The Last Page of History ............................................................................. 158

Thanks to Kevin Godley, Graham Gouldman
and Stephen Lambe

# Introduction: Lights, Action, Sound, Roll 'Em!

The UK winter of 1974-1975 was unusually warm, the mildest in 106 years. If you'd stepped off the train at Stockport Exchange in December 1974, and walked the short distance down Railway Road, you might've felt a balmy breeze as you turned right into Wellington Road, strolled past the Town Hall, left around the corner onto Edward Street, past the courthouse and across Middle Hillgate, past the alleyway to the door of the red brick edifice that was 3 Waterloo Road. Passing through that door you would've entered Strawberry Studios reception, walked through past the toilets and meeting room, along the black painted corridor to the studio control room, where you would've found one unassuming Eric Stewart sitting at the mixing desk, seemingly performing a multiple dental exam as three other guys stood behind the glass all going 'Aaaah' into a microphone – all day! – in the service of a song called 'I'm Not In Love'. If so, you'd have stumbled onto the creative process of 10cc, a unit that had become known as the UK's most arty pop group since The Beatles.

The embryo of 10cc had formed in the meeting of Kevin Godley and Lol Creme as art school students in Manchester, where Kevin cast Lol in his 8mm film of *Dracula*. They became friends, sharing a love of jazz and R&B, spending their time writing songs and contemplating ways they could throw all their artistic interests into one big multi-media cauldron.

Kevin had attended school with Graham Gouldman at Kings Road in Prestwich, Manchester. In 1964, he and Graham formed The Mockingbirds, touting a repertoire of R&B covers and Gouldman's own undeniably commercial original songs. Inspired by The Beatles, he'd taken up songwriting and already written what would become his first success, 'For Your Love', which The Mockingbirds originally demoed. The band's manager, local impresario Harvey Lisberg, submitted the demo to EMI Records stating he'd like The Beatles to record it. The song was rejected with the comment that The Beatles were 'Doing okay in that regard'.

Eventually signing with Columbia and then Rolling Stones manager Andrew Loog Oldham's label, Immediate, The Mockingbirds released five singles through 1965-1966. But real success came in 1965 when Graham's 'For Your Love' and 'Heart Full of Soul' were recorded by and became hits for former blues group, The Yardbirds. A string of Gouldman-penned hits for other artists followed, including The Hollies' 'Bus Stop', Herman's Hermits' 'No Milk Today', and Wayne Fontana's 'Pamela Pamela' which was based on a Godley and Creme poem. Graham eventually recorded his own versions of some of the songs for his 1968 solo album, *The Graham Gouldman Thing*.

Wayne Fontana's 'Pamela Pamela' was a hit in 1966, the year after he left The Mindbenders. In his absence, band guitarist Eric Stewart stepped up as lead vocalist, gaining fame with the band's international hit, 'A Groovy Kind of Love'. In 1968, Eric recruited Graham as bassist for The Mindbenders' final tour, after which the band broke up. But the tour consolidated the friendship of the two.

Now living in London, Godley and Creme started recording, beginning with 'The Best Seaside in the World', a fully-formed effort with solid writing and performance. Even more obvious was the virtually professional arranging and recording ability. You could tell that if these two continued recording, the results would be fascinating. They'd developed their craft early, apparently having disposed of anything truly musically infantile, at least intellectually, while they were in fact still children. Godley and Creme hit the ground running leaving little evidence of an audible learning curve. In January 1968 they released the energetic psychedelic bubblegum pop single 'Seeing Things Green' under the name The Yellow Bellow Boom Room. That year after their demo fell into the right hands, they recorded 'To Fly Away' at London's Advision Studio under producer, Giorgio Gomelsky, and future Yes engineer, Eddie Offord. The track was included on a Marmalade Records sampler but would ultimately be re-recorded in a more stripped-down fashion for the Hotlegs album, *Thinks: School Stinks*.

Meanwhile, preferring to involve himself in record production rather than further pop stardom, Eric Stewart had teamed up with sound engineer Peter Tattersal, to relocate his small Inter City Studios to 3 Waterloo Road, Stockport, just outside of Manchester. The studio was renamed Strawberry, Stewart building the facility from the ground up with a view to providing much-needed high-end recording to the Manchester area. Graham Gouldman was brought in as a partner.

After their time in London, Kevin and Lol returned to Manchester where Graham introduced them to Eric, and they helped set up the new studio. Under the name Frabjoy and Runcible Spoon, Godley and Creme recorded the single 'I'm Beside Myself' b/w 'Animal Song' at Strawberry with Eric and Graham. Released on Marmalade Records in September 1969, it was the first single to bring all four members together, effectively making it a 10cc record.

As the studio found its feet, Graham was commissioned as staff writer by entrepreneurs Kasanetz & Katz to produce hits in New York for their Super K roster of bubblegum acts. Happy in the work, he nevertheless tired of it quickly, feeling he could do a superior job with his team back at Strawberry. It was agreed, Graham returned to Stockport, and the future 10cc became the backing group for many of the Super-K tracks. At Strawberry, they produced surrogate singles under a variety of artist names such as Doctor Father, Crazy Elephant and Ohio Express, the latter an already established American entity existing more as a brand name than a band. The Super-K sessions at Strawberry were overseen by producer and Tommy James and the Shondells' songwriter, Richie Cordell, his presence presumably to ensure that the gum remained as bubbled as possible.

After the three-month commission was complete, Graham returned to New York to continue working for Super-K. Kevin and Lol continued to write, circa this time conceiving the germinal verse that would eventually become their 1985 hit, 'Cry'. But the priority was working with Eric at Strawberry. The three now embarked on the project that eventually found success under the band name Hotlegs, by first recording the accidental hit 'Neanderthal Man'.

# Thinks: School Stinks (1971) – Hotlegs

UK Release date: March 1971. US Release date: February 1971.
Personnel:
Lol Creme: Vocals, Bass, Guitar, Keyboards
Kevin Godley: Vocals, Drums
Eric Stewart: Vocals, Bass, Guitar
Baz Barker: Violin
Mike Bell: Saxophone
Ian Brookes: Trumpet
Cheadle Hulme High School Choir: Vocals
Rod Morton: Tambourine
Peter Tattersall: Piano
Mike Timoney: Organ
Recorded 1970-1971 at Strawberry Studios, Stockport, UK
Producer: Hotlegs
Engineers: Eric Stewart, Peter Tattersall
Arranger: Brian Day
Chart placings: UK: -, US: -.

The commission to produce singles for the Super-K roster got the musicians into the practical habit of using various band names for single releases. Inspiration was everywhere, with the name Hotlegs coming from Strawberry secretary Pam Gilmore and her preference for hot pants.

The 'Neanderthal Man' single's success was a surprise, so after its June 1970 release, the band kept recording. In August they released the entirely superior 'Umbopo' on Pye Records under the name Doctor Father, which sadly sank without a trace. The song was a reworking of 'There Ain't No Umbopo', a 1969 Super-K production under the name Crazy Elephant.

In light of the international success of 'Neanderthal Man', Kevin, Lol and Eric embarked on a Hotlegs album proper. Graham couldn't contribute, being back in New York continuing his work for Super K, though he did play bass on a version of 'Today' eventually released on the 1976 Hotlegs compilation, *You Didn't Like It Because You Didn't Think Of It*. 'Today' was also issued in a completely different version under the band name Festival on RCA Records in October 1972, interestingly *after* the first 10cc single 'Donna' a month earlier.

*Thinks: School Stinks* was a fascinating blend of bubblegum pop, homage and left-field experimentation, often happening simultaneously on a micro-level. Lyrics repeated cult-ish themes alongside the deeper notion of escape for self-discovery followed by return. All three wrote the songs with four by Godley and Creme only. Interviewed by Melody Maker during recording, Eric revealed the band were already planning a future concept album. Full of praise for Godley's vocals, Eric expressed his desire to remain in the background while Kevin got the limelight, Eric's sole lead vocal being the bluesy 'Run Baby Run'.

As good as it was, the lack of traction for *Thinks: School Stinks* was partially due to its style being a world away from that of the hit 'Neanderthal Man' and wasn't what people were expecting. Likely in reaction to this, Philips Records reissued the album in the UK in December 1971, replacing 'Neanderthal Man' with the previously unreleased 'Today'. But the damage had been done on initial album release when a promotional opportunity was lost with some of the band going not on tour but on holiday to Antigua. A tour with the Moody Blues ensued but was cancelled part-way through due to one of their members falling ill. It was too little too late. A million-selling single notwithstanding, at this point Hotlegs were feeling the chill and no amount of exposure could get them arrested.

**'Neanderthal Man'** (Lol Creme, Kevin Godley, Eric Stewart)
Released as a single A-side, 19 June 1970 (UK), 3 August 1970 (US), b/w 'You Didn't Like It Because You Didn't Think Of It'. UK: 2. US: 29. CA: 13. AU: 24. NZ: 15. DE: 1. IT: 1.

Hotlegs' sole hit single had a rather inauspicious birth compared to most, certainly in contrast to its surprise international success. It began life as a bit of meaningless fun as the band started singing for a laugh on a taxi ride one day. In early 1970, in a test of new recording equipment, Kevin laid a basic drum track. Needing something to go with it, out came the nonsense 'Neanderthal Man' singalong. Being merely a test of the new Ampex tape recorder and mixing desk, the vocals were quiet, leaking in via the kick drum microphone.

Dick Leahy from Philips Records dropped into the studio, heard the song, and made the famous exclamation, 'It's a smash!'. What followed was the accidental erasure of the tape by someone or other. This was an irritation, but not ones to give up, the band simply re-recorded the song.

Coming to grips with the new gear as they went, the new recording sounded better. They used the same technique – vocals bleeding through the kick drum mic, albeit quadrupled to make it sound bigger. In an experimental technique, they added a tone generator up-slide to create tension leading to a hammer striking a slab of steel, and 'Neanderthal Man' was born. Unfortunately at mastering, the hammer strike broke the cutting head as, in Kevin Godley's words, 'The equipment was, strangely, calibrated for music, not extreme roadworks.' The faux pas was rectified, likely by an extreme frequency cut at the moment of hammer impact. Philips were never overly happy about the hammer strike or the quiet vocals but after the single began selling like hotcakes, any quibbles faded into the distance.

The band first became aware of the song's popularity on a tent sleepover at a music festival where they woke one morning to hear a familiar noise. Godley has recalled opening the tent flap to be greeted with the sight and sound of a multitude of radios playing 'Neanderthal Man'. It *was* a smash!

It was also the first clear sign that the band, whatever their name was, were moving in the right direction. In the UK, the single was selling 3000 copies a day. After Hotlegs' *Top Of The Pops* appearance, where they were surrounded by the female dance group, Pan's People, it sold 35,000 a day. It peaked at number two in the UK, kept from the top spot by Elvis Presley's 'The Wonder of You'.

London had long been the centre of UK recording. No one could record anywhere else if they wanted success. Hotlegs broke that mold by proving it could be done elsewhere. Strawberry Studios then began to attract many local groups. 'Neanderthal Man' had broken the doors open. It sold two million copies worldwide.

**'How Many Times'** (Lol Creme, Kevin Godley, Eric Stewart)
Released as a single B-side, January 1971 (US), b/w 'Run Baby Run'.

Track two, sung by Kevin Godley, was a comment on the need to be commercial while having an underlying desire to do something else. Brian Day's subtle string arrangement graced the track with exotic moments like the Flat 5 note at 2m:33s and the stronger dissonance building to the final section. There the violins suddenly became country fiddles battling each other in an atmosphere recalling the closing of The Beatles' 'Don't Pass Me By'.

With the album being thought of as suffering from sounding nothing like the single 'Neanderthal Man', 'How Many Times' with its similar feel and bass line towards the end, was the closest thing to it, albeit with *one* drum kit.

**'Desperate Dan'** (Lol Creme, Kevin Godley, Eric Stewart)
Released as a single A-side, February 1971 (DE), b/w 'Run Baby Run'.

A basic rock and roll blues about the *Dandy* comic character, Desperate Dan, the world's strongest man, who, with only one hand, could lift a cow. The song worked well for what it was but was lucky to be given such a prominent position. In its favour, it was unpretentious, as was 10cc's entire 1970s output. Even at their most outrageous and experimental, the band always managed to avoid what some pundits considered to be the damning sin of pretence.

**'Take Me Back'** (Lol Creme, Kevin Godley)
Kevin Godley's soaring vocal got the lion's share of attention in this baroque daydream. As an aid to this, the organ was kept at a respectable size in contrast to the giant Hammond B3's that were beginning to dominate rock of all stripes in 1971. This stopped the song from getting too big for its boots, as did the striking verse two 'la la la' backing vocals. Who'd think something so benign could have such an effect. At the three-minute mark, the move from mellow 12-string acoustic guitar bed to slightly slower drum-laden rock electric solo was welcome.

In the first hint of experimental mixing, the band slowly faded out after over a minute of soloing, leaving the acoustic guitar playing into a sung coda section, then seamlessly returning to the original slightly faster tempo. That was slick. These guys paid attention to detail.

The lyric is an extra layer for contemplation, the narrator either a philanderer or a free spirit playing Devil's advocate by unexpectedly going AWOL. He seems to appreciate the fact that after all he's done wrong, his 'whereabouts are cared about'.

'Take Me Back' was the first real demonstration of Kevin Godley's vocal ability to draw a listener in and keep them there – something that would recur at certain points further down the discography.

### 'Um Wah Um Woh' (Lol Creme, Kevin Godley, Eric Stewart)

Benignly presented as the seeming soundtrack to many a groovy early-'70s movie party scene, a left-field lyric threw this fairly standard rock jam off its axis. It reflected those who at the time traded as hippie gurus and gathered followers, forming cults. The sudden change to the stylized a-cappella group vocals at 3m:38s was pure Godley & Creme, their willingness to explore to the fore.

### 'Suite F.A.' (Lol Creme, Kevin Godley)

In a lyric technique hinted at in 'Take Me Back', 'Suite F.A.' demonstrates the often-told narrative trope known as 'The Hero's Journey', where an adventurer sets out, fighting for some kind of victory, ultimately returning transformed. In this case, it transpires over the course of three movements.

The first movement, 'On My Way', has a long and relatively uneventful introduction. Broken guitar chords enter in the verse, moving first as a variation on Thunderclap Newman's descending guitar line from 'Something in the Air', secondly as an exact replica and thirdly as a clash of the two. The 'I'm on my way' vocal hook follows supported by a guitar line clearly inspired by The Beatles' 'Sun King'. At 5m:18s the first movement is taken out by an instrumental section recalling the Mothers of Invention's early psychedelic jams. It trades places with the above-mentioned chord descents before returning to fade.

Movement two, 'Indecision', adopts a Beach Boys ballad style replete with French horn, before changing to a rock texture. The cherry on top is the marvellous boogie-woogie piano appearing out of nowhere at 9m:28s before the track fades out, ushering in movement three, 'The Return'. A repeated vocal harmony refrain then dominates for the entirety of the closing section in the vocal style of the recently adopted Frank Zappa band members, Howard Kaylan and Mark Volman aka Flo and Eddie.

Eric Stewart later described Hotlegs as a progressive band, which technically they kind of were, applying whatever progressive tendencies they possessed to a pop framework. Kevin Godley described 'Suite F.A.'

as their version of The Beatles' *Abbey Road s*uite. Hotlegs clearly took inspiration from wherever they found it in creating the track. Some cues, like those described above, were at surface level. Other inspiration was more subtle and even subconscious, with original ingredients twisting in borrowed elements.

In light of that, it's important to accept seemingly obvious inspiration or even quotes when exploring this material. In the case of 'Suite F.A.', perhaps the lack of a truly satisfying peak was more of a downfall. It's fair to say that this early in the game, the piece could be considered as a sincere stab at the long-form work the band would increasingly fine-tune.

**'Fly Away'** (Lol Creme, Kevin Godley)
A delicate ballad with minimal instrumentation of acoustic guitar and a short flute solo. The lyric carried another theme of escape, this time more abstract. Kevin and Lol recorded it under the title 'To Fly Away' in 1968 when it was issued on a Marmalade Records sampler album under the artist name Frabjoy and Runcible Spoon. That version was fuller with a double-tracked vocal, organ and bass.

**'Run Baby Run'** (Lol Creme, Kevin Godley, Eric Stewart)
Released as a single A-side, January 1971 (US), b/w 'How Many Times'.
Released as a single B-side, February 1971 (DE), b/w 'Desperate Dan'.

Eric Stewart's sole lead vocal was this straight-ahead blues-rock song that's claimed to be the basis for the 1975 10cc hit, 'Art For Art's Sake'. 'Basis' is a strong word, as the only real similarity are the words 'Gimme a bottle' sung in the same rhythm as 'Art For Art's Sake''s 'Gimme your body' and other phrases, which is neither here nor there. Thousands of songs share minor similarities. I feel the suggestion as song basis insubstantial enough to be non-existent or at least microscopic.

This confessional vehicle for a character who hits the bottle when his 'baby' is away, moves along predictably enough. But the guitar solo brings a pleasant surprise key-change a major-third down, working its way back up for the last verse. Moving back down, the key remains there for the duration until you hear the odd idiosyncrasy of the fade running long enough to hear the final chord anyway.

**'All God's Children'** (Lol Creme, Kevin Godley)
The multi-vocal acoustic approach is like a fore-runner to coming Paul McCartney and Wings singalongs like 'Bluebird'. But 'All God's Children' leaves you thinking, when you realize that the lyric has the theme of a cult-like gathering. That idea lingers after the song is over, a fitting close for *Thinks: School Stinks* – the most serious-sounding album these musicians would make before the departure of Godley and Creme in 1976.

## Contemporary Tracks

### 'You Didn't Like It Because You Didn't Think Of It' (Lol Creme, Kevin Godley, Eric Stewart)
Released as a single B-side, 19 June 1970 (UK), 3 August 1970 (US), b/w 'Neanderthal Man'.

In a McCartney-esque fashion, the 'Neanderthal Man' B-side combines two songs into one. The first half, which can be safely referred to as 'You Can't Keep a Good Man Down', begins with a repeating abstract jazz-like piano vamp, later joined by rock guitar chunks that have a timbre aurally identical to John Lennon's then-recent single, 'Cold Turkey'. It soon becomes a rock slow-burn with a memorable vocal hook moving into the second half, which we can call 'Take Me Away'. This more pop texture consists of the main hook section, followed by a harmonically beautiful central section that slowly winds its way back to the hook.

The 'Take Me Away' half was later reworked as the central section of 'Fresh Air For My Mama' on the first 10cc album where the song's hook section remained intact. Part of the central section was also used but with a lyric re-write.

### 'Umbopo' (Lol Creme, Kevin Godley)
Released as a single A-side under the band name Doctor Father, 14 August 1970 (UK), October 1970 (US), b/w 'Roll On'.

This Lol-Creme-produced single issued under the band name, Doctor Father, had hit written all over it. One thing that might've stopped it in its tracks was the 5m:28s running time which, despite certain forerunners like The Beatles' 'Hey Jude', was still quite long for 1970. But it had the catchiest chorus hook this side of the black stump, wherever that is – presumably in the same place as the mythical Umbopo river of Borneo searched for in the story but never found. Neither is the guy searching for it, the jungle closing behind him.

In 1969 with Graham Gouldman and Richie Cordell at the helm, the band, calling themselves Crazy Elephant, had recorded a faster, shorter and more urgent version of the song under its original title of 'There Ain't No Umbopo'. Released in May 1970, one month prior to 'Neanderthal Man', *that* was the version that should've been the hit, compared to this slower but equally worthy Doctor Father release in August. Confused? Me too. It's a shame with such clear belief in, and multiple efforts put into, the song, that it amounted to little more than being heralded by hardcore 10cc fans and being read about in a book like this. However, I wouldn't be surprised if 'Umbopo' had reached the ears of British singer/songwriter Albert Hammond and influenced his 1972 hit, 'It Never Rains In Southern California', which bears more than a passing resemblance.

### 'Roll On' (Lol Creme, Kevin Godley, Eric Stewart)
Released as a single B-side under the band name Doctor Father, 14 August 1970 (UK), October 1970 (US), b/w 'Umbopo'.

It's difficult not to hear 'Roll On' as perfect material for Eric Clapton. In his hands, it could've been something. But the slow-shuffle and its mutated blues chord progression, sound like a virtual one-take situation. There's even a near false ending at the three-minute mark, that's how familiar the players were with the song format. But in the days of vinyl, B-sides went along for the ride. Expedience was the thing.

The song wasn't without merit. The complaint of insomnia was ideal blues fodder and Eric Stewart gave a more believable vocal performance than on the album track 'Run Baby Run'. Blues was a natural inclination for him, as was slipping to pop and back again with ease.

### 'Lady Sadie' (Lol Creme, Kevin Godley, Eric Stewart)
Released as a single A-side, 3 September 1971 (UK), b/w 'The Loser'.

The follow-up to 'Neanderthal Man' was an adventurous rock single that, even by '70s standards, was going to have a rough ride running the censor gauntlet. The manor master's older daughter sells herself for a dollar with many coming to see her matinees. Oddly, in the end, Dad sells some pictures to the crown and makes a fortune with his studies of the aristocracy.

On the surface, it was a fairly benign rock chug, highlighted by a slick brass section and blues guitar licks whirling through a Leslie speaker. But the subject matter was always going to keep some distance between the disc underside and radio station turntables.

### 'The Loser' (Lol Creme, Kevin Godley, Eric Stewart)
Released as a single B-side, 3 September 1971 (UK), b/w 'Lady Sadie'.

The 'Lady Sadie' B-side was a fast fidgety blues-orientated song of a disrespectful fool in love who gets the boot. Perhaps having more potential public acceptance than its A-side, 'The Loser' was similarly impotent on the lyric front.

> I've tried to make a decent life for you
> Then all you gave me is the heel of your shoe

Virtue existed in the tasteful central drum groove leading to dual guitar harmonies ala the Allman Brothers. Not to mention that wild and feral group vocal sound that would sporadically present itself as far down the track as Godley & Creme's 1979 masterpiece 'An Englishman in New York'.

## 'Today' (Lol Creme, Kevin Godley)
Re-recorded and released as a single A-side under the band name Festival, 6 October 1972 (UK), b/w 'Warm Me'.

Philips Records first released the Hotlegs version of 'Today' in the UK in December 1971 on the reissued *Thinks: School Stinks* album which was re-titled *Song*. 'Today' replaced 'Neanderthal Man', presumably after criticism for the album's lack of cohesion with the successful single.

The new track, sung by Kevin Godley, revealed the band's ever-improving production and arrangement techniques which here included a substantial orchestral arrangement and cutting edge synthesizer, effectively putting the remainder of the album in shadow. The composition itself was their most formally adventurous yet. Two memorable verse sections featuring the title hook were followed by twelve bars of B section leading to a thoroughly through-composed 21-bar C section subdivided by seven and fourteen – a development worthy of a classical piece. The cherry on top was the re-entry of Graham Gouldman on bass, effectively making 'Today' a 10cc track.

The song was a reworking of a Godley and Creme number dating from when they recorded as Frabjoy and Runcible Spoon. The lyric shared with 'Take Me Back' and 'Suite F.A.' a theme of escape, though this time, not the entire body, only the roving eye.

As if that wasn't enough, 'Today' was re-recorded, again with Graham on bass, and released as a single on RCA Records in October 1972 under the band name Festival. This re-recording was a treat, tougher but slightly slower and darker with more focus on the bass and a solid backbone of two simultaneous drum takes. Gorgeous 'Aaah' backing vocals cut through from behind with a thick but watery texture that was completely not loud enough. The band's finest work yet.

Note, this single came one month after the issue of the first 10cc single, 'Donna'. But the style was such a contrast, it was likely decided that the two would not conflict. As it happened, 'Donna' was the success, the 10cc name stayed, and the band settled into the five years of activity that would come to represent the bulk of their chart success.

# 10cc (1973)

UK Release date: July 1973. US Release date: October 1973
Personnel:
Lol Creme: Vocals, Guitars, Piano, Keyboards, Percussion
Kevin Godley: Vocals, Drums, Percussion
Graham Gouldman: Vocals, Bass, Guitars, Dobro, Tambourine
Eric Stewart: Vocals, Guitars, Synthesizer
Recorded 1972-1973 at Strawberry Studios, Stockport, UK
Producer: 10cc
Engineer: Eric Stewart
Chart placings: UK: 36, US: 201

Godley and Creme had felt that they'd unfairly outnumbered Eric Stewart in Hotlegs. But upon Graham Gouldman's return from New York, the four-piece locked in once and for all. They started working on songs for their own pleasure around other booked studio sessions. Most significant was the securing of legendary US songwriter and recording artist, Neil Sedaka, who Graham first met in New York. With Sedaka now on tour in England, the two met again at a Leeds hotel where Graham heard Sedaka's new material with a view to recording his new album at Strawberry with the future 10cc as the backing band. It was agreed to begin with three songs. There would be plenty of room for the musicians to move ideas-wise, but the primary focus was to make Sedaka's songs tangible in the current singer/songwriter style of artists like Carole King. The June 1972 sessions flowered into the full album 'Solitaire'.

Sedaka was encouraging, telling the band they ought to establish themselves as a recording act in their own right. With the project complete, and buoyed by Sedaka's enthusiasm, the soon-to-be-named 10cc got serious about releasing their own material. The first track cut was 'Waterfall', intended as an A-side, followed by 'Donna' as its potential B-side. Submitted as a package to The Beatles' Apple Records, they were rejected two months later. By this stage, it was apparent that the characterful 'Donna' was the stronger number of the two. Eric Stewart figured the track might be of interest to pop singer, impresario and UK Records owner, Jonathan King. Stewart knew him from the Mindbenders days when King would follow the band around in a tatty white sports car telling them he could make them the next Beatles. The band just laughed. But the laughing stopped a few months later when King had a number four UK hit with 'Everyone's Gone to the Moon'. After that, he was taken more seriously.

Invited to Strawberry to hear 'Donna', King loved the track. He signed 10cc to a five-year contract with UK Records and released 'Donna' as the first single. With the band in need of a name, King told them of a dream he'd had three times where he saw in lights the words, '10cc – The Best Band in the World'. The most recent dream had been the night before, the lights this time being above the Hammersmith Odeon. The name was born.

Released in September 1972, 'Donna' reached number two in the UK, after which a follow-up was expected. It came in the form of 'Johnny Don't Do It', which failed to chart. But success returned with the March 1973 release of 'Rubber Bullets' which made it to the Hot 100 in the USA and making it number one in the UK.

UK Records were champing at the bit for a 10cc album, so having just finished a second Neil Sedaka album, *The Tra-La Days Are Over*, the focus was now on completing the 10cc debut. 'Sand in My Face' and 'Fresh Air For My Mama' were in the can. The rest were done at a frantic pace over three weeks, recording sixteen solid hours a day. As soon as someone had a song, it got recorded. The deadline was Kevin Godley's wedding, set for June 1973.

Graham Gouldman's return had provided needed balance. He and Eric naturally paired off to write, but the first album didn't represent two writing pairs as a rule. 'Ships Don't Disappear in the Night, Do They?' was the only new Gouldman/Stewart song cut during the bulk of the sessions. 'Speed Kills', an Eric idea that began life in Hotlegs, was credited to all four. The Godley/Creme/Stewart piece, 'Fresh Air For My Mama', partially dated from the Hotlegs days too as it contained pieces from the 'Neanderthal Man' B-side, 'You Didn't Like It Because You Didn't Think Of It'. That left three Godley/Creme/Gouldman songs – 'Johnny Don't Do It', 'Sand in My Face' and 'Rubber Bullets' – and Godley and Creme's 'Donna' and 'The Dean and I'.

Finding themselves two songs short close to the deadline, they paired off to write them simultaneously. The race was on to see who could complete their song first. Kevin and Lol won, coming up with 'The Hospital Song'. Graham and Eric appeared shortly afterwards with 'Headline Hustler'.

In a 1976 interview, Lol Creme provided some insight into the creation of the debut.

> It's interesting that all the songs in that album were developing a personality then and it was coming up by the last tracks of that first album. An identity was beginning to form, like those very bizarre songs. We were almost seeing how mad we could write, seeing how far we could go, and 'Hospital Song' went quite far. It was a very exciting period and all these things were just arriving, like the way of putting over certain emotions – like the heavy sound or light sounds – the humour.

You could be forgiven for missing the phallic symbol standing proud on the cover of *10cc*. Godley and Creme had taken on the task of illustrating an identity to match the musical one. It was the visual equivalent of the multiple lyrical references that came at you thick and fast – sometimes deep, other times so obvious they were invisible.

The colourful and fun album was released in July 1973, a mere three weeks after completion. This was a high production turnaround that could be attributed to UK Records director, Jonathan King, who Lol Creme at the time heralded as the greatest record executive in Britain.

Otherwise, thanks to their ownership of Strawberry Studios, 10cc were fully independent. In 1973, Eric Stewart told *New Musical Express* that if the band had their own pressing plant, they'd press their own records too. He also mentioned the band's unique approach to live shows with a plan to set the stage up like a recording studio, though he figured this might be more viable in the USA. It wouldn't be long before the USA caught the 10cc bug.
In the meantime, the album peaked at a modest number 36 in the UK, but it had influence in high places. As we shall see, without the 10cc debut, we may not have the Rolling Stones' 'It's Only Rock 'n' Roll (But I Like It), or Paul McCartney and Wings' 'Helen Wheels' – tracks it's fair to say took some influence from *10cc*.

**'Johnny Don't Do It'** (Lol Creme, Kevin Godley, Graham Gouldman)
Released as a single A-side, 1 December 1972 (UK), 8 February 1973 (AU), b/w '4% of Something'.
Released as a single A-side, 1974 (JP), b/w 'Silly Love'.

Like the main character, Johnny Kowalski aka Johnny Angel (a reference to the 1962 Shelley Fabares hit, 'Johnny Angel'), this '50s doo-wop death-song pastiche and second song recorded for *10cc*, was doomed to be unpopular. The character failed to rise above base retribution and the single, 10cc's second, was eclipsed by the 1972 UK re-release of The Shangri-Las' 1964 hit, 'Leader of the Pack'. Without this, 'Johnny Don't Do It' might've done it after all as the 'Donna' single did before it.

But the lack of chart action didn't stop this first Godley/Creme/Gouldman release having musical merit. The rock guitar harmonies really toughened it up and the two-chord repeating turnaround at the end gave the track a more modern flavour. The single discarded the introduction fanfare heard on the album, but had an additional twenty seconds of hook at the end, making it a collector's item. Both 'Johnny Don't Do it' and the prior single 'Donna' were remixed for the album.

As an aside, the lyric mentions Joe's garage, seven years before Frank Zappa's album set of the same name, which was fitting considering Godley and Creme's later Zappa references. The entire song is not unlike his doo-wop pastiche concept for 1968's Mothers of Invention album, *Cruising with Ruben & The Jets*.

**'Sand in My Face'** (Lol Creme, Kevin Godley, Graham Gouldman)
Now the fun zone kicked in with an effective uptempo advertisement for Charles Atlas' 1920s exercise system known as Dynamic Tension. The song was recorded for pleasure before 10cc's debut album was even on the radar. Right away there were the wobbly audio-phonics and vocal dexterity that would characterise much of 10cc and Godley & Creme's discography. Humour

was to the forefront and never more than on the hysterical verse two vocal entry on the first word of the line 'I opened my magazine'.

The story is the karmic tale of a nine-stone weakling whose girlfriend is stolen by 200lb Alex. The weakling answers a TV ad for Dynamic Tension, and in a happy ending, kicks sand in Alex's face and gets his girlfriend back.

From the defined death song genre of 'Johnny Don't Do It' to the comedic kickback of 'Sand in My Face', it was clear that stylistic boundaries meant little to 10cc.

## 'Donna' (Lol Creme, Kevin Godley)
Released as a single A-side, 4 August 1972 (UK), November 1972 (US), 19 October 1972 (AU), July 1972 (NZ), b/w 'Hot Sun Rock'. UK: 2. AU: 53.

There was something indescribable about the sound of Lol Creme singing the words 'Hello darling, yes I love you darling, yes I love you' in 10cc's debut single as it dripped from the radio in 1973. This was no mere doo-wop pastiche alone. Clearly it also drew on The Beatles' 'Oh! Darling' – that ballad being likewise mangled '50s mincemeat. But more than Creme's voice, obviously squeezed through the narrow telephone frequency band straw, it was the character he played. Was it the male or female character singing that line? It could've passed for either. This was typical of what would become part of Creme's modus operandi within the small but distinguished discography of 10cc mark one. With such clearly identifiable and characterful voices as those of his fellow band members' present, a listener might be puzzled by the times they could never quite tell who was singing. That voice was usually Lol Creme, the vocal chameleon and bit player. It was indicative of the half-serious-half comedic journey 10cc were taking you on.

Recorded in May 1972, the doo-wop-influenced single, sung predominantly by Creme, was the perfect dual cherry and bubblegum-popping soundtrack. Originally intended as the B-side for 'Waterfall', that single package was rejected by The Beatles' Apple Records, which was no real surprise considering Apple usually released artists that came in via Beatles relationships, of which 10cc had none, yet. That would change sooner than they thought, if they even thought about it, which they probably didn't. 10cc had a tendency to isolate themselves from what was going on out in the pop world, to concentrate on their own work.

'Donna' had an influence on the burgeoning UK rock & roll revival that would come to be dominated by artists such as Alvin Stardust, Showaddywaddy and the successful studio concoction, The Rubettes. But 10cc never stood still, so by the time the whole '50s craze blew up, they'd already moved on.

Having said that, 'Donna' wasn't pure doo-wop, to begin with. Doo-wop was a convenient handle to carry the song around by when in fact it played fast and loose with genres. The chord progression alone moved beyond the normal patterns. The A (containing the title) and B sections both fit the standard doo-wop mold. But additional C and D sections had their way with the tradition. The C section, starting with the words 'Hello darling', took the song down one key in pitch which was pretty unusual for pop and was unheard of in doo-wop. The D section took the song *up* one key which was more conventional. But that didn't change the key of the entire song, just the key of *that* section, which eventually found its way back to the original key for another verse. Additionally, the D section gave the song a central dynamic departure, bringing in the glam rock flavour that prevailed in the UK charts at the time. 'Donna' was a singular signal filtering through that glam noise.

Under a microscope, the lyric too twists standard doo-wop love/heartbreak fare, showing more than it tells by exposing the inner mind workings of someone obsessed. Besides the character's obvious affection for Donna, he's completely beside himself, unable to remain sitting down, standing up, breaking up or breaking down. But Donna is waiting by the phone anyway, presumably for *him* to call. But he just can't settle down about it. This was the kind of angst-ridden detail that '50s doo-wop left out unless a song was intended as a novelty. 'Donna' was daring. Perhaps not as daring as Frank Zappa's 1968 doo-wop homage and suicide threat, 'Stuff Up the Cracks', but daring nevertheless.

Anyway, the formula worked. Eric Stewart especially was surprised by the single's success. Reaching number two in the UK secured 10cc a *Top Of The Pops* appearance to perform (mime to) 'Donna'. Never short of ideas, Jonathan King suggested the band appear wearing transparent polyethylene uniforms. The response was a resounding 'No.'.

**'The Dean and I'** (Lol Creme, Kevin Godley)
Released as a single A-side, 10 August 1973 (UK), 29 November 1973 (AU), b/w 'Bee In My Bonnet'. UK: 10. IE: 1. AU: 61.

In a 1973 issue of *New Musical Express,* Kevin Godley quipped that this song was written by Godley and Creme and Rodgers and Hammerstein. The gag held water considering the track was recorded in May 1973, a full year after 'Donna', and represented a substantial songwriting development.

Like 'Donna' messed with '50s doo-wop, 'The Dean and I' experimented with the pop song format. Where most pop songs would have two, three or occasionally four separate sections, 'The Dean and I' had no less than seven perceivable sections and three styles, which was quite a feat for a track that clocked in at only 3m:07s. The bridge alone consisted of three sub-sections, each appearing to interrupt the one before. Even the obvious potentially repeatable chorus hook 'Church bells, three swells, the Dean, his daughter and me' was stated only once. The rhythm, also not beyond change, moved back and forth in a McCartney-esque half-time/straight-four swap.

The lengthy three-part 'Suite F.A.' from *Thinks: School Stinks* was one thing, but 'The Dean and I' is where the concept was distilled in a three-minute pop package with all risk-taking intact. The first album could've been thought of as very early in the game for taking such a chance, but 10cc had paid their dues for their first flush of success, not to mention Stewart and Gouldman having already been through the mill as successful pop stars and songwriters respectively. They'd earned the right to do as they pleased musically.

The lyric was no exception – the main character telling his kids how romantic it was meeting their mother, the Dean's daughter. Cut to today and the guy has lost all feeling and wants out. Eventually out, he suddenly gets rich.

Along the way we find nods to '60s pop, not least of all in the extended bridge which takes stylistic cues from Beach Boys songs and from their cover of the Spector/Greenwich/Barry hit, 'Then He Kissed Me', which the Beach Boys re-titled to 'Then I Kissed Her'.

Quoted on the words 'Awol awol awol awol' is perhaps one of the world's most famous melodies, that of 'Westminster Chimes', which was a variation on part of Handel's 'Messiah'. But the ever-restless Godley and Creme changed the second-to-last note, making the melody their own.

'The Dean and I' packed a lot of information into a short time span. Even so, the single edit halved the length of the vocal intro hook 'Humdrum days and humdrum ways'. They must've wanted to get to the good bits. Certainly, Eric Stewart would've wanted to as he didn't love the song, though adding blues guitar licks made it work for him. Conversely, 'The Dean and I' is one of Graham Gouldman's favourite 10cc songs.

**'Headline Hustler'** (Graham Gouldman, Eric Stewart)
Released as a single A-side, March 1974 (US and CA), b/w 'Speed Kills'.

'Headline Hustler' was written quickly, close to the album deadline, when the writers paired off to simultaneously come up with two final needed songs. The first Gouldman/Stewart song on a 10cc album, it was lyrically a conglomerate of trans-Atlantic political scandals, the Lambton Affair and Watergate. This was reflected in the erratic, nerve-wracking and unrelenting drum rhythm. The British-sounding track was a single only in the USA and Canada. But the song was clearly floating around the UK in late 1973 when the Rolling Stones' Mick Jagger and Ron Wood collaborated on 'It's Only Rock 'n' Roll (But I Like It)', which, likely unconsciously, shared a clearly identifiable melodic hook in its verse.

**'Speed Kills'** (Lol Creme, Kevin Godley, Graham Gouldman, Eric Stewart)
Released as a single B-side, March 1974 (US and CA), b/w 'Headline Hustler'.

'Speed Kills' acts as a kind of buffer between the manic 'Headline Hustler' and the panic of 'Rubber Bullets'. Lol Creme told NME in 1973 that the track began in the Hotlegs days as a drum-based piece similar to 'Neanderthal Man'. He added in a typically comedic fashion that Eric kept adding guitars to it over eighteen months, getting heavier and heavier until the studio had to be reinforced several times.

Eric's multiple guitars do grab the bulk of the attention, with the group voices coming across more like backing vocals and containing more than a hint of the Beatles circa *Abbey Road*. Underneath lies a basic blues chord progression, but the middle section is more harmonically abstract and unstable. Some of the guitars are tape-sped up, including the solo which is followed by banks of three-part guitar harmonies, a sound that would become a 10cc signature.

The nine scant lyric lines hold a lot of information, stating how difficult it is to make it, the defined requirements for such then becoming blurred with those for drug-taking.

> One fine day I started writing home
> One finds it's so hard to make it
> It's gotta be the right time
> It's gotta be the right kind line
> It's gotta be the mainline
> It's gotta be
> It better be
> So let it be
> One fine day

This is songwriting economy plus, and it's hidden away inside what could be considered a throwaway compared to the surrounding material. But in many ways the song is more experimental than the following track, 'Rubber Bullets'.

## 'Rubber Bullets' (Lol Creme, Kevin Godley, Graham Gouldman)
Released as a single A-side, 30 March 1973 (UK), May 1973 (US),July 1973 (AU and NZ), b/w 'Waterfall'. UK: 1. US: 73. CA: 76. IE: 1. AU: 3. NZ: 17.

In need of a third single to strike while the iron was still practically hot from the success of first single 'Donna', Stockport's newest stars loaded up 'Rubber Bullets' in time for Christmas 1972, aiming for a March trigger-pull. Originally the BBC weren't interested, taking one look at the title, presuming it to be about Northern Ireland and discarding it. But thanks to *Top Of The Pops* producer Johnnie Stewart inviting the band back on the show, the single hit number one anyway. Jonathan King saw this achievement as a milestone in the British record industry, claiming it was the first single to hit number one with hardly anyone noticing.

Soon more than one BBC representative phoned UK Records asking for another copy of the single, claiming they'd mislaid the first one. That had been a shortened version made especially for them. Now the shoe was on the other foot, UK Records told them they were out of pressings of the edit and they'd have to play the full-length version, which they did. It's mysterious how the song title had been the only issue. There was never any mention of the lyric line 'Balling in the street'. It was believed that the BBC only listened to ten seconds of a song before deciding whether to playlist it. At the time, Graham Gouldman cited Lou Reed's risque 'Walk On the Wild Side' as an example of this. BBC Radio 1 *did* ban 'Rubber Bullets' however, clinging to the conclusion that the title referenced Northern Ireland unrest, which was untrue.

The benign lyric addressed an out-of-control county jail party, based loosely on New York's Attica State Prison riots. Eric Stewart described it as a kind of updated version of the James Cagney movie, *Angels With Dirty Faces*. Kevin and Lol had written the verse and chorus. Not sure if it was any good, they took it to the band. Eric loved it, believing it to be a potential hit. But it needed more. Graham then wrote the mellow middle section. But it does sound like something Kevin might've written, mostly because he largely owned anything he applied his falsetto voice to, his soaring vocal in this case sounding like a forerunner to the more sentimental parts of 1975's 'Une Nuit a Paris'.

The totally unexpected bridge appears like a welcome hallucination amidst the madness, before returning to the party. At that point, we get a definite tip of the hat to the 1964 Beach Boys hit, 'Fun, Fun, Fun', in the group backing vocal lines 'The national guard' and 'The exercise yard'. But though it trod similar territory, the song was much more than simple early-Beach-Boys parody, to which the exquisite bridge can attest.

At the time 'Rubber Bullets' broke into the charts, Eric Stewart was invited to participate in a cabaret tour with a reformed Mindbenders, along with other '60s acts of similar ilk. He declined, thinking nothing could be worse than going back to the bad old days. It's interesting to think that a mere eight years earlier could've been considered the bad old days. That indicates how much the music business had developed from 1965 to 1973.

**'The Hospital Song'** (Lol Creme, Kevin Godley)
One great thing about living and recording in Manchester was that 10cc were in no way slaves to trends or what was hip. They were free to write about American prison mayhem as above, or indeed traverse the existential implications of bed-wetting, which is exactly what happened here. From the perspective of being under, a grumpy patient sings of getting revenge on the matron by wetting the bed when he wakes up. It's pure theatre (excuse the pun) executed from within the comfy folds of a slow semi-funky drum groove.

The bridge melody on the line 'You'll be waiting with a hypodermic needle' is a partial melodic and likely unconscious borrowing from The Beatles' 'Cry Baby Cry'. From there it quickly morphs into one of those opaque instrumental breakdowns that would populate future corners of 10cc's repertoire. Coming to a theatrical climax with the last verse deceleration, we are treated to another chorus of 'I get off on what you give me, darlin', before reaching the final line, 'And when I go I'll die of plaster casting love' – a reference to Hollywood personality and plaster-caster to the stars, Cynthia Albritton.

'The Hospital Song' was the first-completed of the two final songs written close to the recording deadline. The other was Gouldman and Stewart's 'Headline Hustler'.

## 'Ships Don't Disappear in the Night, Do They?' (Graham Gouldman, Eric Stewart)

Rather than going like bats out of hell, Gouldman and Stewart eased into their songwriting collaboration, even less seriously here than in 'Headline Hustler'. That's not to say they weren't serious about being lighthearted.

Blues-rock marinated in slide guitars was the musical foundation for this supernatural black comedy. Horror actors Vincent Price, Boris Karloff and Bela Lugosi all made a lyrical appearance. The virtually instrumental breakdown after the first chorus was of that particular Godley and Creme nature where you can't quite identify all of the sounds, apart from Godley's unmistakable falsetto operating mostly as a wordless texture.

Effort went into this serious spoof, but not so much as to not know when to stop. The minimalist recording benefits from not going too far over any line and is one of those tracks that undeniably demonstrates sonic skill, regardless of what you might think of the song itself. I'd say that the verse at least was a stylistic influence on the Paul McCartney and Wings hit, 'Helen Wheels', recorded during the 'Band On the Run' sessions in Laos, Nigeria, mere weeks after the appearance of 10cc's debut album. I wouldn't be surprised if *10cc* was among the tapes stolen from McCartney at knife-point on that ill-fated trip.

## 'Fresh Air For My Mama' (Lol Creme, Kevin Godley, Eric Stewart)

The precisely-chiselled 'Fresh Air For My Mama' launches with two verses, the second changing course part-way through. Eric Stewart has stated that the lyrics had some basis in reality. Kevin Godley confirmed for me that they concerned the conflicts and attendant responsibilities of leaving home and moving on. Even in that knowledge, they retain a mysterious and impenetrable nature.

A short chorus hook housing the song title emits the tiniest atmospheric glint of the Beach Boys' 1971 masterpiece 'Surf's Up' – the sole obvious reference in this otherwise truly distinctive piece delivered via Godley's soulful vocal.

A part-instrumental four-bar transition then leads to the central section, within which Graham Gouldman suggested incorporating the 'Take Me Away' section of the Hotlegs B-side, 'You Didn't Like It Because You Didn't Think Of It'. He always loved it, thinking it was a crime no one ever heard it when buried away in an obscure B-side. This development, embodying a partial lyric rewrite, is the perfect reinforcement in support of the argument pro song-crafting. Some believe the initial flash of inspiration is best left pure and unchanged, as reflected in author William Burroughs' aphorism, 'First thought, best thought'. Others believe the opposite – composer Igor Stravinsky for example, having stated that composition is one per cent inspiration and 99 per cent sweat. There are pros and cons to both. Certainly chord sequences and melody can be and are combined and developed, whether we like it or not.

But in the case of 'Fresh Air For My Mama', we have actual lyrics flown in from another 10cc song, then requiring some re-writing to make them belong. If you're listening and unaware of this, it all sounds perfectly fine. But if you become aware and think about it too much, your brain can play tricks and overthink it. To assess from that vantage point would be more subjective than objective. Therefore, in this case, I'll opt for the Stravinsky option and give this song its due as high-grade work put together by respected musicians who knew what they were doing.

Partial Frankenstein-monster or not, the album closer is a surprise that leaves you thinking the rest was just a fun lead-up to revealing the real 10cc. This was probably true to an extent.

## Contemporary Tracks

**'Hot Sun Rock'** (Graham Gouldman, Eric Stewart)
Released as a single B-side, 4 August 1972 (UK), November 1972 (US), 19 October 1972 (AU), b/w 'Donna'.

You can think of 'Hot Sun Rock' as quite literally cutting into 'Donna''s underside. The instrumental filler incorporated certain popular flavours of the period. A Led Zeppelin vibe lived in the unison riff that came after the four-bar intro, and the repeating C section recalled 'Hocus Pocus', the 1971 instrumental by Dutch group, Focus. Though not a hit in the UK until 1973, the influential 'Hocus Pocus', well-known in musical circles, was an absolute earworm, allowing for its possible unconscious assimilation into the work of others. That theory could only possibly hold water on an arrangement level though, and maybe not even then, considering 'Hot Sun Rock' began life three or four years earlier as a piece Graham Gouldman was working on for Robbins Music.

**'4% of Something'** (Lol Creme, Eric Stewart)
Released as a single B-side, 1 December 1972 (UK), 8 February 1973 (AU), b/w 'Johnny Don't Do It'.
Released as a single B-side, 16 May 1975 (UK, DE and NL), b/w 'Waterfall'.

Sung by Eric Stewart, the first released Creme/Stewart song was an uptempo blues workout (though not strictly a blues chord progression) bemoaning the musician's struggle to make a living. Within the first year of 10cc's UK Records contract, Eric broached the low percentage issue with Jonathan King, who replied, '4% of something is better than 10% of nothing.'. That response inspired this lyric. It was unfortunately early in the game for such a dispute to rear its head, coming soon after 10cc's quite unexpected initial success with the first single, 'Donna'.

## 'Waterfall' (Graham Gouldman, Eric Stewart)

Released as a single B-side, 30 March 1973 (UK), May 1973 (US), July 1973 (AU and NZ), b/w 'Rubber Bullets'.
Released as a single A-side, 16 May 1975 (UK, DE and NL), b/w '4% of Something'.

Originally intended as a single A-side with 'Donna' on the flip side, that two-song package-demo was turned down by Apple Records. Not strictly an ecology song, the substantial rock ballad nevertheless got back to nature lyrically, getting its day in the sun as a non-US A-side in 1975. But eclipsed by surrounding singles from *The Original Soundtrack*, it failed to chart. Nevertheless, 'Waterfall' was a worthy addition to the discography for the glorious entry of the backwards guitars after the first chorus alone.

## 'Bee In My Bonnet' (Graham Gouldman, Eric Stewart)

Released as a single B-side, 10 August 1973 (UK), 29 November 1973 (AU), b/w 'The Dean and I'.

The character in this straight-ahead rock song has got it bad. He's on his way to meet his love and he's explaining all the ways he's bent out of shape over it. Two of his symptoms are the 'rockin' pneumonia and the boogie-woogie flu', taken from the title of Huey 'Piano' Smith's 1957 hit – a song again made a hit in 1972 by US recording artist, Johnny Rivers.

## 'Warm Me' (Graham Gouldman, Eric Stewart)

Released as a single B-side under the band name Festival, 6 October 1972 (UK), b/w 'Today'.

A predominantly Graham Gouldman vocal, 'Warm Me' had the general feel of early '70s soft multi-vocal singing group hits like those of the early Brotherhood of Man and America's Ray Conniff Singers. Though less overt in approach, this song could've loaned itself to that genre extremely well.

## 'Extracts LP 10cc Side One' (Lol Creme, Kevin Godley, Graham Gouldman, Eric Stewart)

Released as a promo-only 7' single, 1972 (UK), b/w 'Extracts LP 10cc Side Two'.

Not technically a song, 'Extracts' was a single on the UK label which across both sides featured snippets of all songs from the *10cc* album prefaced with spoken introductions. It was given out as promo upon the album's 1973 release.

# Sheet Music (1974)

UK Release date: 28 May 1974. US Release date: July 1974.
Personnel:
Lol Creme: Vocals, Guitars, Keyboards, Percussion
Kevin Godley: Vocals, Drums, Percussion
Graham Gouldman: Vocals, Bass, Guitars, Percussion
Eric Stewart: Vocals, Guitars, Keyboards
Recorded January-May 1974 at Strawberry Studios, Stockport, UK
Producer: 10cc
Engineer: Eric Stewart
Chart placings: UK: 9, US: 81, NL: 15

10cc completed their first UK tour in December 1973, followed by two January 1974 straggler concerts in Newcastle and London. With work about to commence on album three, *Sheet Music*, Eric Stewart phoned Lol Creme out of the blue to tell him he was leaving the band. 10cc were no-nonsense people and Lol's immediate reaction was to get Eric down to the studio for a session. The phone call was a blip. Eric had become so involved with engineering that he felt his guitar-playing had taken a back seat and his performance had suffered because of it. He didn't want to let the side down. The band threw a guitar into his hands and forced him to put a solo on something. Luckily for everyone involved, this fixed the problem.

The material and sound of what became *Sheet Music* were such a development on *10cc* that you could easily believe there'd been an album in-between. Everything the band wanted to achieve musically now came into sharp focus. Experimentation with song forms continued. In 1974, Kevin Godley stated, 'It's trying to get rid of the old assumption that a song has to be two verses, a middle eight and a verse.'. Lol Creme added, 'We're trying to learn about music, we're not trying to cater for a particular market. The only way to learn about it is to try different things.'

Though they had experimented with longer-form material in the Hotlegs days, the opulent 'Somewhere In Hollywood' signalled the beginning of what some referred to as 10cc's epic syndrome. Lol explained.

> We are into epics. We're also into short ditties. We like everything. There are shorties like 'Hospital Song', 'Clockwork Creep' and 'Silly Love'… I mean, those are little ditties. We don't want to be full of short meaningless ditties and we don't want to be full of long epics either.

*Sheet Music* featured every possible writing pairing between the four musicians, Godley and Creme having the most with four songs. Jonathan King was convinced that Creme and Gouldman's 'The Worst Band in the World' was the best choice for the first single. It wasn't his wisest move. 'The Wall Street Shuffle' did much better, peaking at number two in the Netherlands and ten in the UK. The third single 'Silly Love' also hit the Netherlands top ten but halted at 24 back in the UK.

The album fared better in the UK, reaching number nine. Reviews were positive, but the insular rock press made too big a deal of what they considered to be 10cc's influences. The debut had made one or two distinct homages to doo-wop and also wasn't shy with a handful of summery Beach Boys-esque moments. But *Sheet Music* did a much better job of assimilating possible influence into a unique soup sounding unlike anything else currently charting.

Some critics compared the style of 'The Wall Street Shuffle' to Paul McCartney and Wings. They *were* around the *Sheet Music* sessions, working at Strawberry producing the *McGear* album for McCartney's brother Mike, who recorded under the name Mike McGear. Wings worked nights, allowing the proprietors to use their drum kit during the day. McCartney and Wings' presence was surely the best circumstance for some semblance of similarity to be acceptably present. Lol Creme explained sound similarity best in a 1974 interview.

> What happens is that we listen to a lot of music, assimilate it all and then regurgitate it in our own work. That's learning, isn't it? You see, we have got exactly the same set-up as the Beach Boys. We've got our own studios, four guys that do all the singing with a voice range from high to low and we all write and produce our own sounds. We also play all the instruments and engineer the sessions. It's inevitable when four guys do all that in the same way that there are going to be similarities in the sound somewhere along the line.

Press-focus on 10cc's image clouded the issue further. Some critics, unhappy with the band's default civilian presentation, seemed to need some kind of visual uniformity matching the sound. In 1974, Eric Stewart stated how the band had been endlessly hassled about what they should be wearing on stage. 'Someone even got the person who does all Elton John's clothes to design some costumes for us. They turned out so weird they didn't even bother to show 'em to us.'

Thankfully, these trifling concerns didn't alter *Sheet Music*'s popularity one bit. In fact, Eric went as far as to title the album as a pun on an insult contained in an NME review.

Within the band, Graham Gouldman has claimed *Sheet Music* as his favourite 10cc album simply because it was bursting with ideas. It was about the music. At the time, Lol Creme nailed it with the following statement; 'It says a lot for the whole business when the only big obstacle in your way is that you don't have the right sort of image.'.

**'The Wall Street Shuffle'** (Graham Gouldman, Eric Stewart)
Released as a single A-side, 24 May 1974 (UK), August 1974 (US), 15 July 1974(AU), b/w 'Gismo My Way'. UK: 10. US: 103. IE: 9. DE: 43. NL: 1. Released as a single A-side, 1974 (ES), b/w 'Baron Samedi'.

The album opener and second single was conceived in a New York taxi in 1973. Crossing Wall Street, Lol yelled 'Wall Street. The Wall Street shuffle.', to which Eric replied 'Let's do the Wall Street shuffle.'. The phrase was remembered, the song written later as a comment on the current financial climate. Back in Stockport in January 1974, recording commenced on *Sheet Music*, 'The Wall Street Shuffle' recorded first.

Compared by some critics at the time, to the Paul McCartney and Wings sound, the hit nevertheless carried 10cc hallmarks including their ever-unsatiated formal boundary-pushing. The song was made up of no less than five discreet sections and at least one unique transition. Graham Gouldman's hooky low vocal interjections provided contrast against judicious layers of dramatic Mellotron. All keyboards, lead guitar and lead vocals were handled by Eric Stewart.

Though 'The Wall Street Shuffle' was a collaboration with Graham, a lot of the ideas were Eric's. It was his first major piece of writing with the band. This added a dimension, taking the heat off Godley and Creme who realised there was an entirely substantial second writing half to the group.

**'The Worst Band in the World'** (Lol Creme, Graham Gouldman)
Released as a single A-side, 11 January 1974 (UK), 1 April 1974(AU), b/w '18 Carat Man of Means'. UK: 51.

UK Records head, Jonathan King, visited Strawberry all the time. He'd only stay for five minutes usually, poking his head in the door enough to hear what the band were working on. On one particular day when 'The Worst Band in the World' was being made to sound as good as possible considering the suggested circumstances, King appeared, heard the first few bars and simply said, 'The next single'. And it was – *Sheet Music*'s first. It was also Creme and Gouldman's first and only-released writing collaboration.

King not only had an ear, but a nose, for hits. But his instinct was a tad off this time. He couldn't be on the money all the time, as much as it might've been his primary wish for it to be beneath him. It's possible the song title simply put people off. Clearly tongue-in-cheek, 'The Worst Band in the World' sounded serious enough to be ambiguous to an audience wanting to be confident of a song's intention. Surely any song's ultimate intention is to entertain, and if you have to think a bit along the way, so be it. But in this case, the public at large didn't see it that way. Often written off as a non-charter, the song, to be fair, wasn't even issued as a single in the USA. But in the UK it peaked at 51 – not too bad. It was 10cc's least popular UK single of the '70s, sharing that honour equally with 1977's 'People in Love'.

Lyrically, more money-shuffling was involved, this time as a slow rock commentary on the capitalistic record business. Colourful cultural references speckled the lyric, such as 'If Garbo played guitar with Valentino on the drums, Then we'd be nothing more than a bunch of Dharma bums'. The line suggests that if celebrities were in the band, it would be enough to generate sales regardless of their level of musical ability. In verse two the vocals are purposefully sung off-key on the words 'Tune up' as if to hammer home that point. The reference to beat author Jack Kerouac's influential 1958 novel, *The Dharma Bums,* supports the confession 'We've never done a day's work in our lives', followed by the justification of 'And our records sell in zillions'. That does appear to be the character's goal going by the lines 'Up yours, up mine, But up everybody's, that takes time, But we're working on it' and 'Buy me and you play me, Then my plastic turns to gold'. But the lyric's spotlight on the singles-buying public might've all been a bit much when of late they were used to throwing their cash at the likes of Golden Earring's chugging 'Radar Love' and Mike Batt's undeniably musical but positively safe and infant-focused 'Wombling Song'.

For all you completists out there, if you can find it, the single is collectable for containing two whole extra seconds of music at the end of the fade. It was also a slightly different mix with a cleaned-up lyric after the BBC banned the track. On their insistence, the incomplete line 'We're the worst band in the world and we don't give a…' was re-sung as 'We're the worst band in the world and we don't give up'. The less obvious 'Up yours, up mine, but up everybody's, that takes time' was changed to 'I'm yours, I'm mine, but everybody, that takes time'. Wisely, the line advising to leave the roadies in the van was left as is.

### 'Hotel' (Lol Creme, Kevin Godley)
It's what this lyric doesn't say that is the point. The natives have their eyes on the beautiful opposite side of the island. The idea is reflected in a set of descending chords beneath a sentimental and figuratively sympathetic melody. Meanwhile, the Western tycoons are on their way, and judging by their bust-or-rip attitude and the abrupt style change, this can only lead to one thing; havoc – most certainly when the natives focus their appetites on the visitors. It's social comment and anthropology with a whiff of ecology thrown in. Also, it acts as the first tropically-themed 10cc song – a style that would punctuate moments throughout their repertoire.

Another multi-section piece, the verse rhythm recalls Paul Simon's 1972 hit, 'Me and Julio Down By the Schoolyard', even melodically on the line 'We'll get a golden island in the sun made of coconut'. The band's influences were many and they dipped in and out of styles, genres, moods, modes and fads with consummate ease, as they pleased.

### 'Old Wild Men' (Lol Creme, Kevin Godley)
Godley and Creme's 'Yesterday'? Perhaps. This virtually acoustic number with its landscaped landmarks of autoharp, gizmo and synthesizer carried the air of a truly crafted classic, potent for being covered. It dated from the Hotlegs days, an initial demo being recorded after that project's demise. The

idea came as a personalised response to Simon & Garfunkel's 1968 *Bookends* album track, 'Old Friends'. That song's theme of two elderly men sitting on a park bench reflecting on their lives, was here developed into a discourse on musicians fallen into old-age disrepair.

The softly-focused song sat on one style without interruption, the lyric and melody seamlessly intertwined, giving a timeless lullaby atmosphere. Indeed the coda wound things up with Godley and Creme's invention, the gizmo, quoting 'Twinkle Twinkle Little Star' to end. Perfect.

## 'Clockwork Creep' (Lol Creme, Kevin Godley)

Godley and Creme strike! Five energetic and extravagant sections combine here, all occurring within 2m:47s which is even tighter than 'The Dean and I'. The lyric alone is worthy of the early 20$^{th}$ century European Dada avant-garde art movement. The rhythmically manic verses switch between a bomb with a bad self-image telling how he's about to blow up the jumbo jet he's on, and the jet itself declaring his desire to serve and how good he is at his job. The characters are delineated by Creme's clean vocal as the bomb and Godley's distorted voice as the jumbo jet.

The middle section is the voice of an all-knowing narrator building the drama for the listener, interrupted along the way by group vocals of passengers singing 'Oh, no you'll never get me up in one of these again, Cause what goes up must come down'. These vocal lines take on a Beach Boys-style – a hilarious touch further emphasising the possibility of crashing, this time into the water. This section was later edited onto the beginning of 'I'm Mandy Fly Me' as in-flight music covered in jet noise on the left side, tying in with that song's airline theme.

Further along, the second unique bridge section has the plane extolling its own virtues in a slice of theatre worthy of a Rodgers and Hammerstein musical – all in the middle of a pop song. Of course, it takes talent to do *that* well.

It also takes talent to make the dark political comment inherent in 'Clockwork Creep' while keeping the mood positive. Thank heavens for rhyme, onomatopoeia, trills, tangos and sound effects as aids to sneaking a serious topic through. The black comedy culminates in the bomb's clock ticking, making for a dizzying tension to end side one.

## 'Silly Love' (Lol Creme, Eric Stewart)

Released as a single A-side, 23 August 1974 (UK), 14 October 1974(AU), b/w 'The Sacro-Illiac'. UK: 24. BE: 20. NL: 7.
Released as a single B-side, 1974 (JP), b/w 'Johnny Don't Do It'.

An ascending chromatic run ushers in *Sheet Music*'s third single, sounding not unlike the introduction to 'Sand In My Face'. 'Toots' (Lol Creme's nickname for his wife Angie) is turning the male character's legs to water, and in the verses, he waxes lyrical about her. In the choruses, another character describes the behaviour as silly. This is expanded on by Eric in the bridge section, taking this otherwise rock song temporarily into left-field on another island getaway. In the last verse, the chorus characters take over, further expounding their distaste for the lead's decline into sincere romantic cliché. The lyric also acts as a commentary on the mediocre quality of many love songs of the time.

This all reads as quite complicated when in fact the song was as accessible as a 1974 hit could be without lapsing into banality. The lyric was in fact about the inherent compromise necessary when a love song is written by two or more people – typically intellectual for 10cc and there's nothing banal about that.

Recorded in May 1974, mere weeks before the album's release, 'Silly Love' could be construed as an effort to inject some glam wallop into an otherwise mostly mellow and esoteric collection. If so, it worked – a silly love song, two years before Paul McCartney publicly defended such.

### 'Somewhere In Hollywood' (Lol Creme, Kevin Godley)

Known as 'Hollywood Song' during its making, *Sheet Music*'s piece-de-resistance moved through some level of development before reaching its final configuration. In the line, 'A star with the stature of a Harlow', the name Harlow was originally going to be Monroe, but in a 1974 interview, Kevin Godley said the name Monroe was too trendy. He might've been referring to Elton John's then-current hit, 'Candle in the Wind', but songwriting technique would've played a part. The name Harlow falls in the music on strong and weak rhythmic accents as HARlow. For it to be MONroe wouldn't've scanned metrically and these songwriters knew that. It would've been instinctual, as opposed to sitting around analysing and dulling the spontaneity. Not to mention, the Monroe trend thing was probably a more interesting interview story for a press concerned with trivialities like 10cc's clothing.

Lyrically, the story unfolds from a visual perspective analogous to that of the Beatles' 1995 Joe Pytka-directed video for 'Free as a Bird', where an ever-expanding moving wide shot sees all aspects. The narrator knows all, predicting the newborn star's glorious but doomed future, and shows how she is being 'groomed to enrapture' everyone she encounters. This is spelt out through the eerie sonic effect of tap dancers, entering over the half-time drum rhythm. The directive 'Lights, action, sound' leads to a single bar of showtime stomp that moves like a Busby Berkeley choreography extravaganza but in slow motion. In fact, with the exception of the stomp substantially returning later as temporary guitar solo accompaniment, the entire track is a surreal liquid likeness of a subject that was significantly more lively and erratic in reality. It's as if we're in a darkroom watching a photograph develop, at first coming into focus, but receding in clarity, to be replaced by another and another.

I'm certain the line 'Norman Mailer wants to nail her' uses artistic license in a round-about way, referring metaphorically to the writer Mailer's real-life requirement to speak at length with a subject in order to inhabit their psyche. This was for the betterment of his practice known in the 1970s as new journalism.

The expanding zoom-out becomes stream-of-consciousness at the lines, 'He's armed and he's dangerously … Close was the weather'. With increasing abstraction, the narrator suddenly claims that the actress gave him 'A feather from her gown' when he was a kid. He suddenly reveals himself as an actor, claiming he was 'The galley slave who lost his heart when the ship went down.'. In a surprise singular move to the second person, the narrator addresses the actress directly with the line, 'I had a part in the talkies, When you were a little girl'. That's if it's the actress he's addressing. The lyric is cryptic enough that intention, perspective and relationship, are difficult to define. But that's the point. The words combine into a metaphorical mystery – a lyrical moving target you can barely line up conceptually or visually, let alone hit. The moment you think you've got it, it moves somewhere else, ill-defined, but always away. It first woos you in with promise before having its way with you, exactly as Hollywood's been known to do.

'Somewhere In Hollywood' was greater than the sum of its pieces and performances. It was the waking moment of 10cc's first real beast – tame in behaviour and placid in manner, outwardly beautiful but inwardly broken. If he could've talked to the animals, Norman Mailer would've had a field day.

### 'Baron Samedi' (Graham Gouldman, Eric Stewart)
Released as a single B-side, 1974 (ES), b/w 'The Wall Street Shuffle'.

Returning to the tropics, this time Haiti was the location. Baron Samedi is a voodoo spirit purported to be one of the intermediaries between the creator and man. His character is thought to be reckless with a particular fondness for drink, drugs and debauchery. Maybe he could've made a good rock star. 10cc themselves were work-focused and not overly- interested in the by-products of the rock and roll lifestyle. The recreational activities of a supernatural deity were always going to be more interesting lyric fodder.

> Take you up when you feeling down
> When you're sick he will come around
> Take his cures from out the ground
> He's the one who can hypnotise
> And you'll never believe your eyes
> He can cause the dead to rise

Heavy stuff maybe, but the musical atmosphere is not necessarily bleak. The spirit is presented in a manic drum-heavy five-section song that is more celebration than warning. With the exception of the beginning double-verse, it barely repeats itself. If a melody returns, it twists into something else as it unfolds.

The middle bridge section moves into pure early '70s pop mode in a glam rock styling. The third verse line, 'Make it with the living dead', holds the word 'dead' and the pitch is tape-sped up higher and higher to truly comic effect.

Giving semi-dark subject matter a light, even flippant, treatment, achieves the perfect balance. But a hint of potential danger remains as the song closes on a repeating darkly-diminished circular chord turnaround that finally lands on the home key.

### 'The Sacro-Illiac' (Kevin Godley, Graham Gouldman)
Released as a single B-side, 23 August 1974 (UK), 14 October 1974(AU), b/w 'Silly Love'.

Even in a less serious 10cc song like this, there would always be melodies to die for. 'Here's a new dance that you all can do, Baby baby what's he gonna do?'. The flat-five note gives that line its air of mystery, drawing the listener into what was the first-released Godley/Gouldman composition.

It was typical of 10cc to create contrast. The prior track, 'Baron Samedi', about a dark voodoo spirit, couldn't've been more different to this singalong invitation to learn a dance you can do sitting down if dancing's not your thing. It's called the Sacro-illiac because you're sitting on it when you do the dance, which is actually a non-dance.

More contrast came with Gouldman's only lead vocal on the album (Shared with Godley on the middle section), his vocal presence always lifting the mood. The song may not have been quite the A-material that would populate the next album, *The Original Soundtrack*, but its melody was finely crafted – that of 'You want to drown in your cocktail, You want to leave with the laundry', worth the price of admission alone. Plus you got a bonus free non-dance thrown in.

### 'Oh Effendi' (Kevin Godley, Eric Stewart)
Another 10cc first, this time for a Godley/Stewart composition. The fairly conventional rock and roll rhythm section carried the confessions of a middle-eastern gunrunner who detailed his extracurricular schemes. 'Look what I did for the pyramid, I put a pool in and made it pay'.

The middle section (predictably sub-divisible into three smaller sections) moved slightly off-track stylistically. But for the most part, the song stayed on course, sharing with 'The Sacro-illiac', the honour of being *Sheet Music*'s least adventurous production. The ending was unique and original in that it came after re-stating only the first line of the middle section – 'There's no more goodies in the pipeline'. But there were.

## Contemporary Tracks

### '18 Carat Man of Means' (Lol Creme, Kevin Godley, Graham Gouldman, Eric Stewart)

Released as a single B-side, 11 January 1974 (UK), 1 April 1974(AU), b/w 'The Worst Band in the World'.

The second-released track credited to all four band members was a straightforward rock song reflecting the struggling musician's lack of and desire for money. This it shared with the 'Johnny Don't Do It' B-side, '4% of Something'. With everything in its place and a couple of memorable hooks along the way, it was perfectly respectable B-side material.

**'Gismo My Way'** (Lol Crème, Kevin Godley, Graham Gouldman, Eric Stewart)
Released as a single B-side, 24 May 1974 (UK), August 1974 (US), 15 July 1974(AU), 7 June 1974 (NZ), b/w 'The Wall Street Shuffle'.

A waltz-time instrumental, taking a melodic cue from Engelbert Humperdinck's 1967 schmaltz smash, 'The Last Waltz'. The title name-checked the gizmo, but the guitar accessory had an understated role, supplying the silvery string-like background chords.

# The Original Soundtrack (1975)

UK Release date: 11 March 1975. US Release date: August 1975.
Personnel:
Lol Creme: Vocals, Autoharp, Gizmo, Guitars, Mandolin, Organ, Piano, Percussion, Synthesizer, Vibes, Violin
Kevin Godley: Vocals, Cello, Drums, Marimba, Percussion, Synthesizer, Timpani
Graham Gouldman: Vocals, Autoharp, Bass, Double Bass, Guitars, Mandolin, Percussion
Eric Stewart: Vocals, Guitars, Organ, Piano, Steel Guitar
Recorded November 1974 – February 1975 at Strawberry Studios, Stockport, UK
Producer: 10cc
Engineer: Eric Stewart
Chart placings: UK: 3, US: 15, CA: 5, NZ: 37

*The Original Soundtrack* was a soundtrack only to whatever went on within the confines of Strawberry Studios in the winter of 1974-1975. It represented another step up in terms of material depth. Again you got the feeling there was an album missing after the prior *Sheet Music*. 10cc released everything they recorded, but a lot more songs were written than ever made it to the recording stage. Lol Creme ran the interview gauntlet in 1975, telling NME, 'We spend four days writing a song and then we scrap it because all we've done is get the cobwebs out.'. He told *Melody Maker* that year, 'In our category, music becomes the controlling factor. We write music for the love of it. We're not writing specifically to get a top-five hit but we know the people who are. At the very best, those people are going to keep the level of music the same and God knows what'll happen at the very worst.'. Prophetic words indeed.

The record business was riding its crest in 1975, and though it would continue to do so for some time, the other side of the hill beckoned. Recording budgets and percentages would only shrink over time. Still struggling financially, 10cc now locked horns with Jonathan King over the 4% of something their UK Records contract tied them into. King refused to renegotiate. But other labels were interested now. One was Richard Branson's newly-minted Virgin Records who had distribution through Atlantic in the USA. That was almost a done deal, but with the band's Caribbean holiday scheduled, organising everyone to be present for signing was difficult. Management were given power of attorney to sign on 10cc's behalf. But they signed instead with Phonogram for release on Philips Records in the UK and Mercury Records in the USA, claiming it was a safer bet considering Virgin had only one hit under their belt – Mike Oldfield's *Tubular Bells*. Reaching Eric by phone at St Lucia customs, Branson expressed his fury, which was the first 10cc knew of the Phonogram signing. They were mortified, feeling the situation put them in a bad light as if they'd backed out of their all-but-signed Virgin agreement without a word. For some, it was a wound that would never completely heal.

At the time, Graham Gouldman felt that *Sheet Music* had been a bit busy, chopping and changing more than he might've liked. But things settled down for him with *The Original Soundtrack*. The first song attempted was the early bossa nova version of 'I'm Not In Love', which was scrapped. The tour de force, 'Une Nuit a Paris', was then successfully tackled, sparking some talk of a possible concept album which never caught fire. There's no denying the album was eclectic and adventurous, but it stopped tastefully short of blowing itself out of proportion. One way this was achieved was by tailing the hard-act-to-follow that was album-opener, 'Une Nuit a Paris', with the most commercially appealing track the band had ever recorded – 'I'm Not In Love'. Hot on its heels was the medium-tempo grit of 'Blackmail' taking side one out with a crowd-pleasing slide guitar solo. Side two moved through the potentially heavy topics of religion, crime and life experience in a pragmatic way. Then 'Life is a Minestrone' virtually poked fun at the music preceding it, the album ending on the pure self-deprecation of 'The Film of My Love'.

It was quite a journey, with enough light moments to take the heat off and allow for the one serious juncture that was 'Flying Junk'. But even *that* was spiced with wordplay and irresistible hooks. A substantial soundtrack indeed, with no visual required. The band even joked with one American magazine that the movie houses would have to shut down temporarily while hip listeners stayed home listening to 10cc's vinyl movie. With music this colourful, who needed images?

## 'Une Nuit a Paris' (Lol Creme, Kevin Godley)

Taking their families on vacation to Antibes in the south of France, Kevin and Lol hired a villa with a piano. They wished to experiment with a longer composition that developed on what they'd begun with 'Somewhere in Hollywood', while backing away from the Americana with a lyrical relocation.

Originally the song was around 25 minutes long. In 1975, Lol even alluded to it as a section from a musical he and Kevin had written. The tentative plan was for the song to occupy a full album side. But upon playing the magnum opus for Eric and Graham (an event Godley has jested he brought in camp stretchers for), their joint opinion was that the song was overly-lengthy, a bit boring, but undeniably brilliant. So all padding was cut and the piece honed down to a more manageable beast.

When recording commenced, it was with the intention that 'Une Nuit a Paris' would be a movie for the ears. They worked for two weeks, filling the track with every instrument they could think of, only to scrap the lot and move back to a simpler foundation of piano, bass and drums.

### Part 1: Une Nuit A Paris

Sounds of a Parisian street (created in Stockport) usher in 10cc's most expansive and theatrical composition of all. The initial mood is mellow but tense, piano chords commencing with the vocal. Lyrically, humour is to the fore. A tourist takes a room in Paris exclaiming, 'It isn't worth a centime. I'll take it!'. From there, temptation attempts to woo him in the form of the coquette offering her services, and the 'voices of the streets' declaring, 'One night in Paris is like a year in any other place' – the supporting main chorus theme now a slow but bawdy and brash cabaret.

## Part 2: The Same Night in Paris
An assortment of street hustlers accost the tourist in a surrealist montage. 'Is he gonna buy? Is he gonna pay? Or is he gonna fall in love the all-American way?'. Curiosity turns to accusation with 'You know you ain't no Casanova, You can't even do the bossa nova, Or the tango or a samba'. A bed of percussion created by Kevin Godley striking the bass strings of a Steinway piano with soft percussion beaters then turns temporarily to a samba. Becoming a slow rock groove, it twists up to double-time during Lol's repetitive piano vamp recalling parts of Paul and Linda McCartney's 1971 *Ram* album. Returning to the percussion, we then get another round of the main theme chorus, landing on a stopgap into part three.

## Part 3: Later the Same Night in Paris
In an intimate theatrical cabaret style, the coquette tells the tourist of a past club raid that occurred when the chief of police was 'Up in my boudoir with some other fella'. Suddenly the floor clears, and over a solo piano, Kevin Godley delivers perhaps his most achingly beautiful vocal of all for the pure pathos of the story climax.

> When the floor cleared
> A woman screamed to herself
> Henri, though you're not the toast of Paris
> I love you
> Although you bed and beat me
> Henri, leave it alone
> For the Gendarme's just doing his job

Earlier themes then return, developing into an urgent and increasingly chaotic noise choir chanting, 'Notre Dame is ringing her bells, Another Gendarme has gone to hell'. One more rousing statement of the main chorus follows, landing on the final line, 'This night in Paris may be your last', to fin.

From 10cc's point of view, 'Une Nuit a Paris' was a serious composition. Some critics viewed it as just more 10cc fun but longer, when in reality it was a macabre murder mini-opera that had required a mass of hard work to achieve.

The claim that 10cc's magnum opus directly influenced Queen's 'Bohemian Rhapsody' has never been confirmed. On Friday 28 December 1973, the two bands performed together at Liverpool's Top Rank Suite, where Graham Gouldman has since claimed they played 'Une Nuit a Paris'. That seems very early for the song's existence, being even before *Sheet Music* was recorded. Queen's Roger Taylor is also on record as believing Freddie Mercury never heard the 10cc song before writing 'Bohemian Rhapsody'. Even if he did, Mercury absorbed the influence well, his song barely showing a similarity in more than a general way. Whatever is the truth, 23 years ahead of time, Lol Creme definitely stated 'Une Nuit a Paris' to be 'Our tribute to George Gershwin in his centenary year.'.

**'I'm Not In love'** (Graham Gouldman, Eric Stewart)
Released as a single A-side, 23 May 1975 (UK), July 1975 (AU and NZ), b/w 'Good News'. UK: 1.US: 2.CA: 1.IE: 1. BE: 5. DE: 8.NL: 5. NO: 6. CH: 8. AU: 3. NZ: 4. ZA: 17.
Released as a single A-side, April 1975 (US), May 1975 (CA), b/w 'Channel Swimmer'. US: 2.CA: 1.
Released as a single A-side, 1975 (FR, IT and TR), b/w 'The Second Sitting for the Last Supper'. FR: 2.IT: 24.
Released as a single A-side, 1975 (ES and JP), b/w 'The Film of My Love'.
Released as a single A-side, 21 September 1979 (UK), b/w 'For You and I'.

After an early 1975 concert in Manchester, Lol Creme sat backstage with *New Musical Express* interviewer, Charles Shaar Murray, explaining the difficulties of love song collaboration.

> A love song can't be written by more than one person if it's honest. We write in twos. Therefore it's a compromise of two people's emotions. You can't write seriously about someone that you really love, with another person. So when two people get together, you have a laugh and a joke and you try to enjoy what you're doing. You take a humorous point of view and a humorous song develops.

You couldn't describe 10cc's breakthrough global hit as humourous, but it is certainly ironic. The lyric protests too much, and by the end, the lie is out. The initial inspiration came from Eric's wife Gloria. The two met at a Mindbenders gig at the Halifax Town Hall in 1964 and tied the knot in Bradford on Monday 7 March 1966. Gloria's father gave it two years. But he needn't have worried – rather than being the cliché rocker gallivanting and smashing up hotel rooms, Eric has claimed he was more likely to repair a broken shower rail or something if he saw it.

Jump to 1974 when Gloria commented to Eric that he never told her he loved her enough. His view was that if he said it too much, the phrase would become meaningless. Eric took inspiration from the event in taking on the challenge of writing a love song. Graham had the intro chords to which Eric added a verse and lyrics, Graham then filling in with the bridge section. The trick with the lyric was for Eric to say he wasn't in love, and integrate every reason that he was. The deceptively simple song was penned in three hours flat.

But the smooth classic's gestation was extended and anything *but* smooth. The first recording, made in late 1974, was a lightweight bossa nova with acoustic guitar. But the track wasn't sparking. Kevin Godley, especially, was not in love with it, recommending massive change if it was to come alive. The recording was scrapped and the song forgotten.

Work on other material ensued. But the smooth bossa and its haunting hook kept reappearing in the form of studio staff whistling it around the place and asking about its progress. In December, a second attempt was made, Godley coming up with a new rhythmic approach and suggesting the radical idea of orchestrating it entirely with the largest choir of voices you could imagine. Realising the need for some kind of rhythm to sing to, it was agreed to begin with a basic kick drum pattern, played by Kevin on a Moog synthesizer, and a guide electric piano track. But voices would provide the bulk of instrumentation.

With only the bare bones of kick drum and piano, the band already felt that something interesting was going on. Then the hard work began. The question was how to achieve the sheer amount of voices imagined. Lol had the brainwave of the band all singing 'Aaaah' together for every note of a chromatic scale, holding each note for as long as they could. Eric, of course, would engineer. This they would do sixteen times for each individual note. The tracks for one note would be mixed to a separate tape machine which was then looped so the note would play endlessly. That loop would be played and recorded back onto the master tape for the length of the song, and the process would begin again for the next note.

This was a typical example of the kind of time-consuming task 10cc had a habit of entangling themselves in. Someone might have a grand idea that required the use of 50 pianos or something, and no one would ever say no. They'd always try an idea in case it worked. They never knew what they were going to get. That kind of thing could interrupt the flow by taking a day or more in the middle of working on a song, but it was always worth it.
This particular operation took up a number of weeks. Eventually, they had all the scale notes laid out on the master tape, ready to be manipulated, or in fact played via moving volume faders up and down over the course of the song. The four sat at the mixing desk, running the tape until they got a good stereo mix of the choir. These days the multi-voice choir would be much quicker to achieve digitally, but professional singers that could hold all the notes in tune in the first place (which is not as easy as it sounds) would still be a fundamental requirement.

Eric's guide vocal, despite the band's intention to replace it, ended up being a keeper. But there were still ingredients to add. The surreal central instrumental piano melody break replaced a conventional bridge that had brought the song down too much. The lyrics there were to be, 'Don't feel let down, Don't get hung up, We do what we can, We do what we must'. The idea of singing lines there was dumped after it was discovered that the master tape had captured Lol randomly speaking the words 'Big boys don't cry' into a drum mic. But they needed the right voice to speak the words. Enter studio receptionist Kathy Redfern, quietly informing Eric of a phone call, and Lol exclaimed 'That's the voice!'. Kathy scarpered back to reception with Lol in close pursuit intent on talking her into it, which he did. After the final touch of a toy music box playing over the surreal section and ending, the recording was complete.

In the process of mixing, a final sonic masterstroke was added, when every single choir note was left running at a low volume, bubbling and simmering endlessly throughout the song. A snatch of this can be heard at the beginning of the album version for three seconds before the piano enters. Who else would do that?

Ensconced in the recording process, 10cc didn't contemplate the song's single potential. But they knew they had something. The recording stopped them in their tracks. It demanded re-listens for pleasure's sake, to which they happily obliged. The night it was finished, they celebrated their achievement by going out for a curry.

*The Original Soundtrack* was initially sold to Phonogram on the strength of 'I'm Not In Love' alone, but it was decided to hold back the knockout and issue 'Life is a Minestrone' as the lead UK single to give a longer album promotion cycle. The support of ex-The Move and Electric Light Orchestra member, Roy Wood, played a part in the eventual decision to release 'I'm Not In Love' as a single. Eric received the following telegram from him after *The Original Soundtrack* came out.

> You've got to release that song. It's an effing number one um, thank God you guys are around. British music is saved.

In America, Mercury Records insisted on editing the single for radio. They were struggling and took no chances. Rather than them saving 10cc in America, it ended up the other way around when the hit came through.

The song's *Top of the Pops* performance in the UK was mimed to the full length version, the film nevertheless edited after the fact. Though cut in a different spot, it somewhat matched the single length and form, leaving Eric's provocative last-verse raising of the eyebrows at a mystery audience member (probably Gloria) discarded to the cutting room floor.

The huge global hit ultimately received three Ivor Novello awards in 1976 for Most Performed British Work, Best Pop Song and International Hit of the Year. The advanced vocal technique was an ongoing influence on other musicians' work, most notably that of American singer/songwriter, Billy Joel, on his 1977 standard, 'Just the Way You Are', which utilised a similar-sounding, though smaller, bed of voices weaving its way around the recording. But 10cc went to great lengths to keep their process a secret, not revealing it to anyone outside the studio for three years.

'I'm Not In Love' is the song that 10cc are most known for by the vast majority of the public, and yet it represents only one facet of what they did. They were never held back by the so-called need to be formulaic or homogenous, and they never offered the public anything less than their very best work. That wasn't possible due to the commandment they hung symbolically over their work ethic and literally on the studio wall; 'In the pursuit of perfection there is no compromise'.

**'Blackmail'** (Graham Gouldman, Eric Stewart)
Like 'Headline Hustler' before it, 'Blackmail', or 'Behind the Keyhole' as it was originally known, implicated the gutter press in skullduggery and wrongdoings. Inspired by a contemporary scandal, the lyric sees a photographer confessing to sending a high-profile woman naked pictures he took of her through a keyhole. In a letter made from 'Different type from different lines', he threatens to send the pictures to the press.

The act seems particularly malicious as the photographer, aware of her penchant for indiscretion, appears to have no axe to grind or any personal stake in the matter. He's staked her out beforehand. 'But every time she's going down, She never looks around'. It's an act of sheer greed. 'Ooo it'll be so scandalous for the both of them, But mainly her'. The blackmail attempt backfires when she shows the pictures to her husband, who loves them, and sells her to Hugh Hefner, turning her into a *Playboy* centrefold and superstar. The plot is a near-repeat of the one used for the 1971 single, 'Lazy Sadie'.

Aspects of the musical arrangement cleverly reflected the situation. The brisk walking-speed tempo was smug, confident and sure of itself. Predominantly group vocals, some lines were sung in octaves or unison, but no voice was ever left solo, as if to stay in disguise as much as possible. The 'I'm Not In Love' vocal loops were used again, pitched an octave down to comic and practically demonstrative effect throughout the song, particularly in the penultimate verse as accented pairs of sixteenth-notes stood in for x-rated details of specific shots. But Eric Stewart's closing manic slide guitar solo betrayed earlier confidence, mirroring the chaos of the situation.

Sounding more like a Godley and Creme exposè, Gouldman and Stewart's 'Blackmail' testified to the group's objective ability to absorb each other's ideas for the sake of musical democracy leading to the best possible outcome.

**'The Second Sitting for the Last Supper'** (Lol Creme, Kevin Godley, Graham Gouldman, Eric Stewart)
Released as a single B-side, 1975 (FR, IT and TR), b/w 'I'm Not In Love'.

Eric and Graham took this initial idea to the others for help finishing it. With Godley and Creme's input, the message became clearer and the tempo was increased, providing more vitality.

The lyric, an agnostic take on the return of Jesus Christ, was positive and open to the idea. Simultaneously it acknowledged the downward slide of humanity and the phony gurus taking advantage of the situation. The repeated lyric line, 'We think you'd better come down', emphasised the need for a solution, showing just how alone we really are.

Explaining to *New Musical Express* in 1975, Lol Creme saw it as a positive song.

> Three of us are Jewish. But I think that the idea of Jesus Christ is such a fabulous idea. So we said it in a song. I can't get off on the idea of acid, alright? 'A trip from the fifteenth floor' is liable to be a fatal one, so I think that's a fairly positive thing to say. I think there's a lot of money made out of so-called religion – which I think is a positive statement. We're saying that we think it'd be fantastic if a messiah came down and gave us some direction – if that messiah was the kind of Jesus Christ that everybody loves. We said that very positively.

Forward-thinking in its musical arrangement, the song's manic proto-punk attack was combined with all that the coming punk transformation would rail against. The verses were formal pop, the choruses virtually Latin-jazz, and the finale pure and virtuous rock and roll of the sort the advancing punks would accuse of being past its use-by date.

Being 10cc, there would always be the harmonious and the unpredictable. The breakdown chorus and its soaring melody were as memorable and hook-laden as anything they ever recorded.

> The second coming of the holy ghost
> We need a pocketful of miracles
> Two thousand years and he ain't shown yet
> We've kept his seat warm and the table set

Mysteriously, the chorus' first half was skipped the second time around, which was disappointing considering the section was of such a high calibre. But that was just another 10cc trick – to leave you wanting more.

### 'Brand New Day' (Lol Creme, Kevin Godley)

The idea for 'Brand New Day' was in Creme's head all through his wife Angie's pregnancy. Kevin eventually helped with the song. In Lol's words, 'It developed strange. But still a lullaby to my baby, Lalo, to tell him to watch his ass.'

The outcome was easily the next most complex composition on the album after 'Une Nuit a Paris', and certainly the most intellectual. In a semi-stream of consciousness, the lyric reflected on the daily grind of what it is to be human.

> For birds of prey
> You live and learn your life away

But there below your body must go
Against the grain
Like an old mule train
Keeps pulling hard against the
Here boy there boy
The boss got you running everywhere boy

Minus drums except for five bars of kick drum in the second bridge, rhythmic interest was maintained through piano, bass and synthesizer bass accents, percussion and a variety of gizmo, echo and wah-wah effects – and I'd put money on the ending percussion effects influencing the similar cacophony of sound that ends Kate Bush's 1980 single, 'Babooshka'.

### 'Flying Junk' (Graham Gouldman, Eric Stewart)

Graham and Eric told the others that 'Flying Junk' was about antiques, but they were not believed. Graham later said they wanted to write about drugs and shady characters in an ambiguous way, though they didn't stop short of name-checking the once-famous '60s and '70s Kings Road rock star roost, The Chelsea Potter.

From the beginning, the track disorientates with its spinning layers of autoharp. The lead vocal constantly precedes itself through the use of advance echo – a technique achieved in 1975 by turning the master tape over and recording an echo delay on the now backwards-running voice. Turn the tape back over and you hear the voice echoes coming before the voice itself. The sly razzmatazz devil salesman character is pulling one over everyone he deals with, the reverse echo ironically suggesting that you should be able to see him coming. Woe is you if you don't.

The salesman was slick, and so was the slow rock groove. Some drama was built-in through Graham's recurring James-Bond-styled guitar line. If a Hank Marvin mood was required, Graham was your man – he had the Fender Strats and Eric had the Gibsons. But according to Lol in 1975, it was the addition of the zither that brought the track to life and gave it colour. (He was in fact referring to the autoharp, which he actually played along with Graham.)

The overall colour here was of a dark shade indeed – the darkest yet from 10cc. Where they sometimes lightened up a dark subject with humour or an energetic rhythm, here the tone was kept consistent throughout. There was no denying the deliberate turn taken with 'Flying Junk' and the ability it shared with its dangerous protagonist, to sweeten you up with a bitter pill.

### 'Life is a Minestrone' (Lol Creme, Eric Stewart)

Released as a single A-side, 28 March 1975 (UK), May 1975 (AU and NZ), b/w 'Channel Swimmer'. UK: 7. IE: 7. BE: 15. NL: 12. AU: 48.
Released as a single A-side, August 1976 (US and CA), b/w 'Lazy Ways'. US: 104.
Released as a single B-side, 1978 (JP), b/w 'Channel Swimmer'.

Driving home with Eric one night, flipping through radio stations, Lol caught what sounded like someone saying 'Life is a minestrone'. The phrase presented the perfect opportunity to write something lighthearted. Lol even joked with the press about originally wanting to record it in an Italian restaurant. The subsequent low-pressure recording in January 1975, in-situ at Strawberry, must've been a welcome relief after the intensity of 'Une Nuit a Paris' and the technical concentration of 'I'm Not In Love'. Graham Gouldman has since confirmed 'Minestrone' as being great fun to record because the chorus was so gloriously happy. Like 'Brand New Day' before it, the words touched on life and death but mixed them into a goulash of food similes and random wordplay.

> Minnie Mouse has got it all sewn up
> She gets more fan mail than the Pope
> She takes the mickey out of all my phobias
> Like signing cheques to ward off double pneumonia
>
> Life is a minestrone
> Served up with Parmesan cheese
> Death is a cold lasagna
> Suspended in deep freeze

It's obviously total lunacy that demands nothing of the listener. But the real depth is below the topsoil, existing in the minutia of notes and chords. This deserves a quick rabbit-hole-dive, in the hopes of clarifying virtues lost on those who wrote the song off as nothing more than nonsense.

The track balances between two distinct rhythmic feels, from verse (triplet shuffle) to chorus (straight four). The post-chorus instrumental is actually a traditional I-IV-I-V-IV rock and roll chord progression but ingeniously rendered. It feels like the expected final two chords of that well-heeled pattern are skipped in favour of the hard cut to the two isolated intro guitar/piano chords that first appeared ushering in verse one. Due to the mix change and absence of bass and drums on those chords, you don't really notice that they are in fact the two expected closing chords of the traditional pattern. But because we heard them isolated the first time, this second time we're conditioned to accept them as an interruption to flow, the radical mix change throwing us off the scent – not to mention the verse entering a full minor third higher than the traditional progression might suggest as a logical landing point. That makes the complete one-time appearance of the rock and roll progression almost like a joke for the hell of it. When that progression repeats at 2m:46s, the two closing chords are completely omitted, cutting back to the chorus. It's like a 4m:45s art-house movie for audio.

But who needs stuffy Roman chord names? Anyone that's heard a thousand rock and roll or blues songs (and let's face it, who hasn't?) will be able to feel the logic of the traditional progression taking place but being subverted. These guys were just playing with music. They could do anything they wanted, and they did.

'Life is a Minestrone' had such a refreshing lack of pretension as to make other parts of the album seem almost pretentious. 10cc were having a laugh through self-deprecation, but even that wasn't purposeful. The song had depth when experienced within the context of *The Original Soundtrack*. It was as serious in approach as the serious songs were playful in their candour – 'Flying Junk' notwithstanding. But did anyone notice? The clearly finicky purveyors of one contemporary Australian bootleg certainly gave the lyrics not one thought when printing the song title as 'Life is a Milestone'.

**'The Film of My Love'** (Lol Creme, Kevin Godley)
Released as a single B-side, 1975 (ES and JP), b/w 'I'm Not In Love'.

This could well be the funniest song in the entire repertoire of 10cc and Godley & Creme. The romantic hero proudly predicts how 'The film of my love will travel the world, Will travel the whole world over'. We are left in the dark as to the quality or indeed the hue of the film. The lyric brims with glorious movie-making metaphors as an allegory for romance and the performance is a total cabaret send-up. The below stanza says it all.

> A close-up of yours
> A long shot of mine
> Superimposed together
> I'll zoom in on you
> With a love that is true
> In Cinemascope forever

Our hero is so enthralled with the romantic, moving picture that he even anticipates the British Pathe movie preservationists eventually recalling 'The thrill of it all'.

But the genius layer here is the songwriting. 'The Film of My Love' is apparently the offspring of someone who doesn't quite know what they're doing, and that's the entire point. The evidence for it is everywhere, from the lack of economy in the lines 'Co-starring you and co-starring me, Starring us both together', to the repetition of 'Over and over and over, Over and over and over again, Over and over and over'. Overdone lines like that and 'Forever and ever and ever', suggest a novice writer unskilled at filling the gaps, or in fact unnecessarily over-filling them. The irony, full to the brim and spilling over the edges, is that Godley and Creme left those gaps inadequately unfilled (or filled) with consummate skill.

This was all supported by the cheesiest Bontempi toy drum pattern you could imagine, set to a mandolin-choked waltz resembling Engelbert

Humperdinck's 'The Last Waltz'. The song even ended on a stressed three-accent cliché, intended to work better in 4/4 time, forced illogically into place as if that's the only way to end a song like this (and it probably is). This left the joke still well and truly on the hypothetical novice songwriter.

Lol Creme stated in the press that the song was a joke targeting one particular singer whose name he refused to divulge. But the critics didn't get it.

> Every single verbal and musical cliché about movies.
> Charles Shaar Murray, *New Musical Express*

> The only thoroughly dull track they've ever put on an album.
> Phil Sutcliffe, *Sounds*

> Leave it to 10cc to close an album with a piece of warped romantic schmaltz.
> Michael Gross, *Circus Raves*

The song's audibly evident joke at the expense of schmaltzy songwriters everywhere, was lost on the critics. They would've needed to be songwriters themselves to get it (which Charles Shaar Murray *was*), and honestly self-evaluating open-minded ones at that.

When the time came for 10cc to discuss who would sing 'The Film of My Love', their in-house evaluation spoke for itself as the room emptied out. Graham volunteered.

## Contemporary Tracks

### 'Channel Swimmer' (Kevin Godley, Graham Gouldman)
Released as a single B-side, 28 March 1975 (UK), May 1975 (AU and NZ), b/w 'Life is a Minestrone'.
Released as a single B-side, April 1975 (US), May 1975 (CA), b/w 'I'm Not In Love'.
Released as a single A-side, 1978 (JP), b/w 'Life is a Minestrone'.

A conventional, almost '60s-sounding acoustic guitar-based pop approach, in an ABABA form. The A section (presumably Gouldman's) contains the title. The more elaborate B section (presumably Godley's) can be broken down into several sub-sections.

Lyrically, the character is swimming across the ocean to take his love, only to fail. Each chorus ends with the lines, 'Who'd be a channel swimmer, Only a fool like me'. But the song ends on a gag; 'Who'd be a channel swimmer, Only a fool like me… would forget he can't swim'.

There are melodic charms, but the track comes off as recorded quickly, perhaps purposefully to fill the B-side space. But it was regarded highly enough to be re-released as an A-side in Japan in 1978, with the original A-side 'Life is a Minestrone' flipped to the B-side. This qualified 'Channel Swimmer' for inclusion on the Japan-only 10cc compilations, *The Songs We Do For Love* (1978), and *Tropical & Love* (1979).

**'Good News'** (Lol Creme, Kevin Godley)
Released as a single B-side, 23 May 1975 (UK and EU), July 1975 (AU and NZ), b/w 'I'm Not In Love'.

Beginning as a keyboard-dominated love ballad, this B-side is soon revealed to be a medley of two seemingly disparate song pieces, stitched together in true McCartney fashion. The ballad barely gets off the ground before taking a left turn to an acoustic guitar-based island rhythm for the bulk of the track, which is a repeating hook of 'All I need is some good news, To put me at my ease'. It is A-grade B-side material but likely pipped by 'Channel Swimmer' in the staying afloat stakes.

# How Dare You! (1976)

UK Release date: January 1976. US Release date: January 1976.
Personnel:
Lol Creme: Vocals, Guitars, Keyboards, Percussion, Gizmo, Vibraphone, Recorder
Kevin Godley: Vocals, Drums, Percussion, Castanets
Graham Gouldman: Vocals, Bass, Double bass, Guitars, Steel guitar, Dobro, Zither, Glockenspiel, Percussion
Eric Stewart: Vocals, Guitars, Keyboards, Bass, Steel guitar, Whistle
Mair Jones: Harp
Recorded July – October 1975 at Strawberry Studios, Stockport, UK
Producer: 10cc
Engineer: Eric Stewart
Chart placings: UK: 5, US: 47, CA: 5, NZ: 1, NL: 7, FI: 26, NO: 10, SE: 5

High spirits characterised the making of the first 10cc album to enter the US Top 50. Eric Stewart's acquisition of a book titled *How Dare You*, which showed practical ways to respond to insults, was the source of much mirth in dealing with any negative criticism of each other's ideas. Most responses began with the three-word phrase, which was used at any given opportunity. The phrase can be heard quietly uttered by a female voice on the left side of the stereo image just before the first guitar line of the title track.

But along with this, and for the first time, discontent crept in. A previously nonexistent formulaic approach to material selection disgruntled Kevin Godley. Eric Stewart was frustrated by the lyrical brashness of songs like 'I Wanna Rule the World' and 'Iceberg'. Graham Gouldman has since recalled there being some doubt, even self-doubt, concerning song quality. But the first concrete sign of discouragement came in October 1975 towards the end of the sessions, when with 'I'm Mandy Fly Me' in progress, Lol Creme made the offhand remark to Graham; 'I don't think this is what I want to be doing.'. Making matters worse, the pressure to make their best album yet, in order to take advantage of the leverage 'I'm Not In Love' provided in the American market, was an over-riding factor.

It was becoming more and more about business. Eric was concerned about falling into the rut of having to deliver a hit single every few months. As it was, 10cc weren't convinced they had a potential hit living *any*where on *How Dare You!* – the success of first single 'Art For Art's Sake' coming as quite a surprise. Eric wished they could just go away for a couple of years to make an album, without the need for a hit production line. Ironically, as co-author of the gigantic commercial success that was 'I'm Not In Love', he thought the band should be doing more adventurous work along the lines of 'Une Nuit a Paris'. He sensed they were no longer the carefree group of four they'd once been, and he had an underlying feeling that something was wrong.

One something that contributed to (but wasn't necessarily the catalyst for) things going wrong, was the Gizmo. In a positive way, it distracted Godley and Creme. During the making of *How Dare You!*, the pair were already recording experiments that would find their way into their debut album, *Consequences*. Those initial experiments were so satisfying that in the end it simply came down to continuing with 10cc – an extremely pleasurable and successful project that they felt had peaked – or moving on to fresh pastures to develop the Gizmo to its full potential. It sounds simple, but the reality was more complicated. In the meantime, there were two more hit singles and 10cc's most successful American album release yet, to deal with.

**'How Dare You'** (Lol Creme, Kevin Godley)
Released as a single B-side, 12 March 1976 (UK), March (US), April 1976 (AU and NZ), b/w 'I'm Mandy Fly Me'.
Released as a single B-side, June 1976 (FR), b/w 'Lazy Ways'.

Written a few years earlier, the instrumental title track developed from the indigenous-sounding rhythm base. But the appealing, clean slide guitar octaves and well-intended multiple guitar harmonies struggled to imbue enough life, the entire piece crying out to have a song around it. Never adequately developed, 'How Dare You' seemed like a backward step – a 10cc rarity – and its prime position as album-opener was a surprise.
There is the question of whether it was album-worthy at all. Perhaps the B-side would've been it's ideal home. 'I'm Mandy Fly Me' would've made a dynamic alternative opener indeed, which would've rendered its beginning audio snatch of 'Clockwork Creep' and its lyric 'Oh, no you'll never get me up in one of these again' as an appropriate slice of 10cc self-deprecation to open the album on a high note.

The arbitrary crossfade connection to the following 'Lazy Ways' appeared to be based on tempo alone, amounting to little more than a non-complimentary auditory clash, compounding the situation. Although, 'Lazy Ways' itself was prime 10cc real estate, and once it lured you inside, 'How Dare You' was all but forgotten.

The album as a whole might've worked better by keeping the 'How Dare You' opening and swapping out 'Head Room' for the 'Art For Art's Sake' B-side, 'Get It While You Can', despite the incongruous vibe such placement could've given that song.

**'Lazy Ways'** (Lol Creme, Eric Stewart)
Released as a single B-side, August 1976 (US and CA), b/w 'Life is a Minestrone'.
Released as a single A-side, June 1976 (FR), b/w 'How Dare You'.

The track that brings *How Dare You!* to life could well be Eric Stewart and Lol Creme's finest collaboration if we consider the thread that runs to it through '4% of Something', 'Silly Love' and 'Life is a Minestrone'. What surprises might've surfaced had the pair continued with this development?

Deceptively simple and certainly accessible, 'Lazy Ways' actually has six discrete sections – seven if you count the last chord in a new key with the title sung in a different chord degree than before, technically making it a minuscule coda. As was often the case with 10cc, repeat sections would be developed and lengthened. For example, notice the difference between the first and second 'You'll never get up' section. The second one has new lyrics – 'Where nobody cares and nobody tries, Cause a daydream's resting on the back of your eyes', followed by four bars of as yet unheard chordal material.

The instrumentation is rich, but judicious arrangement stops it from ever sounding over-worked. Eric sings, plays bass and provides lead guitar, including the clear nod to Led Zeppelin's 'Whole Lotta Love' guitar lick (which came via Jimi Hendrix' rendition of 'Hey Joe') occurring first at 2m:17s. But not before the descending and ascending five-chord hook later made famous by Andrew Lloyd Webber as the *The Phantom of the Opera* church organ motif that everyone knows. To be fair, Webber messed with the chord thirds, but it didn't stop hardcore 10cc fans from recognising it.

Lol Creme's contribution was substantial, encompassing the typically McCartney-esque vamping piano style Lol employed on 'Une Nuit a Paris', backing vocals, clavinet and the particularly effective and percussive Moog synthesizer part enhanced with analogue delay. But the pièce-de-résistance must be Creme's most expansive demonstration yet of the Gizmo's deeply rich atmospheric drones. A beautiful example occurs at 0m:35s for eight seconds leading into the B-section. At that point, the line 'You'll never get up if you don't get up' brings a rhythm section swap from normal 4/4 time to half-time and back again at verse two for the words 'Hazy days' – another McCartney device if there ever was one.

The recurring verse chords of G and C increasingly reflect the laziness theme, the bass often staying on the G, as if too lazy to make the effort up to C. In verse one the two chords are four bars apart. In the B-section at 'You'll never get up', they are only two bars apart, reflecting the encouragement to stop sitting around. In verse two the advice has been taken and the two chords remain only two bars apart. Section six at 2m:28s sees a lapse into recreation with the chords four bars apart again, compounded by the half-time making it the laziest section. It might all seem a bit complex, but it just goes to show how conceptual ideas can reflect in ways other than lyrics.

Some attention should go to the crossfade that brings 'Lazy Days' in from the opening track, 'How Dare You'. There has always been an issue with how it was ID'ed for compact disc (and now digital streaming) where the first forty introductory seconds of 'Lazy Ways' was kept on the end of the former track. If you want to hear 'Lazy Ways' in isolation, it would be considerably more satisfying with introduction intact instead of entering at the vocal. But this audio bugbear has never been rectified. To at least ID the move to 'Lazy Ways' back at 3m:35s would fix this problem. I'd guess it came about through carelessness at the '80s mastering session for the first compact disc edition, where someone clearly mistook the long resting chord that ends the 'Lazy Ways' intro for being the end of the prior track. I'd also guess that not one member of 10cc was present at that mastering session.

The first CD editions of many pre-existing albums were untouched digital copies of the original two-track masters. Even though these were technically remasters, that was merely to allow for the move from the old format to the new. Even subsequent remasters of *How Dare You!*, the compilation *I'm Not In Love: The Essential 10cc* and the *Tenology* box set, retain the 'Lazy Ways' entry at the vocal. Maybe one day we'll hear a version of 'Lazy Ways' with intro intact minus the fade-out of 'How Dare You' smudged over the beginning. This wouldn't even require a remix if the original two-track tape of 'Lazy Ways' used in the first place was available.

**'I Wanna Rule the World'** (Lol Creme, Kevin Godley, Graham Gouldman)
A military-sounding march beneath a sinister, Orwellian vocal chant, ushers in the first released Godley/Creme/Gouldman song since 'Sand In My Face'.

> I wanna be a boss
> I wanna be a big boss
> I wanna boss the world around
> I wanna be the biggest boss that ever bossed the world around

10cc at their most lyrically adventurous, it is the shocking and aggressive expose of a deranged and idealistic individual with a Napoleon complex, whose unrealistic campaign grows increasingly insane. The song acts like a central link reaching back to 'Sand In My Face' and forward to 'Punchbag' from Godley & Creme's 1978 album, *L*. The three songs share themes of harassment and control.

This dark subject matter headed in a direction Eric Stewart for one had his doubts about. Graham Gouldman had no such qualms, the significant central rant being his idea. Lol Creme screamed the fascist-styled speech.

> A brave new world will rise from the ashes
> And thereupon a rock titanic
> I'll cast a giant shadow on the face of the deep
> And never again will they dare to call me
> A freckled, spotty, specky, four-eyed, weedy, little creep

There were no holds barred with this composition. In its four short minutes and six eclectic sections, its melodies constantly developed. It was as formally complex as the lengthy 'Une Nuit a Paris' from *The Original Soundtrack*. Even the recurring rhythmically straight and rigid vocal chant fought against the more relaxed triplet snare drum march beneath it.

It was all the kind of micro-development and attention to detail that represented 10cc's goal of doing something to circumvent pop music's complete freefall into the dumpster. These efforts, and those of others, served pop music well and helped those that cared cling to some semblance of substance for a time. The disco craze didn't help (at least in the songwriting) and neither did the punk revolution in some ways, although its fallout was particularly inventive. But the second punk revolution, known as the internet, rendered pop invention virtually as extinct as the dodo. Therefore, in hindsight, 'I Wanna Rule the World' stands as a pure example of what was once possible when practitioners with little left to prove worked on narrowing the gap between those two once inseparable concepts, pop and music.

**'I'm Mandy Fly Me'** (Kevin Godley, Graham Gouldman, Eric Stewart)
Released as a single A-side, 12 March 1976 (UK), March (US), April 1976 (AU and NZ), b/w 'How Dare You'. UK: 6. US: 60. IE: 3. NL: 50. AU: 62. NZ: 25.

Eric Stewart has spoken of the original inspiration for the second *How Dare You!* single as occurring in either Manchester or London. Over time the location probably paled into insignificance compared to the vivid image projected when he noticed a tramp on the pavement gazing up at an American Airlines poster with its inviting and even slightly suggestive slogan, 'I'm Cheryl, Fly Me!'.

The American Airlines 'Fly Me' campaign launched in 1971 and caused a bit of a stir, compelling the USA's National Organization for Women to attempt a legal injunction against the ads. They accused American Airlines of lacing their advertising with subtle sexual provocation towards the goal of financial benefit at the moral expense of women everywhere. The injunction failed. Business boomed for the airline and rather than tone down their ads, they ramped them up. But Eric's 'Cheryl' poster image was completely benign and virtuous compared to that of the saucier 'I'm Jo, Fly Me!', and indeed the poignantly chaste brainstorming that gave rise to the ultimate tagline, 'I'm Going To Fly You, like You've Never Been Flown Before!'.

But back to the pavement, the ragged tramp gazing up at the poster and Eric observing this. He was struck by the tragic irony that the tramp would most likely never set foot on an aeroplane, let alone take advantage of whatever benefits the poster offered. From Eric's vantage point, the potential song fodder was obvious.

Back at Strawberry, he threw the 'I'm Mandy Fly Me' idea out to all potential collaborators and Graham bit. He had some chords which he brought to Eric's idea, with the name Mandy chosen simply because it was more singable than Cheryl. But feeling the song was going nowhere fast, they scrapped it. Enter Kevin Godley who suggested that the mellow and floaty piece was a bit bland and stayed on one plane too much (no pun intended). It had it's moments, like the sung title hook clearly designed to simulate a possible jingle. But Kevin felt the song needed a bash around the head, so they added an instrumental section, changing the rhythm completely. In the recording, Graham's urgent acoustic guitars dominated that section, Lol and Eric adding a guitar solo each. Kevin added inspired lyrics, giving heart to the later intro chord pattern repetition; 'The world was spinning like a ball, And then it wasn't there at all, And as my heart began to fall'. This all turned the track around.

The lyric, a surreal dream sequence, has an observer transported inside the poster, boarding the airliner to be waited on hand and foot. Verse two alludes to the advertising innuendo with the character referring to himself as hiding in the small print, inviting Mandy to come fly *him*. Suddenly he sees her walking on the water, where she gives him the kiss of life. He is pulled from the wreckage, but she is not to be found. Then the dream is broken and he wakes up on the street.

Adding an audio segment from the *Sheet Music* track 'Clockwork Creep' onto the introduction was an inspired idea. It set the scene, placing the listener as a passenger hearing the pre-flight canned music over the jet engine noise. If you listen to the right side only, you can hear Godley yell and count the band in (though the audio edit there brought the band in earlier than the count suggested). This is audible only on later editions of the album, suggesting an alternative, contemporary mix was used.

In 1976, Graham stated that 'I'm Mandy Fly Me' was almost his and Eric's way of writing a Kevin and Lol song. They wrote songs in bits and pieces before Graham and Eric ever did. By bringing Kevin into the writing, 'I'm Mandy Fly Me' stood as the only Gouldman/Stewart/Godley song ever released by 10cc. Though oddly, the original vinyl credited Lol Creme as the third writer. Either way, the track was one final development in the multi-writing partnership, and was, by default, the sound of the original 10cc coming to an end. But what a finish.

## 'Iceberg' (Kevin Godley, Graham Gouldman)

Asked by an interviewer in 1976 if he knew what the people on the cover of *How Dare You!* were saying to each other, Lol Creme said yes but revealed no possible contents of the hypothetical telephone conversations. Chances are they might've had something to do with the bleak hot-club jazz fairground waltz that was 'Iceberg'.

Kevin Godley freely admitted in advance to Graham Gouldman that he wished to mess with his mind in forming this showstopper – and stop the show it almost *did* in its original lyrical form. Eric Stewart was most concerned with the content, which Graham later described as 'Dreadfully pornographic and horrible.'. But churned through the 10cc filter, the language was given a lighter shade of black, and a rhythmic jazz frolic enhanced the overall mood. But it still came out sounding happier than Kevin would've preferred.

Considering the song's accessible 3m:40s length, it nevertheless comprises ten sections – adventurous even by 10cc standards. The first seven happen consecutively without any repeats until the chorus comes back after the instrumental. Then there are still two new sections to come, not including a two-bar link to the outro.

Weaving in and out of this rhythmically happy-go-lucky affair are darker surreal segments. The dreamlike introduction creates a whirling carousel effect around the vocal chanting 'Life is a rollercoaster that we all ride'. Even more powerful is the central 'Lie lie lie' section – a darkly beautiful portent of future black diamonds Godley & Creme would chisel from their repertory coalface. In these 24 short measures, you can hear the possible basis for a multitude of bleak and eccentric early-'80s atmospheres wrought by acts like Siouxsie and the Banshees and XTC.

But as could be expected from 10cc, things never stayed dark for long. Even the ominous 'Iceberg' was lightened at one point by the isolated slapstick sound effect of Eric's Levis zip, though in a contemporary interview he gave Kevin the credit.

## 'Art For Art's Sake' (Graham Gouldman, Eric Stewart)
Released as a single A-side, 21 November 1975 (UK),15 November 1975 (US),January 1976(AU), February 1976 (NZ), b/w 'Get It While You Can'. UK: 5.US: 83. CA: 69. IE: 4.AU: 61.NZ: 6.

Graham Gouldman's father Hymie had been a songwriting influence as far back as 1966 when he'd written the opening lines to Graham's song title, 'Bus Stop'. 'Bus stop, Wet day, She's there I say, Please share my umbrella'. Hymie, or 'Hyme the Rhyme' as Kevin called him, used to advise 'Art for art's sake, money for god's sake.'. It was that phrase that Graham and Eric started with when sitting down to write in the music room at Eric's home at Disley near Stockport in 1975. The lyric was a criticism of certain songwriters who chased money, manufactured music like a production line and churned out the same blandness time and time again. But the song also referenced the abhorrent UK tax situation musicians were faced with in the '60s and '70s. With tax rates as high as 95%, many musicians took the Rolling Stones' lead, becoming tax exiles in foreign countries.

> Keep me in exile the rest of my days
> Burn me in hell but as long as it pays

The recording took place in July 1975, early in the album sessions. Eric played bass, sharing guitars with Graham and lead vocals with Lol who sang the bridge section.

Mercury Records in America felt they'd waited too long for a follow-up to 'I'm Not In Love' and heard 'Art For Art's Sake' and it's infectious guitar riff as the obvious lead single. It was certainly the closest thing *How Dare You!* had to an accessible and energetic rock song.

For the single, forty seconds were shaved off the surreal atmospheric introduction and the decision was made to jettison the entire minute of Eric's closing guitar solo, all to ensure tight radio impact. In addition the promotional film eliminated a further 36 seconds from the surreal central instrumental section. But the hooky earworm failed to click with the American public enough to climb anywhere near the Top 40. 10cc were never convinced it was the right single choice to begin with. But Phonogram in the UK shared Mercury's confidence, and the band were totally amazed when 'Art For Art's Sake' redeemed itself by quickly making the top ten its home in Great Britain, Ireland and New Zealand.

### 'Rock 'n' Roll Lullaby' (Graham Gouldman, Eric Stewart)

Kevin Godley described this most submerged of 10cc deep cuts to *New Musical Express* in 1976 as being something 'Even the simplest mind could follow quite easily'. The fairly straight-ahead slow blues/rock shuffle with its slide dobro fills had a directness shorn of anything clever or trite. It occupied a safe middle-ground habitat, ripe for reproductive activity to deliver further offspring for comparatively unadventurous later 10cc albums like *Bloody Tourists* and *Look Hear.*

Surprisingly, Godley heard the song's simplicity as a compliment to the repertoire and fought for its album inclusion. Creme, on the other hand, accused the track of being down and having a lot of holes, clearly seeing it as little more than a digression. Eric Stewart, necessarily modest, admitted to finding the song satisfying on several levels.

For those seeking that signature acerbic 10cc lyrical bite, this lullaby conceals beneath its hot-milk skin, a set of parents hoping their child can, if not get to sleep without bothering them any longer, at least fend for himself. Left like the child, to hibernate, all band members later came to regard the song highly.

### 'Head Room' (Lol Creme, Kevin Godley)

In 1976 there were six basic categories in which records might conflict with the BBC's moral broadcasting standards. They were sex, politics, drugs, death, commercialism (ironic) and bad taste. That year, the UK's *Sounds* magazine accused 'Head Room' of beating about the bush lyrically.

> The birds and the bees of it
> Are weak at the knees
> From making honey every time
>
> I'm throwing my toys away
> I'm leaving the boys to play with the boys
> Gimme girls

How direct were 10cc supposed to *be?* They couldn't win. On one side they were being told what they couldn't say, and on the other to come out and say it. They had no wish to cause broadcast friction, but neither were they willing to censor their lyrics beyond their own standards. So this schizophrenic blues and its strident lyric concerning coming of age and developing a taste for sex, made its plainly obvious point – nothing more nothing less – just like any other piece they wrote. If there was a lyric issue, it was external. The initial banning of 'Rubber Bullets' had oddly worked in 10cc's favour, and who really understood the logic behind banning 'The Worst Band in the World' for a word it *didn't* say? It's not like 'Head Room' was intended as a single. Nevertheless, this time the UK radio chain, Capital Radio, got in on the act and chose to ban it.

On a more macro level, 10cc, along with a host of other international rock acts, were eventually banned in the Soviet Bloc. The band were about artistic freedom from day one. But if there's one 10cc song that unintentionally represents freedom from repression, it's 'Head Room'.

## 'Don't Hang Up' (Lol Creme, Kevin Godley)

Imagine from the camera's viewpoint, Kevin Godley standing at the microphone stage-left. To his right, Lol Creme at the grand piano, Eric with guitar, and Graham engrossed in one of 10cc's most appealing bass parts. This pretty much set the entire six-minute and fifteen-second scene for the 'Don't Hang Up' promo film. Though not a single, 10cc clearly thought enough of the album-closer to use this visual feature to bolster album promotion, even though the public would barely, if ever, see it. Absent from the film was any spice resembling the seemingly coded signals spotted from Lol's hand in the 'The Worst Band in the World' promo film, and Eric's eyes in the 'I'm Not In Love' *Top of the Pops* appearance. 'Don't Hang Up''s tame mime was needless in enhancing the dazzling composing dexterity which was plain to hear.

The colourful showpiece spoke for itself, Eric later calling it one of his favourite 10cc tracks. Both he and Graham later claimed it housed Kevin Godley's finest vocal performance, Graham describing it as technically one of the best vocals he'd ever heard. The production was the perfect marriage of 10cc's two distinct energies – experimentation and pop directness – so well developed and interwoven here as to teasingly suggest further heights they could've scaled had the four stayed together.

'Don't Hang Up' struck a balance by sandwiching a universal breakup message between slices of flashy Latin musicality and lyrical levity that cushioned the story's inevitable hard landing.

> Surprise surprise
> There's a hell of a well in your eyes
> When the barman said 'What're you drinking?'
> I said marriage on the rocks
> I know I never had the style

Or dash of Errol Flynn
But I loved you

10cc mark one's album swansong concluded on a comedic telephone hang-up sound effect, leaving things on a kind of negative upbeat, if that's possible. It was the perfect sonic analogy for the end of the four-piece 10cc. Just like 'Don't Hang Up' itself, to the rest of us it sounded like things were moving along fine. Then suddenly it, and they, were gone.

## Contemporary Tracks

### 'Get It While You Can' (Graham Gouldman, Eric Stewart)
Released as a single B-side, 21 November 1975 (UK),15 November 1975 (US), January 1976(AU), February 1976 (NZ), b/w 'Art For Art's Sake'.
This straightforward but melodic pop song probably deserved more work to relieve its oratory overtones. Two verses and quite a lengthy and substantial half-instrumental middle section set you up to expect another verse that never appeared, so the track seemed a bit short.

The lyric later became historically interesting for hardcore 10cc buffs as it contained phrases re-used in 1978's 'The Anonymous Alcoholic'; 'Everybody's having fun, So why be the one who's out in the cold?'. Those lines were particularly pensive considering the inner-band turmoil that was about to erupt. But the philosophy was correct – you had to get it while you could. And 10cc mark one had certainly done that.

## Song Collaborations
For those interested in the unique songwriting collaborations within 10cc mark one, the below lists them all separately. It's plain to see that the most revered songs were spread out amongst the writers and not always attributable to one of the two dominant writing pairs. But it's also telling how the quotient of high-quality versus mediocre was virtually even in every grouping, which is an impressive hit rate in anyone's book.

It's a shame there were no more Godley/Creme/Stewart songs after the first 10cc album proper. 'Fresh Air for My Mama' was a fine indication of further fruit that could've sprung from that vine. Note also the lack of any Gouldman/Stewart/Creme composition, despite the original *How Dare You!* vinyl album credit error attributing 'I'm Mandy Fly Me' to the trio.

### Godley/Creme/Stewart

| | |
|---|---|
| Neanderthal Man | Think Of It |
| How Many times | Roll On |
| Desperate Dan | Lady Sadie |
| Um Wah Um Woh | The Loser |
| Run Baby Run | Speed Kills |
| You Didn't like It Because You Didn't | Fresh Air For My Mama |

## Godley/Creme
Take Me Back
Suite F.A.
Fly Away
All God's Children
Umbopo
Today
Donna
The Dean and I
The Hospital Song
Hotel
Old Wild Men
Clockwork Creep
Somewhere In Hollywood
Une Nuit a Paris
Brand New Day
The Film of My Love
Good News
How Dare You
Head Room
Don't Hang Up

## Godley/Creme/Gouldman
Johnny Don't Do It
Sand In My Face
Rubber Bullets
I Wanna Rule the World

## Gouldman/Stewart
Headline Hustler
Ships Don't Disappear In the Night, Do They?
Hot Sun Rock
Waterfall
Bee In My Bonnet
Warm Me
The Wall Street Shuffle
Baron Samedi
I'm Not In Love
Blackmail
Flying Junk
Art For Art's Sake
Rock 'n' Roll Lullaby
Get It While You Can

## Godley/Creme/Gouldman/Stewart
18 Carat Man of Means
Gismo My Way
The Second Sitting for the Last Supper

## Creme/Stewart
4% of Something
Silly Love
Life is a Minestrone
Lazy Ways

## Creme/Gouldman
The Worst Band in the World

## Godley/Gouldman
The Sacro-Illiac
Iceberg
Channel Swimmer

## Godley/Stewart
Oh Effendi

## Godley/Gouldman/Stewart
I'm Mandy Fly Me

## The Split

The recording of *How Dare You!*, not without a definite level of fun and good spirit, nevertheless accrued a mounting tension as the two songwriting pairs naturally flowed in opposite directions. Afterwards, there was a vibe of the inevitable about to happen, coming tangible when Godley and Creme expressed a wish to explore beyond the boundaries of new and accessible material like 'The Things We Do For Love' and 'People in Love'.

To lay out the cause of the band-split would be virtually impossible considering 10cc themselves, at least at first, weren't even certain what was happening. I could choose from a multitude of conflicting and confusing stories and opinions. There was talk, even in the press, of Graham Gouldman being included in a Godley & Creme album project. Certain journalists reported Eric as wanting to leave the band, which wasn't strictly true depending on what you read into the concurrent managerial request for Eric to move on, which was overturned a few weeks later as if it had never been uttered. After the fact, it was reported that management tried to keep the band together. So much for reports. The defining moment came in November 1976 when Godley and Creme vacated 10cc, which had an aspect of noble gesture that likely saved a lot of face.

One thing's for sure – there was more influence involved than four guys simply deciding whether to stay together or not. It's murky at best. You had to be there. Ultimately it was suggested that Graham and Eric continue the 10cc name and record the newly-planned album.

# Deceptive Bends (1977)

UK Release date: May1977.US Release date: 25 April 1977.
Personnel:
Graham Gouldman: Vocals, Electric and acoustic bass, Guitars, Dobro, Organ, Autoharp, Percussion
Eric Stewart: Vocals, Guitars, Keyboards, Piano, Organ, Percussion, Whistle
Paul Burgess: Drums, Percussion, Gong, Vibraphone, Piano
Jean Alain Roussel: Organ, Electric piano
Tony Spath: Oboe, Piano
Recorded November 1976 – March 1977at Strawberry Studios South, Dorking, UK, and Threshold Studios, London
Producers: Eric Stewart and Graham Gouldman
Engineers: Eric Stewart and Tony Spath
Arranger: Del Newman
Chart placings: UK: 3, US: 31, CA: 78, NZ: 4, NL: 4, FI: 28, NO: 4, SE: 4

During 1976, Eric, Kevin and Lol all moved down south to Surrey. Eric wanted to build a new studio close to home. With 10cc still a four-piece and intending to record another album, Eric and Graham purchased an old disused cinema building at 61 South Street, Dorking.

After the split happened, Eric and Graham grabbed their usual additional touring drummer, Paul Burgess, and christened the new Strawberry Studios South by recording 'The Things We Do For Love'. Released as a single in December 1976, it quickly caught on with British and American radio, climbing the charts, causing Phonogram to apply pressure for the completion of a new album. But Eric and Graham dug their heels in, taking their time in order to be happy with the results themselves. Quicker working patterns developed anyway, due to not having to run things past two extra people. Even so, Eric felt they were missing the crazy off-the-wall ideas that Kevin and Lol had always brought to the table.

Additional musicians were kept to a minimum. Ubiquitous session keyboardist Jean Roussel contributed piano and organ to 'You've Got a Cold'. Jazz piano moves on 'I Bought a Flat Guitar Tutor' came courtesy of Strawberry South engineer, Tony Spath, who also played the oboe on 'Modern Man Blues'. Some sources, including Eric's memoir, *Things I Do For Love*, list contemporary Frank Zappa drummer, Terry Bozzio, as playing somewhere on *Deceptive Bends*. But Graham Gouldman confirmed for me that Bozzio appears nowhere on the album.

For the first time, a string section was used on a 10cc record, courtesy of British arranger, Del Newman. He'd conducted George Martin's score for Paul McCartney and Wings' 'Live and Let Die', and supplied orchestral arrangements for the Elton John album, *Goodbye Yellow Brick Road*. 10cc utilized Newman's particular talents for the third *Deceptive Bends* single, 'People in Love', and the lush album-closer, 'Feel the Benefit'. The orchestral recording took place at the Moody Blues' Threshold Studios at the Decca Records complex in north London. Eric was particularly pleased with the depth and richness the new element provided.

With recording finished, all that remained was to find an album title. Eric borrowed 'Deceptive Bends' from a road sign he passed every day driving to the studio. London graphic designers, Hipgnosis, responsible for such striking cover images as Led Zeppelin's *Presence* and Pink Floyd's *Wish You Were Here*, were commissioned for the album artwork. They cleverly translated the concept of 'bends' as the consequence of deep-sea diving. For the cover image, they photographed a diver in full regalia carrying a model down a jetty. Initial shots had the model naked, but this was decided against. The photoshoot was lengthy, the diver eventually suffering exhaustion from holding the woman for so long in a full diving suit in a lit environment. In the end, a different and clothed model was used, requiring it all to be repeated.

*Deceptive Bends* was a sleek and lean machine. 10cc had retained their most audibly recognisable vocalist and it's fair to say that the casual listener, unaware of developments, would've barely noticed a difference. 10cc's signature eclecticism remained – Graham even stating later that there were moments when he felt he and Eric were trying to be Kevin and Lol. This might've referred to the formal expanse of 'Feel the Benefit'. But the quirky energy and erotic overtones of 'Honeymoon With B Troop' were the obvious collective touchstone and worthy heir to any Godley and Creme residue. But the song wasn't forced at all, appearing as totally natural in the context. But it didn't change the fact – Godley and Creme were gone. There's a feeling around the whole thing that it could've so easily been rectified. But where Eric and Graham were concerned, Kevin and Lol could agree to disagree but couldn't disagree to part.

### 'Good Morning Judge' (Graham Gouldman, Eric Stewart)
Released as a single A-side, 1 April 1977 (UK),23 June 1977(AU), March 1977 (NZ), b/w 'Don't Squeeze Me Like Toothpaste'. UK: 5.BE: 20. DE: 23.NL: 12. AU: 7. Released as a single A-side, July 1977 (US), b/w 'I'm So Laid Back I'm Laid Out'. US: 69.

Eric Stewart developed the second *Deceptive Bends* single from the guitar riff. The lyric was based on a news story he'd read about a guy who kept committing crimes to get himself sent back to jail. The track was fun but deceptive in itself, not really hinting at the depth of material to follow.

A promo film was made on the streets of Soho, London, with studio scenes showing a courtroom and cell with Eric and Graham playing all parts of judge, defendant, jury and cellmates. The highlight was the costumed pair trading guitar solos. Technically slick for its day, the tongue-in-cheek film suffered from timing, appearing as little more than a slapstick cat amongst the punk pigeons enjoying their heyday.

### 'The Things We Do For Love' (Graham Gouldman, Eric Stewart)

Released as a single A-side, 3 December 1976 (UK), December 1976 (US, CA, AU and NZ), b/w 'Hot To Trot'. UK: 6.US: 5. CA: 1. IE: 2. BE: 24. NL: 13. AU: 5.NZ: 23.

A small mixing desk with pieces hanging out of it sat in the control room at the under-construction Strawberry South in November 1976. The studio's main board was still to arrive, so the band made do with this hand-me-down from the Rolling Stones mobile recording unit. The engineer was forever at the back of it fixing something, but in Graham Gouldman's words, 'Boy did it sound good.'.

In the writing, 'The Things We Do For Love' came from Graham's opening chords, over which Eric's initial idea was to write a lyric about suicide. Graham convinced him the music was too happy, so the lyric was sidetracked to a more positive love angle with a universally understood meaning; Boy wants to contact girl but boy is stuck in the snow and the phone lines are down – a strictly 20$^{th}$-century predicament which had actually befallen Eric years before.

They presented a more blues-styled version to Kevin and Lol just prior to their departure. They were unimpressed, but understandably their heads were somewhere else, with Gizmo experiments that would lead to their triple album *Consequences* already in progress. Kevin suggested speeding the song up to give it some beef. He was right. It wasn't that he and Lol didn't know what to do with a song like this, it's just that they didn't want to do it. But Eric and Graham ran with the tip, ultimately turning the song into their most popular stateside single yet.

Listening today, the lyric stands out as tight and economical. The plot is universal, putting an interesting twist on everyday romantic hurdles. Another ingredient that contributed to the song's ubiquitous appeal was Eric's guitar solo. Composed in advance, he first sang the solo onto tape as a guide before recording the guitar. Further to that, they layered many complex backing vocals which pushed the recording into another realm. Graham has since spoken of a tipping point occurring when Eric sang one particular backing vocal part, after which Graham made the comment through the console to Eric's headphones, 'That song has now become a hit.'

The single was mixed specifically to come across as radio-friendly. Eric has said there were two ways to do it. You could either mix a track for the guy with big speakers and a superb system or mix it for 99% of the public who listened to the radio and had reasonable stereos. In this case, he mixed for the latter and got one of 10cc's biggest global hits out of it. Though not charting as high as 'I'm Not In Love' in the US, it was a bigger seller.

### 'Marriage Bureau Rendezvous' (Graham Gouldman, Eric Stewart)

Boundary-pushing experimentation now held less importance for 10cc. In hindsight, 'Marriage Bureau Rendezvous' signalled a kind of conventional stylistic formula that would soon become the norm. But the song was still interesting, having two separate middle bridge sections in-between its recurring verses, all which had new lyrics. In fact with the exception of chord patterns and the slide guitar harmonies recalling John Lennon's 'Bring On the Lucie (Freda Peeple)', the song had no obviously recurring hooks whatsoever. Even the title was never fully stated. It's as if the song was an uneasy step from artistic depth backwards to directness (or forwards depending on your viewpoint). This completely listenable track showed a 10cc in the process of that transition.

The lyrics were kept uncomplicated as simply a single man looking for love. Perspective maintained interest by the character talking right at the listener, at other times shifting the listener to an observer of the character's side of a date conversation. This all pointed to an unconscious level of experimental defiance while still avoiding listener alienation. The lever between the two extremes had certainly shifted in favour of the latter and over time would shift even further in that direction.

Instrumentation was kept to a minimum with a bed of bass, drums, rhythm guitar and electric piano, beneath block backing vocals, slide guitar lines and Graham Gouldman's strong lead vocal. Gone were the three-dimensional audio surprises that once slapped the listener's face, replaced by more subtle musical gestures like the organ pedal note carrying the bass part at 3m:03s, suggesting a marriage ceremony environment. The sonic beauty was now subtle and mostly inconspicuous, allowing the new 10cc sound to give way to a more crowd-pleasing cream that would hopefully sweeten up the charts.

**'People In Love'** (Graham Gouldman, Eric Stewart)
Released as a single A-side, August 1977 (UK, AU and NZ), b/w 'I'm So Laid Back I'm Laid Out'. AU: 74.
Released as a single A-side, May 1977 (US), b/w 'Don't Squeeze Me Like Toothpaste'. US: 40.
Released as a single A-side, June 1977 (CA), b/w 'Don't Squeeze Me Like Toothpaste'. CA: 90.

More than the bone of contention that was 'The Things We Do For Love', the ballad 'People In Love' could be accused of being at least the musical catalyst for the 10cc split in that the original four-piece lived with it longer and even recorded a version of it. Known as 'Voodoo Boogie', that initial version found its eventual release on the 2012 box set, *Tenology* – that version's entry below.

As for the official release – the album's third single, it took the sweetness of the above 'Marriage Bureau Rendezvous' to a more saccharine extreme. The string section, the first on a 10cc record, was the highlight of the track, arranger Del Newman adding that dramatic spin he was so adept at.

But somehow the track didn't capture the imagination. Love as a topic alone could hardly be blamed, as love is love like an orange is an orange. The performances were superlative. So what blocked the appeal? It's something to do with a combination of overt love lyrics, whimsical accompaniment and good old timing. Even the great success of American soft pop duo, The Carpenters, had peaked by now. The '70s were in a hurry to move on. The Sex Pistols now had three hit singles, the last two still in the UK chart at the release of 'People in Love'. The lyric was lost in a quicksand of infatuation that 'Marriage Bureau Rendezvous' saved itself from with levity and deftness. But 'People in Love' refused to come up for air.

Mercury in the US certainly thought the song had a chance, choosing it as the second single there, presumably to maximize the leverage provided by the extremely successful 'The Things We Do For Love'. But the plan failed. 'People In Love' scraped the top 40 for only one week – the sole similarity to 'The Things We Do For Love' being the appearance at 2m:13s of that song's exact opening chord (G/A), almost causing you to think you're about to hear it. The single made the top 100 in Canada and Australia but wasn't the chart-stormer hoped for. You can't win them all.

**'Modern Man Blues'** (Graham Gouldman, Eric Stewart)
Side one's blues/rock closer puts a new twist on traditional blues woes with the male kicking his heels up in relief after his lover abandons him.

> Now time goes marching on
> And it won't wait for you
> You've gotta take it when it's offered
> And get it when it's due
>
> Now a man can move much faster
> Without a millstone around his neck
> So if you get the chance to lose it
> You've gotta drop it and run like heck

The track initially smokes slowly along in a Pink Floyd lope, sounding cooler and more relevant than the two preceding ballads. The echo-delayed oboe is an unexpected touch that provides an eerie left-field twist. But the mood improves with each happy, relieved and progressively frantic refrain of 'She's gone, I'm so glad that woman's gone'.

Today some might view this lyric as daring. But emotion aside, it's a classic example from a time when topic and attitude were up for grabs, and either an apple, an orange, or an unwanted other half were accepted as simple real-world subject matter, as deserving as any other of exposure within the bounds of a creative work.

**'Honeymoon With B Troop'** (Graham Gouldman, Eric Stewart)
If you find yourself drawn to the early 10cc's more demented moments, side two's manic opener ought to scratch that itch. Graham Gouldman has referred to he and Eric unconsciously channelling Godley and Creme in the making

Relaxing pre-gig in 1975. (*Alamy*)

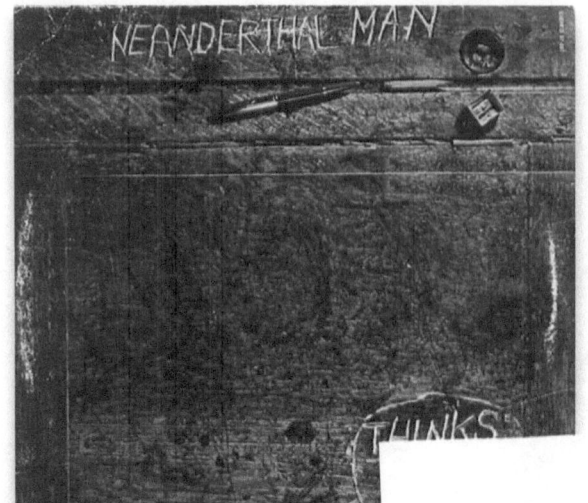

**Left:** One of many covers for the Hotlegs single, 'Neanderthal Man', here taking the aesthetic of the *Thinks: School Stinks* album cover, both a precursor of Alice Cooper's 1972 *School's Out* cover image. (*One Way Records*)

**Right:** Godley and Creme's cover art for the debut 10cc album. This glorious piece swept past all potential censors, and rightly so. (*7Tc*)

**Left:** From 'The Worst Band in the World' promo film 1974.

**Right:** *Sheet Music* – The 1974 album title that was 10cc's self-deprecating response to certain negative reviews of the debut album in the rock press. (*7Tc*)

**Left:** *The Original Soundtrack* (1975) – With music this colourful, who needed hue, or images at all? (*Mercury*)

**Right:** *How Dare You!* (1976) – 10cc mark one's swansong. (*Spectrum*)

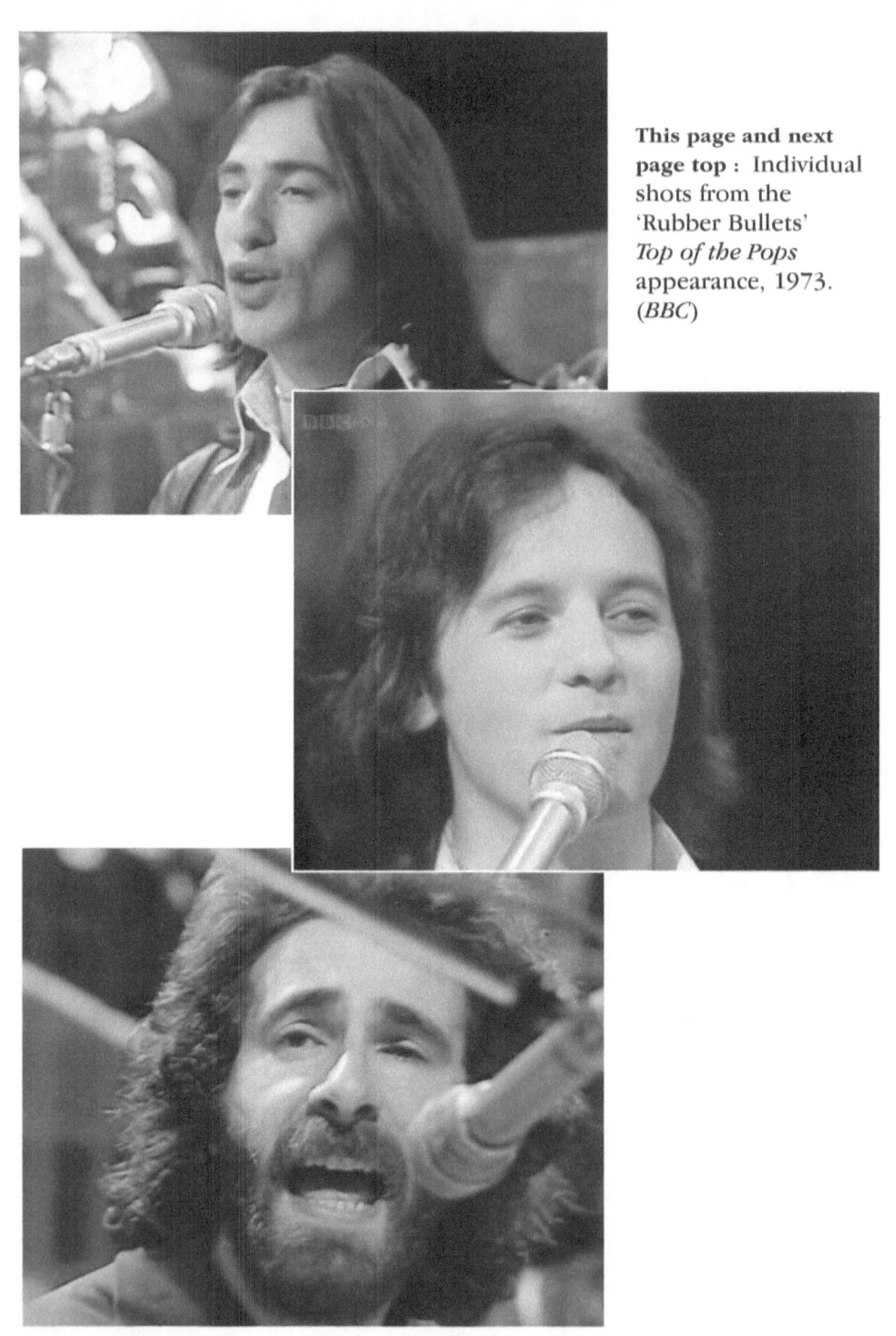

**This page and next page top:** Individual shots from the 'Rubber Bullets' *Top of the Pops* appearance, 1973. (*BBC*)

**Left:** Eric Stewart struggling to control his mirth miming to 'I'm Not in Love' on *Top of the Pops* in 1975. (*BBC*)

**Right:** Eric commits to the surreal tale for the 'I'm Mandy Fly Me' promo film, 1976.

**Left:** The triple behemoth – Godley & Creme's *Consequences* (1977). (*Caroline Records*)

**Right:** The *Consequences* back cover credits. (*Caroline Records*)

**Left:** Lol Creme plays the Gizmo, much featured on the *Consequences* album, live in 1974.

**Above:** Godley, Creme and Peter Cook during the making of *Consequences*, 1977.

**Below:** Jazz singer, Sarah Vaughan – Guest vocalist on *Consequences*. Kevin Godley described her as arriving at The Manor, 'Standing out like a shot of neon.'

**Left:** *Deceptive Bends* (1977) – The debut of the Gouldman and Stewart-led 10cc mark two. (*Mercury*)

**Right:** *Bloody Tourists* (1978) – 10cc mark two here expanded to a six-piece. (*Mercury*)

**Left:** Eric solos in 'Feel the Benefit' live at the Hammersmith Odeon, 1977.

**Above:** Eric, Rick Fenn and Graham in the 'Dreadlock Holiday' video, 1978. (*Mercury*)

**Below:** Graham Gouldman in the 'Dreadlock Holiday' video, 1978. (*Mercury*)

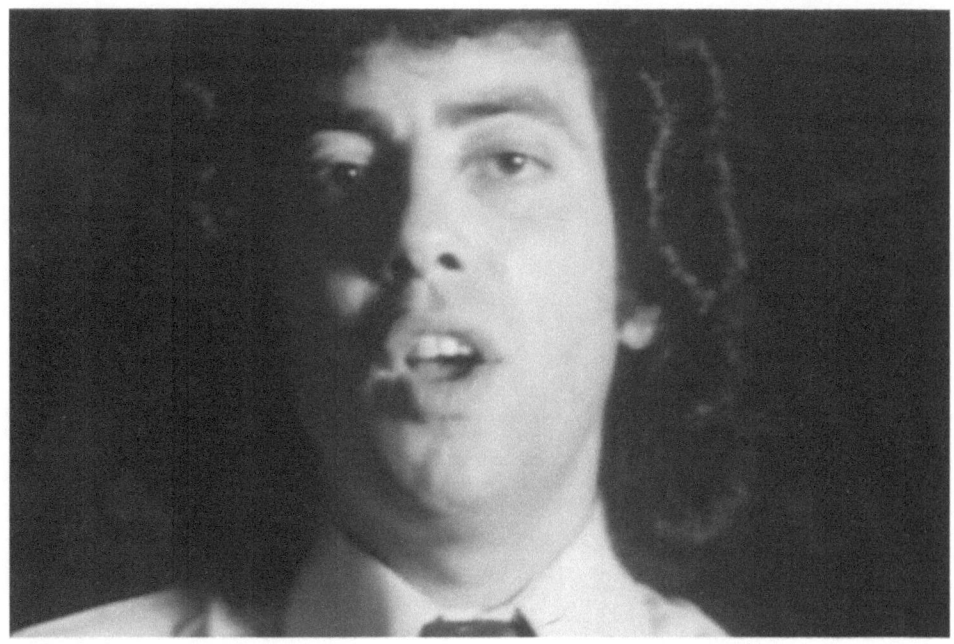

**Above:** Stuart Tosh in 'Dreadlock Holiday', 1978. (*Mercury*)

**Below:** Godley, Creme and backing singers in the 'Wedding Bells' video, 1981.

**Above:** Kevin Godley in the Derek Burbidge-directed video for 'An Englishman in New York', 1979. (*Mercury*)

**Below:** Lol Creme, the other Englishman in the 'An Englishman in New York' video. (*Mercury*)

**Left:** *L* (1978) – Symbolic of Godley & Creme teaching themselves how to make records again. (*Mercury*)

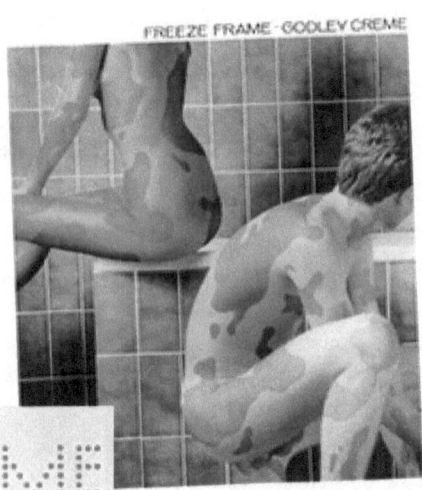

**Right:** *Freeze Frame* (1979) – Arguably G&C's finest 38 minutes, at least in a pop sense. (*Mercury*)

**Left:** *Ismism* (1981) – Containing G&C's most successful UK hit, 'Under Your Thumb'. (*Polygram*)

**Above:** G&C's 'Under Your Thumb' video for *Top of the Pops*. *(BBC)*

**Below:** Godley & Creme, circa 1982.

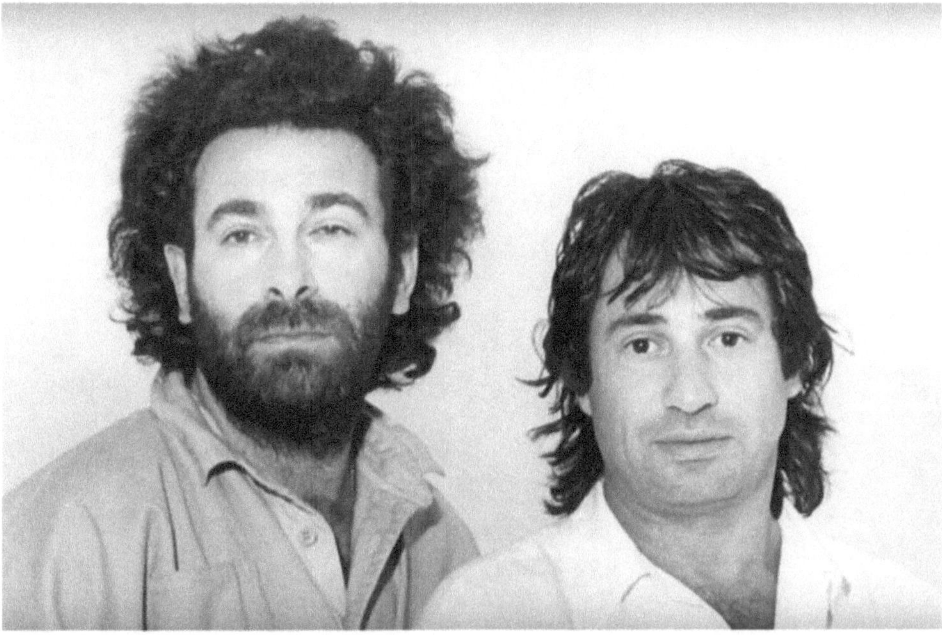

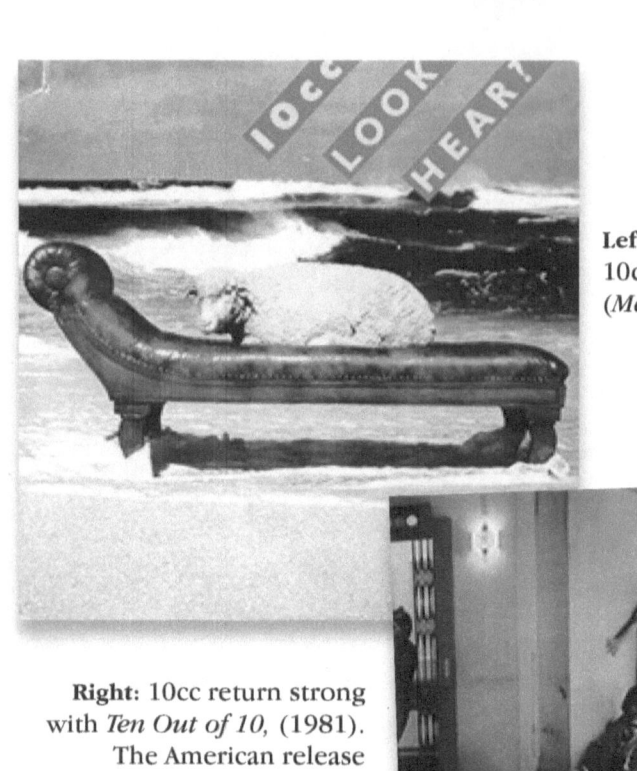

**Left:** The American cover for 10cc's *Look Hear?*, (1980). (*Mercury*)

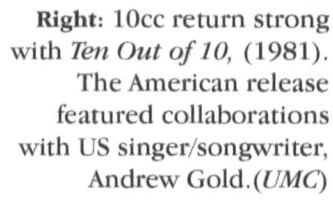

**Right:** 10cc return strong with *Ten Out of 10*, (1981). The American release featured collaborations with US singer/songwriter, Andrew Gold.(*UMC*)

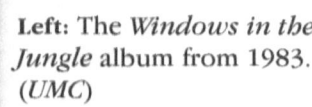

**Left:** The *Windows in the Jungle* album from 1983. (*UMC*)

**Right:** Godley & Creme's *Birds of Prey,* also from 1983. (*Polydor*)

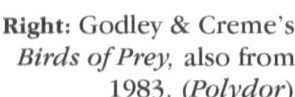

**Left:** *The History Mix Volume 1* (1985) – G&C's penultimate album release. (*Polydor*)

**Right:** *Goodbye Blue Sky* (1988) – G&C's appropriately fatalistic swansong. (*Polygram*)

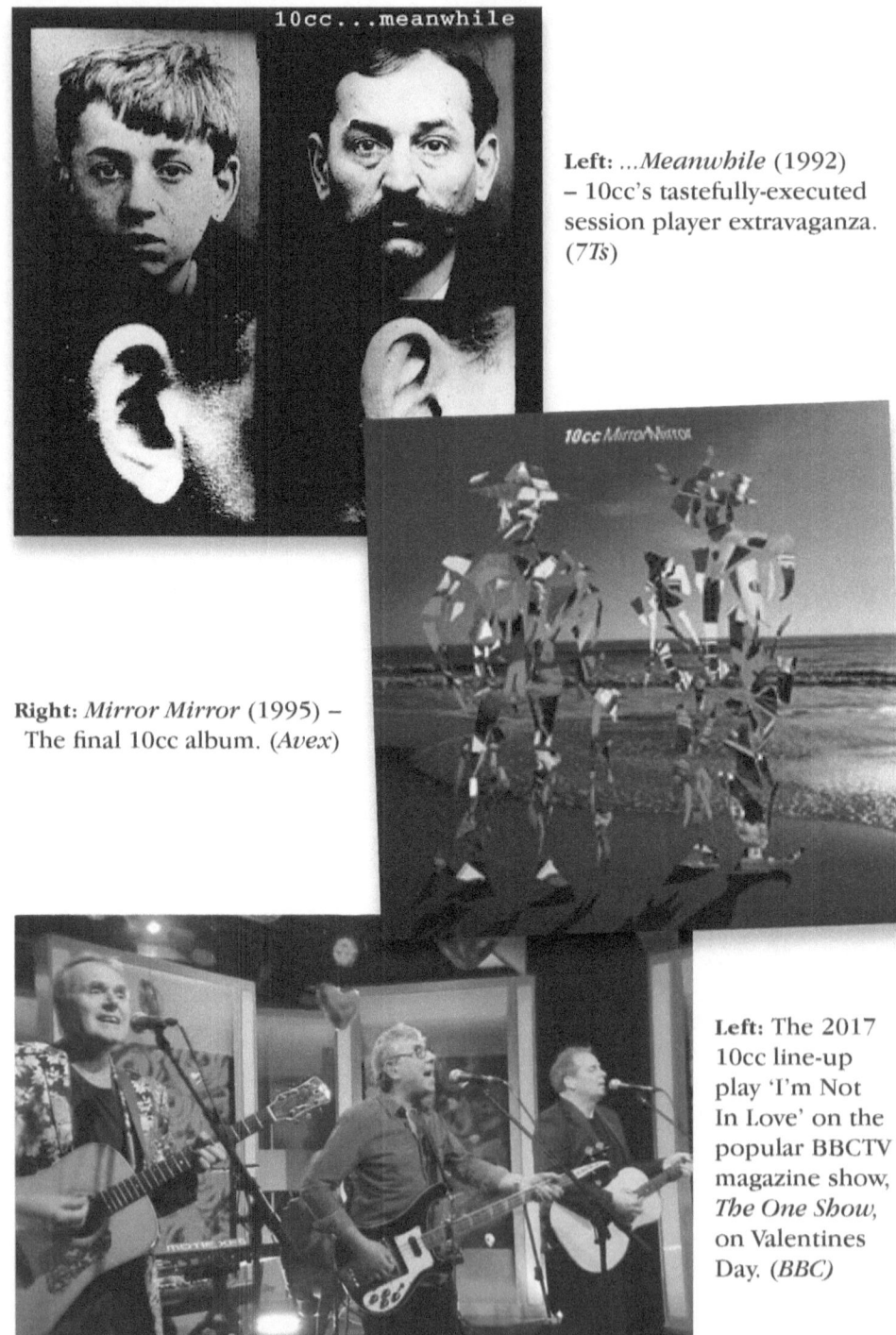

**Left:** ...*Meanwhile* (1992) – 10cc's tastefully-executed session player extravaganza. (*7Ts*)

**Right:** *Mirror Mirror* (1995) – The final 10cc album. (*Avex*)

**Left:** The 2017 10cc line-up play 'I'm Not In Love' on the popular BBCTV magazine show, *The One Show*, on Valentines Day. (*BBC*)

of *Deceptive Bends*, and there's no clearer possible example of that than here. The intro guitar line and its later deranged ornamental development echo 'The Dean and I' quirks, and the track as a whole regurgitates stylistic 'Clockwork Creep' peculiarities.

Inventive instrumental details skillfully embellish the track, like verse two and three's comedic double-tracked consecutive backing vocals and drummer Paul Burgess' divine bubbling vibraphone arpeggios. Pure 3D sonics appear when a jamboree, complete with kazoo and military snare drummer, marches across the soundstage at the one-minute mark. It's a Frank Zappa moment for sure, which leads me to *Deceptive Bends*' most enduring myth. Many sources list contemporary Frank Zappa drummer, Terry Bozzio, as playing on this album. One source credits Bozzio with membranophone – a generic term that covers many varieties of handheld or beater-struck instruments that resonate through a vibrating skin. Surprisingly, this includes the kazoo – a member of the membranophone mirliton group – with a skin that resonates when the instrument body is blown through. It's a good argument for Bozzio's inclusion, but Graham Gouldman has now confirmed it as a myth.

Lyrically, the main character's lazy and crazy girlfriend is an eye magnet that plays hard to get. Her topless sunbathing eventually drives him to propose marriage, in a scene that suggests a symbolic but undeniable level of bondage and discipline, if only to prevent her from escaping. It all amounts to *Deceptive Bends*' most adventurous excursion, and perhaps 10cc's final moment of pure carefree madness.

**'I Bought a Flat Guitar Tutor'** (Graham Gouldman, Eric Stewart)
If 'Honeymoon With B Troop' was *Deceptive Bends*' most insane passage, the jazz-inflected saunter that is 'I Bought a Flat Guitar Tutor' was certainly its smartest. A basic knowledge of music theory helps in fully understanding the inner workings of this showpiece, which spits out lyrical wordplay that both symbolically and literally reflects what's happening on a technical music level at any given moment. See below a line-by-line blow-by-blow of what's exactly going on – my comments in brackets.

> I bought a flat (Moves from A to A Flat)
> Diminished responsibility (Moves from F sharp diminished to E)
> You're de ninth person to see (Moves from D9 to C)
> To be suspended in a seventh (Moves around B Suspended to A7)
> Major catastrophe (Moves from A Major to E)
> It's a minor point but gee (Moves from A Minor to G)
> Augmented by the sharpness of your (Moves from G Augmented to G Sharp Augmented)
> See what I'm going through (C Sharp)
> A to be with you (Moves from A to B to E)
> In a flat by the sea (Moves from A Flat to C)

It's like a pop music exercise, or an etude if you like. The entire second half is instrumental, decorated by engineer Tony Spath's piano solo doubled by Eric on guitar. In the last few bars, he breaks out on his own briefly, only to be silenced by the ending.

There's a lot going on in its brief one minute and 43 seconds, which along the way includes a 2/4 bar and even an evident key change as detectable separately from the generally constant key modulations anyway. All of the above renders the song worthy of inclusion in the jazz Real Book.

### 'You've Got a Cold' (Graham Gouldman, Eric Stewart)

This ode to the common ailment could've made a more accessible single than 'Good Morning Judge', as long as the included '50s American slang term 'badass' didn't upset the censors. Unwell or not, Gouldman and Stewart were probably sick of running the censor gauntlet. When in doubt, use whatever word you want and sacrifice the potential radio-play. Integrity intact.

Possibly the closest thing to disco yet from 10cc, it was certainly their funkiest moment, regurgitating as it most certainly did, part of the synthesizer bass line from Stevie Wonder's 1974 hit, 'Boogie On Reggae Woman'. 'You've Got a Cold' was a creature of its time, thanks mostly to bass guitar wah-wah on the choruses placing the track fairly and squarely in 1977.

### 'Feel the Benefit' (Graham Gouldman, Eric Stewart)

The album finale borrowed from both outside and inside the square. Borrowed time was also a factor in making the 11m:28s colossus. Progress was steady, but delays occurred due to ongoing studio construction. One day, half-way through recording Eric's vocal, the entire studio began to shake violently. Investigation revealed the cause to be a power roller levelling out the parking lot. Half a day's work time was lost as a result.

In an assessment of the rock ballad album-closer, it's too easy to use the term Beatlesque as a jumping-off point. Sure, the Beatles' 'Dear Prudence' cast an unmistakable shadow over the introductory clawhammer guitar-picking style. But John Lennon borrowed that from British folk singer, Donovan, who in turn had taken it from American folk group, The Carter Family.

But the Beatles influence prevailed in a more general way. 'Feel the Benefit' resembled side two of their *Abbey Road*, at least in the intention to move through eclectic sections by the use of hard cuts and crossfades, and by carrying the weight of an earnest philosophical bent as an album climax. But arranger Del Newman's sensitive orchestral accompaniment kept things light, as did what sounds suspiciously like some of the 'I'm Not In Love' vocal tape loops in the bridge section at 2m:30s.

In contrast, the lyric, based on Eric's thoughts and worries about the state of the human race, stated its concerns quite clearly in 'Part I: Reminisce and Speculate'.

> If all the people in the world lost their reason
> What would we see?
> Where would we be?
> If all the entertainers in the world lost their music
> What would they play?
> What could they say
> To pacify the crowd
> To justify themselves?

You could argue that Eric's fears have now come to pass, making 'Feel the Benefit' less '60's pastiche and more 21st-century premonition. It's all down to the interpretation, which is less strenuous in 'Part II: A Latin Break'. Here the music goes on a welcome island getaway, the Latin-American style of which hadn't appeared since the uncomfortable tropical honeymoon of 'Don't Hang Up'.

> Ooh when you smile it's like a holiday
> Ooh pack your bags and we can getaway
> We'll float on a Queen down to Rio
> There's no need to shave
> We'll be stinking like rum in a punch

By this point, you're expecting to be gathered up for a conga line and invited to limbo. But instead, you're led to eight bars of instrumental music I'd claim to be (along with general historic passages of oblique and ironic lyrics) responsible for the band's occasional flabbergasting comparisons to the American group, Steely Dan. By 1977, the ears of any respectable musician would've been well-acquainted with Steely Dan's recent album, *The Royal Scam*. The imprint of this can be detected in 'Feel the Benefit' at the five-minute mark when the drums temporarily desert the Latin feel for a tight and impressive sixteenth funk beat as a basis for guitar and bass improvisation swaps. But the solo machine barely gains momentum before twisting back via an unresolved and distinctly un-Steely-Dan-like guitar lick. The Latin feel returns with a final verse featuring further social invitation and care-taking from the locals.

Part II slowly wends its way around to a crossfade into 'Part III: Feel the Benefit'. It's a return to Part I with new lyrics suggesting we'd all benefit from all people singing together. This conceptually ties-in the song's three parts, making it all a bit early-'70s-Coca-Cola and a smidgen over-boiled.

By now the idea had run out of steam with two and a half minutes to go. In a skilful move, interest was reinstated by the rousing and anthemic repetitions of a four-bar guitar harmony refrain with solo, increasing in intensity until the track's sudden end. But not before 11m:17s when a singular guitar quote borrowed from 'Lazy Ways' (in turn taken from Led Zeppelin's 'Whole Lotta Love') is heard as if waving goodbye to the past.

## Contemporary Tracks

### 'Hot To Trot' (Graham Gouldman, Eric Stewart)
Released as a single B-side, 3 December 1976 (UK), July 1977 (US),23 June 1977(AU), March 1977 (NZ), b/w 'The Things We Do For Love'.

The gaping abyss between this B-side and its popular A-side couldn't be wider. The lyric let the song down and the title said it all by buying into the modern disco parlance. As a song, it was indicative of any B-side's necessary value.

Performance-wise, the band were tight, funky, and the multiple guitar harmonies finely executed. Graham's voice worked well, emitting an attitude that seemed to rise above as if treating the song as a joke. But if you must have a 'hot to trot' in your collection, I'd go for the Commodores 1977 single, 'Too Hot ta Trot', or at least Wild Cherry's less impressive 'Hot to Trot' from that year.

### 'Don't Squeeze Me Like Toothpaste' (Graham Gouldman, Eric Stewart)
Released as a single B-side, 1 April 1977 (UK),23 June 1977(AU), March 1977 (NZ), b/w 'Good Morning Judge'.
Released as a single B-side, May 1977 (US), b/w 'People In Love'.
Released as a single B-side, June 1977 (CA), b/w 'People In Love'.

A neither/nor semi-country pop waltz that suits its B-side status perfectly. The man wishing not to be squeezed is being mistreated and threatens to leave. But by the end of the fairly interminable three minutes and 35 seconds, he's still there, his pleading now turned to masochism. Best left unsqueezed.

### 'I'm So Laid Back I'm Laid Out' (Graham Gouldman, Eric Stewart)
Released as a single B-side, August 1977 (UK, AU and NZ), b/w 'People In Love'.
Released as a single B-side, July 1977 (US), b/w 'Good Morning Judge'.

This is more like it. *Deceptive Bends*' finest B-side. The drum rhythm is alive, uptight, and clumsily trips on itself every bar as if looking for somewhere to hide. The mood simulates a '70s cop show TV theme, with a James-Bond-style repeating guitar figure that gives an over-distinguishing aspect to a character who is nothing more than completely lazy.

> The rent needed paying
> The insurance was due
> The roof needed fixing
> And the rain was coming through

> But the forecast is sunny
> So I'll stay here on my back
> Tomorrow is another day
> It's cozy in the sack

Even a house fire couldn't move this guy – an opening plot device that would've worked better at the end.

> The people were running
> The place was on fire
> The smoke was a-growing
> And the flames were getting higher
>
> The fire chief was shouting
> As he knocked down my door
> He said you better move your butt boy
> Or you'll knock on heaven's door

This semi-mysterious novelty takes itself less seriously than its A-side and is definitely album-worthy. It even trumps the lesser material on the coming *Bloody Tourists* album.

### 'People In Love (The Voodoo Boogie)' (Graham Gouldman, Eric Stewart)
Released in the Tenology box set (2012).

Hearing Kevin Godley's solid drum feel and Lol Creme's startling backing vocals on this first attempt at the third single makes it starkly obvious what was lost when the two departed. Those vocals added an unsettling edge that was missing from *Deceptive Bends* as a whole, though they were perhaps inappropriate to the song and had the feeling of being a large square object being forced into a rather minuscule round hole. The division is audible. You can feel the unit scrambling like a fish out of water and you can hear Eric Stewart struggling to keep the song on track as the simple ballad it was.

The bizarre backing vocals make this version work for me though. For a consumer, a detail like that can be enough to satisfy. But for the originators, issues can run deeper, making overdub indecision a moot point that merely contributes to what can, and in this case did, result in a deal-breaker.

None of this was helped by the lack of an adequate mix – the *Tenology* version's battle with harsh hi-mids and over-compression suggesting the source was a tape cassette. Taking that into account, it's plain to hear that a serious final mix would've made this a perfectly respectable version of a song that lost its mojo in 10cc's transition.

## Lead Me In With a Count of 17! – Consequences (1977)

If sometime in 1976 or 1977 you happened to be driving across Salisbury Plain in the UK and heard the explosive sounds of a fireworks display, it's possible it was Godley & Creme punishing their eardrums for their art. They must've planned on making a racket if they required one of the largest pieces of open grassland in northern Europe to capture the sounds for their new project. They hired fireworks manufacturers Paines Wessex to build the display. Sadly the experiment failed due to – according to Kevin Godley in 1977 – 'The fruity and colourful comments of the roadies as the various fireworks exploded.'. So they were re-recorded later in a Stockport field.

Likewise, hopefully you didn't panic if you were the innocent driver of a Manchester taxi that Kevin Godley narrowly missed while trying to record a Doppler effect from the horn of his moving vehicle. Or perhaps a policeman held back your vehicle, allowing two grown men the privilege of throwing multiple buckets of water at a Manchester wall in silence in the middle of the night. Yes, that was Kevin and Lol too.

How did it come to *this*?! To answer, we must return to the conclusion of *How Dare You!* and the dawn of *Deceptive Bends*. The magic was disappearing. Godley and Creme simply had no wish to repeat themselves. For them, recording *How Dare You!* had all the hallmarks of such a repetitive exercise. They'd done what they'd set out to do and they didn't want to do it again.

In preparation for a new 10cc album, they gathered around the piano at Strawberry to hear Eric and Graham's new song, 'People In Love'. In his memoir, *Spacecake*, Kevin Godley describes the experience as a feeling of dread descending.

It was time to go back to the Gizmotron, which can partially be blamed for the transition from 10cc mark one to Godley & Creme recording-entity-outright. In their heads, 10cc had become stale and predictable. They still wanted a challenge and the Gizmo provided it. To develop the device and its associated recording project felt like it required leaving the band to achieve. All members have since noted that to merely take a break to allow for individual projects, could've worked. That became a pattern for many bands in the '80s and '90s, but in 1976 it was yet to become the norm. The two separating parties merely stuck to their respective guns and the parting occurred.

Kevin and Lol were free to continue their work, which fit more appropriately into the field of avant-garde than experimental, if you consider avant-garde to refer to pushing boundaries within an already well-established square, and experimental to refer to attempting something completely original outside of any square. What Godley & Creme did next probably did both.

## Consequences (1977) – Godley & Creme

UK Release date: October 1977. US Release date: October 1977.
Personnel:
Lol Creme: Vocals, Guitar, Piano, Tubular bells, Gizmo, Percussion
Kevin Godley: Vocals, Drums, Percussion
Mel Collins: Saxophone
Judy Huxtable: Dialogue
Peter Cook: Dialogue
Andy Peebles: Dialogue
Sarah Vaughan: Vocals
Peter Wheeler: Dialogue
Recorded 1976-1977 at Strawberry Studios, Stockport, UK, and The Manor, Oxfordshire, UK
Producer: Godley & Creme
Engineer: Martin Lawrence
Chart placings: UK: 52

'Lead me in with a count of 17 Mr Stapleton. Then wave...your...baton.' Thus spake Mr Blint introducing *Consequences*' closing multi-movement piece, 'Blint's Tune'.

According to the original album liner notes by rock journalist, Paul Gambaccini, *Consequences* was the story of man's last defence against an irate nature. In recording a single to demonstrate their invention the Gizmotron – a device that attached to a guitar bridge enabling notes or chords to be bowed – Messrs Godley and Creme had the eureka moment revealing the fundamental craving that only expanding the single to a triple album could satisfy. Exiting 10cc, armed with a Gizmo prototype held together with tape, they entered Strawberry North at Stockport with engineer, Martin Lawrence, and commenced recording proper, with the full financial backing of Phonogram. It was they who suggested bringing in comedian, Peter Cook, as a way to add extra distinction to the project.

The skeletal structure of *Consequences* was Cook's hilariously dark play about a divorce lawyer conducting business in an attic beneath which lives and works Mr Blint, an eccentric composer, mostly always visible through the permanent hole in the attic floor. Meanwhile, a monstrous apocalyptic hurricane has its way with the outside world, causing increasing strain. Luckily, some relief is at hand thanks to Mr Blint's wisdom and guidance from such statements as, 'Just one bit of advice you might be able to use. 17.'

The significance of the number 17 in the play can't be overstated. It takes place on April 17th. Blint's bath takes eleven minutes to fill and six to empty. Even the original catalogue number of the album itself was CONS17. Manifestations of the mysterious number occur throughout.

Recording took place over sixteen months in 1976 and 1977. Work on side one and two was particularly intensive and time-consuming. With

Godley and Creme having recently moved down to Surrey, they temporarily relocated back, staying at Manchester's Piccadilly Hotel every night instead of somewhere in Stockport.

Part-way through production, it was decided to assure management of the soundness of the project by bringing them into the studio. Arriving on Monday 14th February 1977, the composers insisted that listening be at full volume in the dark, themselves retiring to another room for the duration. Management eventually came out raving of the audio brilliance they'd just experienced. But when they disappeared into the live room to discuss business, an open microphone relayed their conversation to Kevin and Lol in the control room. Comments included 'What was that?', 'What the hell are we going to do?' and 'It's not 'I'm Not In Love'.'. Kevin and Lol just laughed, not considering for a moment that the project could potentially miss the mark.

Due to Strawberry being a working commercial studio with bookings coming in, recording was relocated part-way through to Richard Branson's residential Oxfordshire studio, The Manor. Godley stated in his memoir that 24-hour days made little sense to him and Lol, that they needed 48-hour days and were willing to pay people to sleep for them. It was at The Manor that Peter Cook, his wife – actress Judy Huxtable – and American jazz vocalist, Sarah Vaughan, made their contributions.

As Godley, Creme and Cook worked seven days a week for three months, syncing of schedules was an issue. Cook was always up-and-at-'em, showered and raring to go at eight AM, whereas after working till 2 AM every night, Kevin and Lol were dead to the world till eleven. There would be a constructive meeting of the minds each day between about eleven and one, at which point the alcoholic Cook would behead his first bottle of the day, progressively declining from there.

Ever the professionals, when work occurred, it was swift and productive. They'd start with the subject matter, and Cook would go in and often virtually improvise dialogue recorded on the spot. The rest of the day would be spent setting music to it in response. The next day Cook would conceive a dialogue response to the music made the night before, and so the cycle continued. Once all the dialogue was complete, all that was left was to return to Strawberry Stockport to record side six, which consisted solely of the monolithic 'Blint's Tune'.

Out in the world, life was continuing much as it always had, except for one thing; Punk had arrived. Seeing pictures of the Sex Pistols in magazines, Kevin and Lol realised a cultural shift was happening – a shift completely at odds with the project they'd just bled sixteen months of their life onto. Punk was a real kick in the guts for the massive artistic endeavour that was *Consequences*. Godley has described him and Creme as coming 'Blinking out into the light of day like a couple of soldiers lost in the forest during World War II.'. It was a different world and *Consequences* was a beast out of its habitat.

To launch the album, Phonogram threw a playback party at Amsterdam's Sonesta Hotel. Godley, Creme and Cook witnessed the event from the balcony – the Gizmo placed proudly onstage inside a glass case atop luxurious black velvet. There was no doubt that the device was an achievement and its abilities were the star of the show. But the track 'Sleeping Earth', containing the sound of Kevin Godley snoring, summed up the entire evening. The creators suddenly realised they'd worked eighteen months on something that was going to be a hard sell.

A recuperation period followed the sobering realisation that *Consequences* was ill-received. Godley was gutted, whereas Creme took it in his stride, saying that all of his work was more about the journey than the destination. One positive outcome was the request from cigarette company, Benson & Hedges, to use part of side one for a commercial. This led to a request to provide music for a short film. It wasn't a huge leap from there to future music video work. Godley later stated that *Consequences* was really the work of frustrated filmmakers who didn't yet have the tools to make a proper one.

Video work was inevitable. In some ways, the project helped lead them to it, so all was not lost. After all, the audio *was* something to behold, and the play was hilarious. Not to mention the hours of work put into the artwork. *Consequences* actually reached number 52 in the UK – a detail often overlooked and respectable by any standard. Something had to come from an album that ate £250,000 and hit the market at £12 per unit – exorbitant for 1977.

One single, 'Five O'Clock in the Morning', was released, but consumers slept through the alarm. A single promo album titled *Musical Excerpts from Consequences* was sent to radio in 1977, but not until February 1979 did Mercury issue a single album, *Music From Consequences*, to gain further attention for the ill-fated triple-set. But by then the snooze button had been hit for the final time. The lack of appreciation of *Consequences* was a crime. If nothing else, it deserved awards for purely technical reasons.

In the below track outlines, space prevents giving a detailed blow-by-blow account of either the story, history behind the album artwork or every sonic embellishment (which could fill a book in its own right just for 'Stampede' alone.). Also, many tracks after disc one are titled 'Dialbgue' and consist of only that. Many of those tracks are omitted. Should you wish to dive deeper into associated *Consequences* detail, I direct you to Kevin Godley's memoir, *Spacecake*. Further in-depth history can be derived from Giles Booth's splendid online presentation, 'Mr Blint's Attic'. http://www.suppertime.co.uk/blint/.

## 'Seascape' (Lol Creme, Kevin Godley)

The introduction to the triple-set is a textbook example of Gizmotron tone variety. Of course, the tone is determined pre-gizmo by a combination of instrument and amplification and pre or post by equalisation or any number of other effects. But it's fascinating how much difference the envelope – or ASDR – of the notes can make to sound perception. ASDR is electronics terminology referring to attack, sustain, decay and release. It's usually applied to synthesizer use but is convenient to use in relation to the gizmo considering the device primarily affects how notes actively begin, progress, and to a lesser extent finish.

The word seascape is a good description. Gizmo tones flow in and out, their attacks sometimes gruff and cello-like with a constant bowed sustain. Other times notes softly ease in to a hollow brass-like tone. But those are subtle comparisons. Gizmo tones can suggest the presence of strings, horns, organ or even woodwinds, but still maintain their unique and individual character. At some moments a Mellotron might come to mind, but that monstrosity's limited-length audio loops paled compared to the living, breathing and varying development of a sustained gizmo tone. So allow for the above description to suffice for many general tones applied throughout *Consequences*.

**'Wind'** (Lol Creme, Kevin Godley)
Drums made their entry this time. But the star of the show was the rather ingeniously-created talking wind voice representing the violent hurricane swirling outside. This remarkable effect was achieved by mangling the studio vacuum cleaner. The gizmo string section was played through a speaker and sent through the hose to a smaller tube held in the mouth. As the sound came down the tube and out the mouth, the words were mouthed into a microphone. The result was a cross between a vocoder, like you would've heard on the Lipps Inc hit 'Funky Town', and a guitar talkbox as popularised by British guitarist, Peter Frampton. The message was ominous – 'I am the wind and I'll blow you away, Bye-bye everyone'.

**'Fireworks'** (Lol Creme, Kevin Godley)
The fireworks recorded on a Stockport field are mixed here with various gizmo, vocal, timpani, snare drum, percussion and delay effects.

**'Stampede'** (Lol Creme, Kevin Godley)
Percussion effects here support a substantial melodic theme. A brief disco section interrupts with a DJ voice and simply perfect vocal harmonies wailing 'Burn baby burn', a phrase that just that year had branded itself into the disco lingo, thanks mostly to the Trammps hit, 'Disco Inferno'. The substantial theme returns briefly, followed by the gizmo simulating the buzzing of flies and bellows of elephants. Even the comical whinnying of an actual horse can be heard.

At 1m:52s, the main theme is sent through a noise gate by a snare drum playing the melody rhythm. Instead of the snare sound coming through, the beat of the drum triggers the gizmo sound underneath. Blowing above this is what sounds like a saxophone but is actually a guitar playing through the vacuum cleaner (see 'Wind' above), this time with tissue paper at the hose-opening to simulate a sax's mouthpiece reed rasp.

At the vocal entry on the word 'Fire', an instrument track is sent through a noise gate triggered by multiple tracks of popping bubble-wrap, creating the audio illusion that the music itself is crackling fire or vice versa. From the third utterance of the word 'fire', the vocals too are run through the gate, repeating to a slow fade. Multiple vocal tape loops and butchered vacuum cleaners were one thing (or in fact more), but this use of the noise gate was ingenious innovation and upper-echelon stuff for 1977.

The Theremin was an electronic musical instrument invented in 1928, whose constant pitch was controlled by frequency oscillators sensing the movement of the hands around an antenna. The track's closing section at 3m:52s presents gizmo-as-Theremin. The shaking vibrato was achieved by placing a small piece of sellotape on the tape recorder wheel at the playback head, causing the tape to speed up at every turn of the wheel, resulting in an authentic Theremin effect. Not that that was the goal, but it was certainly the outcome.

**'Burial Scene'** (Lol Creme, Kevin Godley)
The sounds of a rainy burial scene with preacher are heard from inside a coffin. The sounds get progressively quieter with each landing shovelful of dirt until there is no sound. This was recorded by placing a mic and assistant under the studio stairwell, covering him with a board and shovelling dirt onto the board. A lush set of piano chords then waft in coated with various gizmo textures including the earlier Theremin-like sound, leading to the solo piano playing part of the later piece, 'Honolulu Lulu'. This slowly fades to end side one.

**'Sleeping Earth'** (Lol Creme, Kevin Godley)
Partially due to the included snoring, this track had some people squirming at the *Consequences* playback party. Mellow guitar lines, vibes and congas largely made up the lengthy textural piece. Dramatic, thickly layered gizmo lines entered halfway through providing extra interest, but probably not enough to justify the full six minutes and 40 seconds. Strangely, the track was included on the 1979 *Music from Consequences* compilation.

**'Honolulu Lulu'** (Lol Creme, Kevin Godley)
The first singing on the entire set is the hurricane introducing itself via a complex choir. Banks of vocals are backed by piano and splashes of a Hawaiian guitar. A theatrical movement commences, communicating the necessity for conscription via vocals recalling those of Howard Kaylan and Mark Volman in Frank Zappa's 1971 musical movie, *200 Motels*. Various internal themes return and collide, made dramatic by urgent gizmo octaves and xylophone.

**'The Flood'** (Lol Creme, Kevin Godley)
Released as a single B-side, 2 December 1977 (UK), November 1977 (US and CA), b/w 'Five O'Clock in the Morning'.

The sound of pieces of Plasticine being thrown into a bucket of water was the source of a constant singular water drip slowly multiplying into eventual rowing sounds. They were then played at varying speeds from tape loops. Music enters at the halfway point with a bass motif including finest gizmo cello likeness. Layers of Lol's tight and funky rhythm guitars then play to a percussive track created using the water drop sounds. This would've been a painstaking process done with tape in the days before samplers.

The earlier bass motif then expands to a rock band in a live concert situation concluding with audience applause, and someone yelling 'Thank you, good night.' and 'Hey if you think really hard, maybe we can stop this rain'. Audience screams follow a tsunami-like catastrophe after which we hear a heartbeat as if from underwater, progressively slowing down to a stop – an appropriate close to side two.

### 'Five O'Clock in the Morning' (Lol Creme, Kevin Godley)
Released as a single A-side, 2 December 1977 (UK), November 1977 (US and CA), b/w 'The Flood (Edit)'.

Kevin and Lol's *Top of the Pops* appearance for this gentle ballad, the album's only single, had a sense of fallout from the 10cc departure. The recording was suitably minimal but combined with the visual you could be forgiven for thinking it was an unfinished piece waiting for Eric and Graham's contributions. Lol, completely un-phased of course, looks as carefree as ever, his vocal near-perfectly mimed. Audio-wise, Kevin's bridge-section vocal from 'Shifting through the gears' onwards was no less than the typically finessed performance he always gave.

The TV audio mix was slightly different. The album's bird noises were absent from the introduction, and the block vocals somewhat thinned out at the words 'Get up, Get out' – the lower register harmonies stronger and more effective.

Lyrically, this first substantial *Consequences* vocal song took a seemingly mundane morning routine and brought it to life with surrealism.

> The faces on the curtains
> All the Jekylls and the Hydes are gone
>
> It's six o'clock in the morning
> You're only half-awake
> The other half is shaving
> And the toothpaste like a snake
> Has slithered out the door of the bathroom
> And it's hissing in your ear
> Get up, Get Out
> Get out of here

Though not a charting single, 'Five O'Clock in the Morning' was included on the 1998 US compilation, *10cc – The Singles*.

### 'Dialogue 1' (Lol Creme, Kevin Godley)
The play begins with this first substantial section of dialogue. It is best appreciated in context, so I defer from any spoilers. Suffice it to say that Peter Cook's magnificent one-liners come at a fairly blinding rate, so be prepared to laugh.

Introduced here is the recurring singular vocal chord that punctuates dialogue throughout *Consequences*. The three-note E Flat Minor chord, with the fifth of the scale on the bottom, ascends as B Flat, E Flat and G Flat. The tuning could come across as being a quarter-tone out depending on your location, standard tuning differing slightly between the UK and Europe.

### 'When Things Go Wrong' (Lol Creme, Kevin Godley)
A basic rock rhythm rolling along beneath one basic kalimba chord pattern that varies around a static bass line is the foundation for this collection of complaints. British saxophonist, Mel Collins, steals the show throughout with a selection of licks ranging from cliché rock lines to the most exquisitely rendered melodic jazz contours.

### 'Dialogue 2' (Lol Creme, Kevin Godley)
Two substantial musical pieces worth mentioning play beneath the dialogue here, the first a mellow piano-based groove with lyrics reflecting the plot's divorce. Secondly, a rhythmic vocal-based nonsense chant repeats and varies, revealing one lyric line: 'Keeping a date with the rain'.

### 'Lost Weekend' (Lol Creme, Kevin Godley)
American jazz singer, Ella Fitzgerald, was the first approached to sing on 'Lost Weekend' but sadly her work commitments scuppered the possibility. However, the presence of jazz vocalist, Sarah Vaughan, was an equally-prized acquisition. In his memoir *Spacecake*, Kevin Godley described her on arrival at The Manor as standing out like a shot of neon.

The backing track, Kevin's lead vocal and all the choral vocals were pre-recorded. So it was just a matter of a rehearsal, placing Vaughan behind the microphone and witnessing her magic do its thing. Three takes were recorded and one complete take used for the final mix. The personality she gave the track was beyond measure, topped off with that exquisite closing high F.

Credit must also be given to Godley and Creme's formidable choral vocals, sounding every bit plucked from somewhere in '40s Hollywood. The vocal arrangement builds harmonic tension through major/minor/diminished wire-walking, leading to the precipice of that seductive flat-9th carrot dangling just long enough to barely stand it as you're dumped down only to repeat the entire cycle. Talk about playing with emotion.

A major guest appearance can, in many cases, obscure multiple other project virtues the guest is not responsible for. So as ardent and profound as Sarah Vaughan's contribution indisputably was, her possible absence would've nevertheless left 'Lost Weekend' as predisposed to being *Consequences*' pre-eminent recording.

## 'Dialogue 3' (Lol Creme, Kevin Godley)
Side four and the second disc of the CD edition begins with an expansive six minutes and twenty-five seconds of gut-busting hilarious dialogue. It would also be absolutely criminal to ignore the brilliantly recorded jingle for Ladbrokes gambling company, that answers the telephone.

> Ladbrokes, good morning
> Gambling is our trade
> Sorry, no racing
> No flat or steeple-chasing
> The course is running
> No dog racing
> They cannot find the dogs

Towards the end, composer, Mr Blint, plays singular chords, attributing them to play characters. For some reason, the C# Minor representing Lulu is played as a B Major. The G Major allotted to her husband adds a dissonant C# note.

## 'Rosie' (Lol Creme, Kevin Godley)
This mournful ballad is Mr Blint's plaintive cry to his wife, lost when their street was bombed in World War II. In the Music Hall section, he recalls his youth in the service. Peter Cook plays the part alarmingly straight, all humour temporarily absent, Kevin Godley's vocal expressing the anguish perfectly.

## 'Office Chase' (Lol Creme, Kevin Godley)
Bass, drums, percussion and harmonised guitar created a frantic chase atmosphere. In the process, Kevin Godley let his hair down in a drum solo showing him to be every bit the virtuoso, which the usual priority of serving-the-song could often stifle considerably. The percussion eventually transformed into an army of multiple typewriter key and carriage sound effects. But also vying for attention again were the wind noises of the trusty studio vacuum cleaner.

## 'Cool, Cool, Cool' (Lol Creme, Kevin Godley)
A goldfish belonging to the increasingly intoxicated character, Mr Haig, commits suicide by jumping out of the window. What follows is 'Cool, Cool, Cool' – its eclectic genre-jumping surrealism worthy of Brian Wilson's originally ill-fated Beach Boys project, 'Smile'. Beginning as a multi-vocal

ballad, it moves via the chorus through a slow gospel-based rock feel to a creepy smoky-jazz swing coda. Of note is the line 'Like a cat on a hot tin roof' which, except for one note, is a (likely unconsciously borrowed) fragment of melody from the *How Dare You!* song, 'Head Room' – though difficult to detect, being in a different key.

> Like a cat on a hot tin roof
> Like a mouse on the run from the owl
> When you're caught like a rat
> In the empty top hat of the night
> Even shadows have shadows and a long silhouette
> All the black notes of pianos
> Play a strange cadenza

As confirmed at the end by Mr Blint; 'It's not a good omen when your goldfish commits suicide.' The single line is given its own seven-second track as 'Dialogue 6', followed by an absolute audio repetition of the chorus as 'Cool, Cool, Cool (Reprise)'.

### 'Sailor' (Lol Creme, Kevin Godley)
One mark of melodic skill is the ability to unfold an interesting line across a static harmonic state. (Or write a good tune across one chord.) This has been achieved in spades in this haunting lament, where the chords appropriately rise and fall above the root bass. It has the air of a standard, with a lyric that works outside the story.

> Sailor, I love you
> But you only love the sea
> Sailor, What's happening to me
> Like a ship in a bottle
> You ache for the sea
> Sailor
> Ache a little for me

The middle section messes with the harmony by effectively modulating to a diminished climate over the same root, moving out completely for the short two-bar transition back to the verse. Technical maybe, but unlike many dry-sounding musical explanations, this musical move actually sounds to the ears like a million bucks.

### 'Mobilization' (Lol Creme, Kevin Godley)
A lot was thrown in the pot for this brief gizmo-dominated instrumental. Interesting melodies unfurl over an almost cowboy feel. At times taking seeming stylistic classical cues from composers like Saint-Saens and

Mussorgsky, the piano even plays a verbatim melodic quote from Henry Mancini's famous 'Peter Gunn' TV theme at 0m:28s. Further snatches of melody ring a bell later on. The hard chord that interrupts and repeats up a key at 0m:40s is like a precursor to future audio samples like the famous 'Orchestra hit' that punctuated so many singles in the '80s – Godley & Creme ahead of themselves, again.

### 'Please, Please, Please' (Lol Creme, Kevin Godley)
A slow rock instrumental bar one backing vocal word – 'Please'. It bears chordal similarity to 'Funky City' – the Godley/Creme/Gouldman B-side to the 1972 Manchester City F.C. single, 'Boys in Blue'. Dialogue occurs fairly consistently over the top.

### 'Blint's Tune – Movements 1-17' (Lol Creme, Kevin Godley)
The lengthy 17-movement concerto composed by Mr Blint (not technically a concerto at all), uses a hard-cut/block composition technique. A more formal approach would've required multiple transitions. Some people, like me, find the sudden moves from one mood or style to the next, quite thrilling. It's all about the rub intensity – a kind of musical sadomasochism if you like. Or sadomusicism.

1. This monolith begins with three thickly-layered multi-octave gizmo accents accompanied by the sound of a violin trying to tune-up to an out-of-tune piano. A cowboy-pizzicato rhythm appears beneath, while pitched-down human laughs trigger the tail of the third accent. A gizmo melody descends, repeated by piano with elaborate trills.
2. 0m:45s hard-cuts to a more sparse section suggesting Mr Blint was a neo-romantic – that is, like Rachmaninov in the 20$^{th}$ century, who failed to embrace modernistic approaches, clinging to Liszt and Chopin for dear life. But as 'Blint's Tune' progresses, Mr Blint, in fact, reveals himself as more of a post-modernist. (Anything goes.)
3. 1m:45s. The cowboy-pizzicato returns adorned by purely modernistic piano chords punctuated by xylophone and swooping gizmo.
4. 2m:28s cuts to a pulsing softly-attacked chord followed by a short sharp three-note layered gizmo motif.
5. 2m:40s. A mellow but tense soundscape consisting of distant percussion, vocal noises, gizmo drones and vibraphone, leads to gizmo and piano decoration. A slow melodic piano theme enters, repeated to the accompaniment of pizzicato rhythm with gizmo and glockenspiel melody backup. A brief chromatic chord transitions to movement six.
6. 4m:44s. This incredibly effective and scattershot construction was achieved by cutting chunks of chord attacks out of the master tape, and splicing them back together at random.
7. 5m:22s. For more than a minute, gizmo resembling the tone of an Indian dilruba rides across piano clusters and military snare drum. Piano lines

hint at Stravinsky, leading to elaborate choral layers recalling those in 'Lost Weekend'.
8. 6m:35s. A faster, more percussive middle-eastern-sounding section supports a sophisticated melody partially following an octatonic scale. Included are dual chord and snare attacks sounding like the ones cut to pieces in movement six.
9. 7m:06s. Slow rhythmic piano chords march with and without military snare drum.
10. 7m:26s. Six deliberate and aggressive chord and percussion accents sound, followed by several seconds of pure rhythmic and melodic mania.
11. 7m:42s. The closest *Consequences* gets to the disco that was unavoidable in 1977. Funky layered guitars groove over a percussion bed of woodblock, timpani, gizmo, shaker, rototoms and snare drum.
12. 8m:30s. The page turns.
13. 8m:36s. A substantial melodic piano progression acting as the centrepiece of the entire 'Blint's Tune'. It could've made a good vocal song, with the repetitive section at 9m:41s acting as a potential chorus.
14. 11m:25s. Twenty wacky seconds of heavily percussion-based Zappa-istic mania.
15. 11m:46s. A bed of rhythmic pizzicato carries a delicately adorned piano melody.
16. 12m:10s. More tape cut-ups as in movements six and eight appear, this time sounding more specifically constructed. They lead to a brief and effective piano cadenza, speedily ascending and descending to land solidly on a final held B Flat major chord.
17. 12m:37s. The final chord crossfades into a one-and-a-half-minute sea of sonic drones, bird noises, and soft hurricane breezes, if such a thing is possible. In Godley & Creme's world, anything was.

# L (1978) – Godley & Creme

UK Release date: August 1978. US Release date: November 1978.
Personnel:
Lol Creme: Vocals, Piano, Rhodes, Guitar, Bass, Acoustic bass, Gizmo, Organ, Clavinet, Drums, Percussion
Kevin Godley: Vocals, Drums, Bass, Clavinet, Xylophone, Percussion
Paul Gambaccini: Bad samaritan voices on 'This Sporting Life'
Jonathan Handelsman: Saxophone
Andy Mackay: Saxophone
Recorded March-June 1978 at Surrey Sound Studios, Leatherhead, Surrey, UK
Producer: Godley & Creme
Engineers: Chris Gray and Nigel Gray
Chart placings: UK: 47

*L* was recorded simultaneously with the debut Police album, *Outlandos d'Amour*, at Nigel Gray's Surrey Sound on Kingston Road in Leatherhead. The story is often told of Police mentor Miles Copeland intermittently arriving at the studio and deriding the band's efforts with contempt until he heard 'Roxanne' and took the polar position. Thankfully, Godley & Creme were insulated from such extreme pressures and could make choices as they saw fit. First on the agenda was studio choice. Post-*How Dare You!*, Strawberry Stockport fitted the Eastlake recording system, which Kevin and Lol deemed characterless during the making of *Consequences*. Likewise-fitted was Strawberry South, so they opted for Nigel Gray's obscure 16-track hideaway close to home.

They'd reached the point where it felt necessary to relearn how to make records again – a point many acts reach if they continue activity across cultural change. The expectations that come with following up a hit were absent, though record label preference for hits went without saying. The duo were effectively starting from scratch, thus the L plate. The idea was to downsize, and the decision made to dump the commentary approach of their 10cc work and focus on personal experience.

They intended to record the album in three weeks. Commencing at the rate of one track a day, they caught themselves with the realisation they were merely working in contrast to the slo-mo of *Consequences*. Taking a more balanced view, they gave it three months, affording a chance to – as Kevin Godley put it – look under rocks for new audio species.
But the unveiling of 'Art School Canteen' for manager Harvey Lisberg was greeted with an air of scepticism. Ongoing, people kept asking if they'd done any singles yet. In 1978, Lol Creme gave *Melody Maker* the following quote.

> 'These people wanted us to be 10cc, a pop group. But they don't even know what 10cc should be now, when in fact that's what they've got, the spirit of what 10cc was in the early days, good ideas and hooks and they don't realise it.'

The new tracks fulfilled individual functions. Some, obviously experimental, remained completely listenable, like 'This Sporting Life'. Others, like 'Group Life', were simple on the surface, the acumen more deftly integrated.

**'This Sporting Life'** (Lol Creme, Kevin Godley)
Proceeding from a slow, cool, swing-jazz feel, 'This Sporting Life' is a fine example of experimental-meets-accessible. More than *Consequences*, it's a movie for the ears. Its thirteen unique modular sections click into place, encapsulating style changes from slow prog to funky fusion, each join more satisfying than the last. Along that journey, we get the audio equivalent of a chase scene and even perspective camera changes.
A narrator asks the simple questions.

> Are you bored?
> Are you jaded?
> Has all enthusiasm faded?'
> Are you one of those people
> Like glazed fruit
> Who sit there in shell-shock
> Till the dot on your screen disappears?

It sounds surreal, but that was an actual thing in the mid-20th-century, to switch the TV off and see the tiny central white dot eventually give up the ghost. The lyric shows a suicidal individual contemplating those very questions, who gives up the ghost himself. Booking into a hotel, a rapid James-Bond-goes-new-wave rock feel hauls him to his room where he calls the 'Bad Samaritans', who only encourage him to 'Wait until there's a crowd down below, Give a little when you go'.

The tempo slows and the arrangement thins to a peculiar reggae. The perspective shifts to that of the crowd below, craning their necks up to the balcony holding the individual, their cries of 'Why are we waiting?!' egging him on. The narrator returns, telling him, 'You ain't gonna be on *This Is Your Life* tonight'.

So what happens? Does he jump? You'll have to go listen to find out.

**'Sandwiches of You'** (Lol Creme, Kevin Godley)
Released as a single A-side, 19 January 1979 (UK), b/w 'Foreign Accents'.

The innovative duo were well into alternative territory here, which might've been the thinking behind 'Sandwiches of You' as a single. It could've quite rightfully been aimed at the growing population of Avant post-punkers, its angular pitch-adjusted guitar and xylophone lines used as bait to lure them back unsuspecting into a post-hippie realm of Zappa-meets-Aldous-Huxley in a happy concentration camp. That kind of twaddle could've been written about it at the time anyway, for the arty world of critical prose was then as overblown as ever, and an abstract slice of audio culture like this supplied the perfect opportunity for pundits to sharpen pencils.

But the funny thing is, we must face the fact that riding on the duo's use of an effective (and rhythmically oblique) drum loop was, in reality, a love song. Guy is keen on girl. Girl says papa won't approve. Guy just wants to talk. It's like the plot of a '50s doo-wop ballad running in reverse. But as we'd come to know from 10cc outings like 'Donna' and 'Johnny Don't Do It', Godley and Creme's brand of doo-wop was the skewed, edgy kind. What exactly was this character capable of? His intentions seemed pure and he was doing the right thing. But there was still the issue of his cannibalistic tendencies.

**'Art School Canteen'** (Lol Creme, Kevin Godley)
Jazz and folk thought they were friends for a while in the '60s and continued to liaison, sometimes secretly, in songs like this. That makes 'Art School Canteen' nostalgia, not just for a time, but a vibe – a vibe captured beautifully. This may be Lol Creme's finest recorded piano performance. The instrument certainly *sounds* expensive as it ably avoids treading on any acoustic guitar or bass toes.

But it was the playing of this sumptuous track to manager Harvey Lisberg that put a stick in the mud and caused some outside paranoia re potential Godley & Creme singles. Maybe the opening lines 'Let me tell you what it's all about, Walking 'round with your talent hanging out' was considered too provocative. Maybe the line 'I'm feeling ragged as a scrubber's tights' caused some additional doubt. Maybe actually name-checking Zappa this time was deemed too obscure for the populace, or a line like 'So I lied about the funeral, I was really playing chess' was thought too arty to be seen as commercial, despite it being entirely appropriate. Perhaps the lyric overall just didn't move through a universal-enough situation, and merely communicated aspects of art student life in an overly dispassionate way. Who knows.

The UK charts at the time showed success for folk-crossover songs like Renaissance's 'Northern Lights' and Lindisfarne's 'Run For Home'. So to paraphrase Godley & Creme's fellow Mancunian entertainer, George Formby; If consumers like them, liked songs like those, why wouldn't consumers like *these?*

**'Group Life'** (Lol Creme, Kevin Godley)
At its most basic, 'Group Life' sounded like some guys having a jam with little thought for the results. But the microscope slide told a different story, one of modernistic harmony. The instrumental parts were lean and wiry, built from separate keys that snaked around each other. The bass part, which Kevin spent all night getting right, stayed fairly static key-wise, but the vocal against it sounded as if a fourth of the scale lower than it should've been. The chorus vocals moved up a key while the bass stayed put. Wherever the two were in relation to each other, the piano occupied a third independent harmony zone of its own.

This was wild stuff. The duo had distilled decades of early 20th-century musical development down to a four-minute morsel. It was contrapuntal Cup-a-Soup. It was Bach for punks!

The middle section, where lines from the 10cc song 'Donna' were sung, was the most harmonically stable area, especially when the saxes came in line with the bass. But the piano stayed adventurous throughout that section. Harmonic stability soon deteriorated completely as various voices and parts inhabited different keys. At 3m:12s an unusually sloppy tape edit signalled the block 'group life' vocals, which re-stabilized everything into one key, though the saxophone harmonies perceived as being caged in it, took up modal extensions, attempting a breakout.

But did it all *sound* any good? If you liked poly-tonality, it did. Certain cherries sweetened the deal, like Kevin's low bass voice, expertly mixed as even deeper and resonant than the bass itself. More musicality came from saxophone virtuoso, Jonathan Handelsman, using both alto and soprano sax, taking the song out with jazz-fusion character.

On the upper level, a set of stark and abstract lyrics coldly listed details of band life, interpreting them collectively as repetitive tedium. A degree of humanity was present, but ironically the constant cycle of recording and touring was here pared down to little more than an analogy of still life.

### 'Punchbag' (Lol Creme, Kevin Godley)
No punches were pulled with the subject matter on *L*. Suicide was alluded to right out of the gate, and next came Jewish persecution from the perspective of a schoolboy. The victim is so acclimatised to it that he admits, 'I torture myself in private, To prepare me for the pain'. He even talks to himself in public. But the slow rock calmness soon becomes an irritable swing-jazz, heightening tension to an all-out chase scene sounding akin to 'Spirit in the Sky' on steroids. The oddly negative outlook of the eminent school song 'Guaduamus Igitur' booming around the corridors only aggravates the boy's attempted escape. He tears through the obstacles and a dozen song sections like his life depends on it.

The rhythm reflects the ever-mounting tension, whereas the harmony is kept, like the boy, semi-stable but tenuous. Melodic repetition is scant, but some that do come are developed.

Spoiler alert! The boy gets caught and is left on the ground asking for permission to get up. I would guess it's just another day, possibly at greater Manchester's North Cestrian Grammar School sometime in the late '50s.

### 'Foreign Accents' (Lol Creme, Kevin Godley)
Released as a single B-side, 19 January 1979 (UK), b/w 'Sandwiches of You'.

A lively 12/8 drum unit shuffle with integrated electronic bleeps and handclaps underpins *L*'s sole instrumental. Roxy Music saxophonist Andy

Mackay's two-part harmony figure repeats every two bars, becoming three-part by halfway through. Piano accents interrupt occasionally, but Mackay's solo wails over everything throughout, in that woody timbre befitting the two-tone ska music soon to become popular.

The primary attraction is the indirect Frank Zappa influence – more specifically, that of his intimidating percussion composition, 'The Black Page', just released at the recording of *L*. An angular snare drum, bass and xylophone unit plays fast and loose with the harmony in cross-rhythm, stopping short of ever entering the truly poly-rhythmic territory of Zappa's colossal precursor. 'Foreign Accents' is best heard in the original vinyl or CD editions, its dynamic 3D audio splendour lost on the brick-walled digital streamed masters.

**'Hit Factory/Business Is Business'** (Lol Creme, Kevin Godley)
Industrial and machine-like percussive noises begin the two-part album closer, topped with a descending chromatic melody line and tailed with ominous gizmo pedal tones. Unison voices sing the 'We're all working in a hit factory' hook, as if in protest, which Godley and Creme at least partially were.

In one of the few *L* moments where you think you've found your musical bearings, a solo piano drowned in flanger plays a satisfying theme. Suddenly you're hurtled askew by the explosive kick-in of 'Business Is Business'. Now we're talkin'! That's the kind of satisfying modular surprise that Godley & Creme's hard-cut edits were all about.

Ironically, this most accessible track was a scathing retort on commercial expectations.

> Force-fed on half-dead melodies
> Dragged up from the archives
> Playing on your sympathies
> 
> Throw 'em the bones
> But freeze the meat
> 'Cause the meat goes off
> But the beat goes on
> Business is business

With a regular drum unit pattern and several vocal hooks to choose from, this potential single could've kicked *L* up the ladder into top 40 album territory. In those days the public would tolerate almost any lyric line, if they even noticed half of them. This lyric proved that Godley & Creme knew what was required for a hit single. After all, they'd had a few.

> Keep it simple
> Keep it neat

Aim your hook at the man in the street
M.O.R is good
M.O.R is safe

I'm being brainwashed
And don't know how to block it
'Cause something in the chorus
Burns a hole in my pocket

Kevin and Lol would record their 1985 hit 'Cry' with producer, Trevor Horn, who by that time had conquered global charts himself with his Frankie Goes To Hollywood production, 'Relax' – a hit so ubiquitous that t-shirts bearing its title are worn to this day. Despite the doubt bred by manager Harvey Lisberg's negative reaction to 'Art School Canteen', Godley & Creme were in fact so in touch with what was commercial that 'Business Is Business' virtually predicted 'Relax'. Ahead of the game, again. Even the dance rhythm, if a little slower, was virtually identical. And in a coincidental quid pro quo, 'Business is Business' offered the closing suggestion, 'Maybe you can think of a way to turn me on', and 'Relax' replied, 'Relax when you want to come'.

## Bloody Tourists (1978) – 10cc
UK and US Release date: September 1978.
Personnel:
Graham Gouldman: Vocals, Bass, Guitar, Zither, Percussion, Whistle
Eric Stewart: Vocals, Guitar, Keyboards, Piano, Organ, Percussion
Paul Burgess: Drums, Percussion, Marimba, Glockenspiel, Vibraphone, Concert bass drums, Backing vocals
Rick Fenn: Guitar, Fretless bass, Organ, Synthesizer, Saxophone, Backing vocals, Rick Fenn's Dorking Horns, Percussion
Duncan Mackay: Synthesizer, Piano, Electric piano, Organ, Violin, Taurus bass pedals, Backing vocals, Steel drums, Percussion
Kate Spath: Cello
Tony Spath: Backing vocals
Stuart Tosh: Vocals, Drums, Percussion, Trombone
Recorded in 1978 at Strawberry Studios South, Dorking, UK
Producers: Eric Stewart and Graham Gouldman
Engineers: Eric Stewart, Keith Bessey and Tony Spath
Chart placings: UK: 3,US: 69, CA: 75, AU: 3,NZ: 2, DE: 12, NL: 2,FI: 26,NO: 4,SE: 3, JP: 58

Walking the streets of London in 1978, it wasn't unusual to see lapel badges claiming on behalf of their wearers, 'I'm not a bloody tourist. I Live Here!'. This sight provided the title for the second 10cc mark two album. In hindsight, the prior *Deceptive Bends* can be viewed as transitional, being as its core components were the minimal trio of Stewart, Gouldman and drummer, Paul Burgess. Meeting guitarist, Rick Fenn, on the set of TV show, *So It Goes*, Burgess recommended him for the live band. Adding Pilot and Alan Parsons Project drummer Stuart Tosh to the line-up for the *Deceptive Bends* world tour, 10cc were now a six-piece – the largest formation yet. Added for the new album was recent Steve Harley and Cockney Rebel keyboard player, Duncan Mackay.

The new-look 10cc had quite a pedigree and the potential was astonishing considering between them they consisted of three drummers, three bass players, three guitarists, four keyboard players and six singers. Additionally, Burgess and Mackay had a range of substantial melodic percussion instruments under their belt. Fenn, Mackay and Tosh also contributed violin, saxophone, steel drums and trombone between them. How they decided who did what is anybody's guess. There were times when one member or another would sit out of a session.

A further evolution came from Fenn co-writing 'Last Night' with Graham, and Mackay and Tosh each co-writing with Eric. Tosh took the lead vocal on their song, the second single, 'Reds In My Bed'.

Where *Deceptive Bends* had been a professional second wind, *Bloody Tourists* was a musical one, with all the hallmarks of a sparkling debut. It reintegrated surprise elements and supplied 10cc with their final number one hit, 'Dreadlock Holiday'.

## 'Dreadlock Holiday' (Graham Gouldman, Eric Stewart)
Released as a single A-side, 21 July 1978 (UK), September 1978 (US), October 1978 (CA and NZ), August 1978 (AU), b/w 'Nothing Can Move Me'. UK: 1.US: 44.CA: 30. IE: 2. AU: 2.NZ: 1. BE: 1.DE: 11. NL: 1. CH: 5.

As with many song lyrics, the 'Dreadlock Holiday' story was combined from the experiences of multiple people in separate locations. On holiday in Barbados, Eric Stewart saw a white guy on the street who walked in-between a small group of Afro-Caribbean locals, one of which yelled, 'Hey man, don't you walk through my words!'.

Forward to Eric and Moody Blues member, Justin Hayward, on a parasailing raft on the ocean off Barbados. Eric went off water-skiing, leaving Hayward behind with some locals, one of which tried to hustle his silver chain off him for a dollar. Hayward replied, 'It's worth a lot more than that and it's a present from my mother.'. The hustler responded, 'If this was Jamaica, I'd cut your hand off for that.'. On Eric's return, Hayward did some hustling of his own, recommending they remove themselves.

Graham Gouldman's contribution to the tale was lighter. On holiday in Jamaica, he asked a local if he liked cricket. The man replied, 'I don't like cricket.', paused and continued, 'I love it.'

Back in England, Graham and Eric combined their separate experiences of the West Indies, writing 10cc's perhaps most enduring earworm. Recorded in February 1978, its summer release secured it number one spots in the UK, Belgium, the Netherlands and New Zealand. Continued popularity later earned the song placement in Guy Ritchie's 2000 movie, *Snatch*, 2010's *The Social Network*, and as regular cricket match theme on the Sky network. With the single's success appearing on the brink of the video revolution, an accompanying Jamaican-themed promo starred the band as The 10cc's Combo, filmed on the relatively safer location of the Dorset coast.

## 'For You and I' (Graham Gouldman, Eric Stewart)
Released as a single A-side, January 1979 (US and CA), b/w 'Take These Chains'. US: 85. CA: 82.
Released as a single B-side, 21 September 1979 (UK), b/w 'I'm Not In Love'.

An A-side single in America and Canada only, this ballad dented the American charts no higher than number 82, likely due to the lack of an obvious hook – a virtue the first single 'Dreadlock Holiday' had in spades. But the message, that every human has beauty inside them if you look hard enough, was powerful and recurred in side two's 'Old Mister Time'.

A successful single or not, the musical merit couldn't be ignored. Duncan Mackay's particularly dexterous keyboard moves punctuated the track, the central instrumental section opening out into pure '70s multi-guitar harmony layers over two chords virtually reiterating the 'I'm Mandy Fly Me' 'spinning ball' pattern. Topping it off was Eric's dazzling mix – state-of-the-art for British pop in 1978.

## 'Take These Chains' (Graham Gouldman, Eric Stewart)
Released as a single B-side, November 1978 (UK and EU), October 1978 (IE), b/w 'Reds In My Bed'.
Released as a single B-side, December 1978 (AU and NZ), b/w 'From Rochdale To Ocho Rios'.
Released as a single B-side, January 1979 (US and CA), b/w 'For You and I'.

Linda McCartney had suggested a song title to Eric – 'I'd Love to Love You But My Hands Are Tied'. It was strong enough to deserve a song of its own, but he eventually incorporated it here as a first verse line.

Like 'Marriage Bureau Rendezvous' on *Deceptive Bends*, 'Take These Chains' signals another step down in vitality. The bulk of it seems unworthy of such a prime album position when you consider the superior material that would follow. But again, pleasing musical moments prevail. The intro states typical moody mid-'70s chords roaming over a static bass note, and the chamber-pop bridge section *a la* Brian Wilson certainly enhances the song, if appearing as misplaced. '50s rockabilly style backing vocals jump out of the choruses, offering up yet another of several reasons why 'Take These Chains' tries to be all things and doesn't quite work.

## 'Shock On The Tube (Don't Want Love)' (Eric Stewart)
The sheer eclectic virtuosity of these musicians, capable of turning on a dime at a moment's notice, held *Bloody Tourists* together. But with the material being mostly conventional, such treatment wasn't always required – 'Take These Chains' for example, with its Beach Boys midriff ejecting the song from its home ground. 'Shock On the Tube' too revealed their influence in the introduction's fine a capella vocals. But the track was overblown, moving through a recurring prog-style transitional guitar lick, chicken-pickin' guitar pecks, a barroom piano section and a double-time eruption resembling the most frantic moments of 'The Second Sitting for the Last Supper'. 'Shock On the Tube' tried too hard. Instrumentally, 10cc mark two were every bit as versatile and accomplished as the earlier band, but the new material didn't live up to it.

It would be unfair to constantly compare the new material to the old, though. It's too easy to pitch 'Shock On the Tube' style changes against those of, say, the eccentric 1976 track 'Iceberg' and come up short. But if 'Shock On the Tube' was the first 10cc track I ever heard, I'd be most impressed with the eclecticism and willingness to demonstrate such within the bounds of a three-and-a-half-minute pop song. By the time you arrive at *Bloody Tourists* it's come down to expectation and acquired taste, which can be dangerous things. So from here on, I'd be best to get a grip and realise that the band changed, but utilised past techniques as an ingredient in that change.

Inspired subject matter had always been an aspect, and this song was no exception. In conversation with Eric in 1978, *The Old Grey Whistle Test* host, and by now *Melody Maker* editor, Richard Williams, told him of getting a shock on the tube on his way home the night before. Eric nabbed the idea, turning it into a lyric where a train passenger observed the girl opposite him, falling into a dream scenario that included her. When he woke, she was gone. Shades of the 'I'm Mandy Fly Me' concept were not far from the surface. Old habits were dying hard.

### 'Last Night' (Rick Fenn, Graham Gouldman)

Sexual philosophy was a new angle for 10cc. But I guess the opportunity to expose the ritual games humans can play towards achieving what sometimes amounts to an ultimately empty experience, was ripe for the taking. Either that or it was an example of something that happened on tour, not staying on tour.

Stewart/Gouldman songs were usually integrated to the extent that it wasn't clear who wrote what. But this Gouldman/Fenn collaboration had a more Lennon/McCartney feel in that it seemed more obvious where each writer took over from section to section. True or not, it worked. The sections integrated seamlessly, giving interest without sounding over-produced.

This time Stuart Tosh played the drums, Paul Burgess given the album credit of 'Didn't turn up!'. More rhythmic flow might've helped – the spasmodic and loose funk feel possibly putting off disco punters. But as we know from *Sheet Music*, dancing wasn't everything, and if all else failed there was always the Sacro-illiac.

### 'The Anonymous Alcoholic' (Graham Gouldman, Eric Stewart)

An ambling blues/rock feel ushers in a one-sided conversation pointing a finger at the listener, reminding him of the night he jumped off the wagon. It clearly paints the transition from straight non-drinker through intoxicated party groper to ejected sidewalk dweller. It's an embarrassing story best forgotten, and so well written that by the end you're beginning to believe it even though you can't remember it.

The first bridge section borrows a lyric line from the 'Art For Art's Sake' B-side, 'Get It While You Can' – 'Everyone is having fun, So why be the one who's out in the cold?'. Besides that, there's no connection between the two songs.

When the drunk character (still the listener) decides to hit the dancefloor, the central disco section opens out, and as corny as that sounds, it *is* the point. Between Rick Fenn playing Moog synthesiser brass and real saxophone along with Stuart Tosh on trombone, you get a pretty good semblance of an American funk brass section.

Eventually waking up feeling like old leather, the character (you or me) heads back to the bar. The track's ending chord then utilises an audio gimmick where the stereo master tape is stopped minus the brake, allowing the chord to unnaturally wind down in pitch to a full stop, as if to reflect a hangover.

Side one's closer was inventive, but not single material by any stretch. But there was still plenty of time for *Bloody Tourists* to pull out the big guns, and it would.

### 'Reds In My Bed' (Eric Stewart, Stuart Tosh)
Released as a single A-side, November 1978 (UK and EU), October 1978 (IE), b/w 'Take These Chains'.

The Eric Stewart/Stuart Tosh co-write really stepped things up a notch lyrically. There was a noticeable depth in contrast to the other extremes of 'Dreadlock Holiday' and 'The Anonymous Alcoholic'. Tosh took the lead vocal too, which along with his lyrics showed real future promise for him within 10cc. But it wasn't to be. Tosh contributed only minimally to the next album, *Look Hear?* and never even sat behind the drum kit for that.

This slice of political intrigue about an Englishman being followed while having an affair with the Russian commissar's daughter was a serious left-turn. Heavy subject matter perhaps, but the lighthearted and brisk musical treatment averted any austerity. In fact, the repeated refrain, which really acted as a second unique chorus, was poppy enough that to change the song title to its main hook line 'Let Me Go Home' might well have ensured some chart action and even a stateside single release.

### 'Life Line' (Graham Gouldman)
Side two is the serious side of *Bloody Tourists*. 'Life Line' starts as a mellow ode to a friend who is ten thousand miles away. It eventually breaks into a light reggae ramble beneath the hook 'Don't go talking in your sleep' that could've gained the song respectable single status.

Not essentially a verse/chorus song, 'Life Line' was a generic AABA structure – two verses containing the title in the last line, followed by a bridge and return to the verse. There was a second unique bridge, making the track denser, but many popular songs have done that – The Police' 'Every Breath You Take' for example.

One of two *Bloody Tourists* tracks solely written by Graham Gouldman, 'Life Line' is a fine, if reasonably conventional, specimen, at least compared to 10cc's previous wild left-turn excursions. Followers were getting used to the idea that such experimentation was now less likely for 10cc – replaced by a more surefooted craftsmanship. There was still plenty to like though – Gouldman's fine vocal for example. And how 'bout those second verse synthesizer harmony clusters?

### 'Tokyo' (Eric Stewart)
Further to the above entry, musical adventure wasn't completely out of the question. The bountiful 'Tokyo' straddled Lennon-esque psychedelia, jazz and world music. Rick Fenn's fretless bass combined with Duncan Mackay's

echoed Fender Rhodes gave the introduction a solid jazz-fusion flavour, flowing through the verse punctuated by ethnic-sounding plucked zither tones. It all supported Eric's simple message of general admiration for Japan.

The bridge section opens out into 'I Am the Walrus'-style string accents, spoiled briefly by three pitchy bass notes clouding the issue at 2m:05s. The section-repeat has a bass variation that reveals the culprit to be an instrument (rather than player) problem on the open low E bass note. I'd bet that didn't go unnoticed on the session. But the mood is secure, heightened by the increasing level of what sounds uncannily like 'I'm Not In Love' vocal loops, especially at 2m:54s.

At 3m:23s a dissonant riff rockets through a virtual progressive space-rock stratosphere with perhaps a hint of piano inspiration from the closing of Peter Gabriel's contemporary track, 'Slowburn', only to be dumped back at the verse thirty seconds later. A return trip through it and the ride is over. Drummer, Paul Burgess, must surely have enjoyed the trip, being given the track credit of 'Watched again!'.

### 'Old Mister Time' (Duncan Mackay, Eric Stewart)

Another deep cut standout, this semi-progressive ballad is the tale of an ageing tramp living in a railway shack. Teased by local youth who soon realise there is more to him, the tramp builds a machine from junk found at the dump and transports himself to another dimension.

The track came as a surprise after the substantial 'Tokyo', but the sequence worked. It also fits thematically with 'For You and I' and its advice to look closer for the depth in people. But irony prevailed when someone wrote the humorous album liner notes crediting Kate Spath's cello performance to engineer Tony Spath's 'smarter sister'.

### 'From Rochdale To Ocho Rios' (Graham Gouldman)

Released as a single A-side, December 1978 (AU and NZ), b/w 'Take These Chains'. AU: 65.
Released as a single B-side, 23 May 1980 (UK), b/w 'It Doesn't Matter At All'.

Sharing the 'Dreadlock Holiday' vacation vibe, this perfectly-crafted piece of tropical pop outlines the frustrations of spending half your life on tour. From Greater Manchester to Jamaica and back is quite a round-trip, and is reflected formally by the main hook section taking a break for the better part of two minutes via the semblance of a rock concert, through to Duncan Mackay's steel drums solo and back again. A two-minute break from the main hook is brave in a song that's only 3m:40s long anyway. But as we've established, 10cc were still playing with song forms, if no longer risking total listener alienation through overly-eclectic genre-jumping.

The Australasian single-release could've been an experiment, as pre-21st-century, the territory was often used as a testing ground for UK and USA singles before deciding whether to issue them across the Atlantic. In this case, it was decided against, the single closely by-passing the Australian Top 40 on a similar trajectory to an unexpected comet.

### 'Everything You've Wanted To Know About!!! (Exclamation Marks)' (Eric Stewart)

The adventurous album closer wasn't adventurous enough to spell out the word 'sex' at the end of the title. But that didn't stop the subject matter from playing devil's advocate by sitting on a censor's knife-edge.

A young green and inexperienced guy tells the story of coveting Deborah on the streets of Piccadilly, taking rooms with her more than once. In the closing lines, he states, 'Where would it end?, You'll never know', leaving *Bloody Tourists* with a final dramatic minute of increasing musical tension through a stomping drum rhythm beneath laughing saxophones and whirling and shrieking synthesizers. It all finally winds down through slowly descending piano chords to a lustrous solo bass lick.

10cc had plenty of mojo left. Like their early classic album run, *Bloody Tourists* was to have an influence into the '80s. Where specifically? One possibility is in the music of American crossover superstar, Prince, who made no secret of his admiration for classic trans-Atlantic pop and rock of all stripes. Except for one note, you'll hear an uncanny musical quote from 'Everything You've Wanted To Know About!!!', as the main musical hook in Prince's 1984 *Purple Rain* track, 'Computer Blue'. It's worth persevering with a song to get a potential future honour such as that. Lucky 10cc drummer Stuart Tosh (who didn't play on this) hung around the studio to 'shout encouragement'.

## Contemporary Tracks

### 'Nothing Can Move Me' (Graham Gouldman, Eric Stewart)

Released as a single B-side, 21 July 1978 (UK), September 1978 (US), October 1978 (CA and NZ), August 1978 (AU), b/w 'Dreadlock Holiday'.

You can hear the John Lennon influence here, thanks to the vocal's slap echo. His unbridled love of rock and roll is also shared, the whole point being 'Nothing can move me like my rock 'n' roll do'. In support of that simplistic idea, we don't even hear a second chord until the end of the chorus, but the second chorus invites a few more in. 10cc were capable of keeping it very simple when they wanted to. Eric Stewart's blues/rock influence always had a grounding effect on anything it touched.

# Freeze Frame (1979) – Godley & Creme

UK Release date: 30 November 1979. US Release date: 1979.
Personnel:
Lol Creme: Vocals, Piano, Synthesizer, Guitar, Bass, Xylophone, Vibraphone, Gizmo, Harmonica, Percussion
Kevin Godley: Vocals, Drums, Percussion
Phil Manzanera: Guitar
Paul McCartney: Backing vocals
Rico Rodriguez: Trumpet, Tuba
Recorded in 1979 at Surrey Sound Studios, Leatherhead, Surrey, UK
Producers: Lol Creme, Kevin Godley, Phil Manzanera
Engineer: Nigel Gray
Chart placings: UK: -, US: -, NL: 21

With *L*, Godley & Creme had proven to themselves that they could still make records, so they launched into *Freeze Frame* with new-found confidence. The 16-track Surrey Sound was again chosen as the recording location. The smaller, stripped-down process was invigorating. Songs were tackled one at a time, as opposed to most people's MO of cutting all the rhythm tracks and then overdubbing everything else.

Kevin's next-door neighbour, Roxy Music guitarist Phil Manzanera, came in as co-producer and player on three tracks. His thought process and working methods had a considerable effect. With Kevin and Lol used to meticulous construction, Manzanera brought an element of chance to the work.

Paul and Linda McCartney appeared for part of the process too, when Paul sang backing vocals on 'Get Well Soon'. That just left Cuban ska trombonist, Rico Rodriguez, who layered brass parts on 'An Englishman in New York'.

Two other significant events occurred in 1979. Cigarette company, Benson & Hedges, used part of the *Consequences* track, 'Wind', for their 'Iguana' TV ad. It's likely the most glamorous cigarette commercial ever made; A helicopter flies a single B&H cigarette packet into a remote location, leaving it seductively dripping and draped half-open at poolside.

The other event was the making of Godley & Creme's first video promo, for their single, 'An Englishman in New York'. The single was a success in several European countries, mostly wherever the video was aired. The album, sadly, charted only in the Netherlands, which was surprising. Somehow the hit single failed to elevate the album to its full chart potential.

Some consider *Freeze Frame* Godley and Creme's finest work. Considering the limited amount of recording tracks at their disposal, the album was an accomplished production. Themes of science and exploration were everywhere, giving an edge that synchronised with the times. Side one was certainly a flawless knockout sequence. Oddly, some early pressings included the B-side 'Silent Running' between 'I Pity Inanimate Objects' and 'Freeze Frame', though the track was not listed on the sleeve. It would've certainly interrupted the flow. But with or without it, *Freeze Frame* stands as the one Godley & Creme album where it all came together – sophisticated songwriting and production, flawless performances, spectacular cover artwork by Hipgnosis, plus a hit single. Not to mention the influence the album would have on coming work by acts such as The Residents, Talking Heads and Laurie Anderson. *Freeze Frame* may not have bothered the album charts, but it deserves cult status. It just goes to show that commercial sales and success are no measure of actual merit.

### 'An Englishman In New York' (Lol Creme, Kevin Godley)
Released as a single A-side, 26 October 1979 (UK),1979 (EU), March 1980 (AU) b/w 'Silent Running'. AU: 17. BE: 4. NL: 7.
Released as a single A-side, 4 March 1980 (DK and DE), b/w 'Mugshots'. DE: 25.
Released as a single A-side, 1980 (ES), b/w 'Get Well Soon'.
Released as a single B-side re-titled 'Strange Apparatus (An Englishman in New York), 22 February 1982 (UK), 21 June 1982 (AU), b/w 'Snack Attack'.
Released as a 12' single B-side re-titled 'Strange Apparatus (An Englishman in New York) (Extended version), 22 February 1982 (UK), b/w 'Snack Attack (Extended version)' and 'Wide Boy'.

Even when Godley & Creme weren't necessarily attempting to push envelopes, they were forced to solve practical problems that as yet had no solution. This was the case here recording the vocals and Rico Rodriguez' brass parts. Enough parts were involved that it would've been labour-intensive and time-consuming to play them all more than once to cover repeating song sections. What they needed was digital audio editing ability, which would've allowed them to copy and paste track segments around the recording. But there was no choice but to mix the horn and vocal parts off onto a separate tape recorder and then manually play and record that new tape back onto the master tape in the appropriate places.

As usual, it was all worth the effort to achieve the result, which was an exuberantly arranged concoction of dark, dissonant, merry and jubilant impressions of New York City. Mostly courtesy of Kevin Godley, the lyrics were packed with information.

> Demented New York athletes
> Staggering 'round the block
>
> Devoted collectors of paraphernalia
> Out walking the rock
> Battle and bitch for the ultimate kitsch
> Of a crucifix clock

And don't forget the hilarious double pun; 'Sexual athlete applies for audition, Willing to make it in any position'.

The track's completely upbeat atmosphere was created through a combination of the Roland CR-78 drum machine (Or rhythm box as some called it), Lol's frantic xylophones, multi-octave vocals, and playful piano. The choruses sounded oddly hollow due to the piano being mixed at low volume, not unlike the effect of the quiet vocals on the 'Neanderthal Man' single.

Approaching Polygram with the proposal to make a promo film for the territories where they wouldn't appear personally, Kevin and Lol were surprised when the company embraced the idea. But considering the pair had no experience in directing promo films, the caveat was to bring in director, Derek Burbidge. On the day allotted for the TV studio shoot, they absorbed themselves in the entire process, effectively learning how to make what would become music videos.

The video and the song were important for Godley & Creme. The joyous single was a European success, and considering the lyric's complex religious irony and lack of sugar-coating, it was quite a coup.

### 'Random Brainwave' (Lol Creme, Kevin Godley)
Something of the scientific permeates the *Freeze Frame* lyrics, and never more than in this advanced sonic statement co-produced with Roxy Music guitarist, Phil Manzanera. There's an aspect of scientists around a subject – a kind of Dr Frankenstein meets the Greys, with lines like 'Low-key discussions, Rumble 'round the test bed, Eggheads in a huddle' and 'Are you looking through a broken pair of eyes? Are you ill-equipped to hear me?'.

The intimate acoustic guitar pattern topped with electronic overtones is consistent until interrupted at 1m:09s by four fine bars hinting at jazz-rock fusion in one of Kevin Godley's most intricate drum parts ever. Strings of scattershot vocals twist around it like DNA strands, spelling out the word, P-e-r-s-o-n-a-l-i-t-y. The guitar pattern then returns, increasing in intensity through guitar and gizmo lines towards the end.

More links 'Random Brainwave' to the following 'I Pity Inanimate Objects' than the mere hard edit between the two. The multiple verse vocal harmonies all run in their own unique one-note monotone with the exception of the melody itself which weaves around the other harmonies. This monotone technique would find its full flowering in 'I Pity Inanimate Objects', where the lead vocal, originally sung on one note, was subjected to further technological development.

### 'I Pity Inanimate Objects' (Lol Creme, Kevin Godley)
Released as a single B-side, 4 April 1980 (UK and EU), b/w 'Wide Boy'.

Kevin Godley has referred to this fascinating lyric as a robotic take on empathy and an exploration of immobility in a moving world.

> I pity inanimate objects
> Because they cannot move

From specks of dust to paperweights
Or a pound note sealed in resin

Some things are better left alone
Grains of sand prefer their own company
But magnets are two-faced
No choice for sugar
But what choice could there be
But to drown in coffee or to drown in tea?

It's as if Kevin said, 'If you want existentialism, I'll give it to you.'. He successfully took that idea, whether consciously or not, to the nth degree. A lyric like that needed a vocal to match. A tall order. But of course, Kevin and Lol went the extra distance, finding a vocal sound that potentially outshone the lyric but didn't. The lyric and the vocal sound were of equal invention. Despite the striking overall sound, the lyrics themselves were impossible to ignore – the two an ingenious match.

The vocal sound was achieved via a new piece of kit, the harmoniser. They are commonly used today either to falsely create a vocal or instrumental harmony by re-pitching the original or to effectively re-pitch or 'fix' a sharp or flat note – otherwise known as Autotune. But this was a little different. Godley & Creme's new gadget had a keyboard attached. Thinking laterally as usual, they decided to sing the vocal all on one note in monotone, then send that audio signal through the harmoniser, Lol improvising a melody on the fly with the keyboard while listening to the vocal. Amazingly, note durations stayed the same and only pitches changed. That was done more than once, Lol playing different notes each time, the final take compiled from them all.

With the vocal melody complete, they next used the harmoniser for its exact designed purpose, adding vocal harmonies to chosen lines, at the octave above or below or both. They sent the vocal through the harmoniser at different pitches, adding harmonies to thicken up the title line and 'I pity them all'. As if that wasn't enough, the final touch was to split it through a stereo delay left and right, to make it all sound even bigger. An occasional mangled-sounding electric guitar interjected, soloing as if an inanimate object being tortured, which in a way it was!

Considering this was recorded in an age of musical exploration and originality, very few were doing it anywhere near on this level. In fact, I'd say 'I Pity Inanimate Objects' remains unsurpassed in its year for sheer technical originality and invention. And it wasn't even 1980 yet.

**'Freeze Frame'** (Lol Creme, Kevin Godley)
You can always rely on two drum kits for impact, and that's exactly what you got with the title track, the closest thing here to a straight rock song. The

memorable guitar riff's minor-key gave a hint of darkness, not helped by the dilemma of the narrator recalling, or reinterpreting, his childhood.

> I cried myself to sleep
> Because they wouldn't leave the light on
> I clawed the rails
> With broken nails
> Now there's nothing left to bite on

Sections acted as verse and chorus, but the title hook was saved for the bridge section's repeating title refrains. The bridge also brought a shift to a more adult perspective with the double whammy of, 'Splendour in the grass, Freeze frame, A splintering of glass, Steam train, Stop you're going too fast'.

Two intriguing sonic tricks add much interest. At 2m:33s on the word 'freeze', the entire track freezes. Engineer Nigel Gray achieved the feat while attempting to freeze audio the way a single movie frame could be frozen. A completely different and surreal audio scene then came in over the top of the freeze.

> I asked my mum about the stains in the kitchen
> She said 'Bang, You're dead.'
> And truth is stranger than fiction

A further freeze occurred near the end after the line, 'Follow my phobia down', sounding like two simultaneous freezes of different lengths. It had the effect of audio sample loops, though no sampler was used on this album. Nigel Gray's trick was to recycle molecular fragments of audio. (Worthy of its own book.)

Though quite an intellectual piece, the track was hook-laden and would've made a potentially successful second single. Worthy of name-checking again was the Hotlegs hit; 'Going up, Like a body rejecting a heart, Going down, Like 'Neanderthal Man' in the chart'. This might've added further commercial appeal if too much time hadn't elapsed since that single's success. After the impact of 'An Englishman in New York', 'Freeze Frame' as a follow-up could've provided the second blow of a one-two punch, giving the album the added injury of a right kick up the charts.

### **'Clues'** (Lol Creme, Kevin Godley)
Side two's abstract opener, co-produced with Phil Manzanera, developed on the static harmonic mode idea used in 'Group Life', this time staying on one chord for the duration. The intro's layered guitar hook stretched the harmony in opposite directions like a rubber band. But the bass line beneath all this remained fixed. That's when it was there of course, as all musical parts appeared to be recorded for the entire track length, judiciously mixed in and out as the creators pleased. This, of course, was a year before Talking Heads

would fill their *Remain in Light* album with similar techniques, being granted the credit for such innovation into the bargain.

The lyric was an abstract collection of ideas relating to a crime investigation. Quite a story could've been made from them. But the vocal prize must surely go to the multi-harmony hook, 'Hear no evil, See no evil, Speak no evil', appearing here in an apparent resurrection of the *Consequences* singing vacuum cleaner. However, Kevin Godley confirmed for me it was likely a vocoder and he doubted Surrey Sound even had a vacuum cleaner.

A separate audio scene of xylophone, double bass and wiry guitar slid in over the fadeout, creating a contrasting 3D mix as a kind of coda.

## 'Brazilia' (Wish You Were Here)' (Lol Creme, Kevin Godley)

Like 'Clues', *Freeze Frame*'s most mysterious audio artefact moved over one basic melodic guitar riff beneath a series of disconnected phrases pointing at the title. But it differentiated itself by being mostly in the time signature of 7/8 and bringing elements of world music to the table.

Further departure came in the application of chance techniques thanks to Phil Manzanera's suggestion. He, Kevin and Lol contributed their parts separately, listening to nothing but the Smoke-On-the-Water-like guitar riff. No one heard anyone else's parts until they played them all back together. As a result, the track feels like a landscape you can walk around in. Happy accidents happen such as the initial 'White heat' section's liquid guitar chords against the 'Wish you were here' vocals in a different key.

But halfway through the track comes a left turn, transitioning to a more Latin-American groove beneath a texture comprising gizmo, xylophone, harmonica and flamenco guitar attacks. A faster, carnival atmosphere develops, eventually returning to the 7/8 groove, now in a different key. But that doesn't stop the original 'Wish you were here' vocals from sounding, creating a new harmonic friction.

With the general public exposure of American avant-garde artist Laurie Anderson a couple of years away yet, it's easy to imagine her being aware of 'Brazilia' and taking a cue from Kevin Godley's monotone lyric recitation.

## 'Mugshots' (Lol Creme, Kevin Godley)
Released as a single B-side, 4 March 1980 (DK and DE), b/w 'An Englishman in New York (Edit)'.

Developing from the germ of the title alone, the nimble 'Mugshots' became the ecstatic confession of a guy falling for a girl who leads him into a life of crime. The rockabilly guitar and vocal slap echo gave the track a '50s feel, though against an almost South African township rhythm – Godley & Creme up to their usual mixing and matching tricks.

Like many *Freeze Frame* tracks, 'Mugshots' plays out over one harmonic chord base. But the low wiry guitar harmonies unit attempts a breakout after the first chorus. Not content to be locked up, it makes a sudden comical return at the end of the song fade, as if checking around a corner that the coast is clear.

## 'Get Well Soon' (Lol Creme, Kevin Godley)
Released as a single B-side, 1980 (ES), b/w 'An Englishman in New York (Edit)'.

*Freeze Frame* left one of its strongest tracks for last. The narrator of this slow-mover is sick in bed with his transistor radio, listening to Radio Luxembourg and flicking around whatever stations he can pick up. 'Lousy words and drab percussion, Fading in and out of Russian'. His reading of music magazine, *Fabulous 208,* soon becomes entangled in a bout of delirium.

> 208 fabulous
> 208 fabulous
> 208 contagious
> Flu cold faint contagious
> 208 contagious flu

This is what he got for sacrificing his evening out to the musical, *Ipi Tombi.*
Paul McCartney was invited to sing backing vocals on 'Get Well Soon'. Kevin Godley has described this as a major thrill. McCartney arrived with his wife Linda and spent an afternoon on the vocals. His parts were smooth and so subtle you wouldn't even know it was him. The rich track, with its swooping gizmo lines, was a fitting close to the album and certainly left you wondering what on earth would come next.

## Contemporary Tracks

### 'Silent Running' (Lol Creme, Kevin Godley)
Released as a single B-side, 26 October 1979 (UK),1979 (EU), March 1980 (AU) b/w 'An Englishman in New York'.

The slow shuffle of 'Silent Running' appeared on early pressings of *Freeze Frame* on side one between 'I Pity Inanimate Objects' and 'Freeze Frame', but barely measured up to the surrounding material. The lyric was a lecture on getting your act together and being open to possibilities. The track seemed as if abandoned before it really found that one ingredient to make it fly. In its favour, the clean electric guitar solo was particularly interesting, harking back to early R&B via a Frank Zappa prism.

### 'Wide Boy' (Lol Creme, Kevin Godley)
Released as a single A-side, 4 April 1980 (UK and EU), b/w 'I Pity Inanimate Objects'.

Released as a 12' single B-side, 22 February 1982 (UK), b/w 'Snack Attack (Extended version)' and 'Strange Apparatus (An Englishman in New York) (Extended Version)'.

The contrast to the above B-side couldn't be greater. The uptempo and clearly new-wave-focused 'Wide Boy' featuring guitar by Wings member, Laurence Juber, was a hit waiting to happen. It had hooks galore. Even the bridge hook, 'Wide boy, What is your secret?, Wide boy, You better fill me in', was strong enough to be an alternative chorus. But the song's obvious sonic appeal was likely stopped in its tracks by a judgmental lyric, despite the undeniably skilful wordplay.

> Everybody knows when the sewer overflows
> He'll be the one that always comes up smelling like a rose
> With one foot in your doorway
> And one hand on your heart
> He'll never do it your way

The Madness-style saxophone hook earworm was also hard to shake. The entire track had that maddening hit quality that stays with you after one hearing. It would be too easy to suggest that a few lyrical changes could've redirected the song's destiny. What would've been the point? Godley & Creme were more interested in music than manipulating you into buying their stuff, and it's a shame the hit gatekeepers were more interested in nicety than quality.

### **'Submarine'** (Lol Creme, Kevin Godley)

Released as a single A-side, 19 September 1980 (UK), b/w 'Marciano'.

1980 was quite late in the game for a Shadows-style single, but using the then-popular ska rhythm as a base was a smart move. The '60s spaghetti western schtick worked, even though that particular horse had bolted and the golden age of the instrumental was going with it. But the track was given a second chance the following year when vocals were added and it was re-released as the 'Under Your Thumb' B-side, 'Power Behind the Throne'.

### **'Marciano'** (Lol Creme, Kevin Godley)

Released as a single B-side, 19 September 1980 (UK), b/w 'Submarine'.

This avant-garde and modernistic instrumental was total B-side material considering it was more texture than composition. Though it lacked a melody, the fast-moving sequenced bass line could've technically passed for one if you could keep up with it, which I guess is where '50s heavyweight boxing champion, Rocky Marciano, came in. Like its A-side, 'Submarine' – not out for the count and resuscitated the following year – 'Marciano' the B-side was also worthy of another round.

# Look Hear? (1980) – 10cc

UK Release date: 28 March 1980. US Release date: March 1980.
Personnel:
Graham Gouldman: Vocals, Bass, Guitar, Percussion
Eric Stewart: Vocals, Guitar, Electric piano, Percussion, Vocoder
Paul Burgess: Drums, Percussion, Marimba, Timpani
Rick Fenn: Vocals, Guitar
Duncan Mackay: Synthesizer, Electric piano, Clavinet, Organ, Harpsichord, Tubular bells, Vocoder
Stuart Tosh: Percussion, Timpani, Backing vocals
Recorded in 1979 at Strawberry Studios South, Dorking, UK
Producers: 10cc
Engineers: Eric Stewart and Tony Spath
Chart placings: UK: 35,US: 180, CA: 72, NZ: 40,DE: 40,NL: 21,NO: 3,SE: 14

Waking up in Redhill hospital, Surrey, in January 1979, Eric Stewart heard a nurse's voice say, Eric, Eric, Paul McCartney is on the phone and wants to talk to you.' Eric apparently said, 'Paul *who?*'. McCartney had called Eric to wish him well after hearing of his car accident. One night in January 1979, on the seven-mile drive from Strawberry South to his home in Walton Heath, Eric hit a spot of black ice at Reigate and crashed into a tree. Being woken to take the phone call was the next thing he remembered and he has said that the call had a positive effect on him.

But the accident changed everything. Eric fractured his skull, lost the sight in his left eye and temporarily the hearing in his left ear. 10cc's upcoming tour of Japan and Australia had to be cancelled. It was months before he could consider working again, in which time he couldn't go near anything loud, which counted out music and his beloved motor racing.
By the time he was ready to work, the 10cc machine had slowed, and the music scene was continuing to undergo radical change. Right under their noses, Manchester post-punkers, Joy Division, had cut their debut album *Unknown Pleasures* in 1979, right there on the floor at Strawberry North while Eric lay at home in recovery. Several weeks later, as if to add insult to injury, Joy Division were on the bill of a show called *Stuff The Superstars*, taking place a few miles from Strawberry North at the seedy Mayflower Club on Birch Street in Gorton, Manchester. Not that 10cc would've considered themselves superstars, but the writing was by now well on the wall (quite literally in many cases), and for the old guard to be out and the new to be in was a given.

To get back into the swing of it, Eric produced the album *Facades* for UK band, Sad Cafe, which yielded the huge single 'Every Day Hurts' – one of the biggest UK hits of 1979. Work had also begun on the new 10cc album, *Look Hear?*. Eric was still technically recovering, and by this stage, he and Graham were recording many of their own 10cc songs separately. As a result, *Look*

*Hear?* was a smaller production than *Bloody Tourists* with less contribution from the other band members. Drummer Stuart Tosh, for example, played no kit anywhere. Credited with percussion and backing vocals only, he would skip an album to return for 1983's *Windows in the Jungle*. Rick Fenn stuck mostly to guitar and some vocals, as opposed to his colourful *Bloody Tourists* multi-instrumentality. Fenn and keyboardist Duncan Mackay co-wrote 'Welcome to the World', and Fenn's 'Don't Send We Back' was also included, making *Look Hear?* the first 10cc album since the split to include songs featuring neither a Stewart nor Gouldman credit.

Playing the finished album for Phonogram, Graham Gouldman has said he had a bad feeling. After the last track finished, the label representative said, 'Okay, now have a listen to *this*.', and played some of the new Dire Straits album, after which Gouldman felt the 10cc goose was absolutely cooked.

*Look Hear?* hit the top 20 in several European countries, peaking at number three in Norway. In America, it was 10cc's first album on Warner Brothers, who changed the cover art to a sleeve detail, thinking the words 'Are You Normal' emblazoned across the cover would cause album title confusion.

### 'One-Two-Five' (Graham Gouldman, Eric Stewart)
Released as a single A-side, 29 February 1980 (UK), b/w 'Only Child'.
Released as a single A-side, 31 January 1980 (EU), b/w 'Only Child'. NL: 29. NO: 9.
Released as a single A-side, April 1980 (AU and NZ), b/w 'Only Child'. AU: 94.

Like 'The Anonymous Alcoholic' and 'From Rochdale To Ocho Rios' from *Bloody Tourists*, the semi-disco 'One-Two-Five' creates one particular scene where you feel you're experiencing a live band. It's not as obvious as in the former songs, but the chat-up lines that go along with it leave no question as to where you are in this party song about a good night out. There are no lyrical pearlers as came from the 10cc of old, but I can't give them too much of a drubbing when lines like 'Hey, can I take you home tonight?' and 'We can dance by the light of the moon' are more-or-less appropriate – even if the latter is more fitting a '40s movie.

The performances were tight and worthy of a listen for drummer Paul Burgess' playing alone. His grooves by now were well-oiled, and like many drummers in 1979, seemingly under the spell of American session player, Jeff Porcaro, the imprint of whose monstrous fills could be felt in the fade-out of 'One-Two-Five'.

Further to this, was the sonic apparition of Redbone's 'The Witch Queen of New Orleans' slowly gliding across the reggae bridge – hoodoo custom also bestowing a strong visual impact (and a throwback to 'Baron Samedi') at that point in the otherwise banal promo video. This begs the question; If 10cc fitting the changing times was an issue, why didn't they take note of what way the winds were blowing? Considering their penchant for tropical rhythms, they could've ditched the MOR and made a more direct commitment to the ska direction of bands like The Specials and Madness. Such a move could've also comfortably contained the 10cc sense of humour.

### 'Welcome to the World' (Rick Fenn, Duncan Mackay)
Apocalypse is not something you often think of in relation to 10cc songs. But band members Rick Fenn and Duncan Mackay were let off the leash for the first 10cc track since the split minus a Gouldman or Stewart credit. However, Graham and Eric sang the song, their recognisable timbres freshly resonating against sobering political lines like 'We're still delivering ten thousand souls a day, And disproportionately packing them away' and 'You've all got bodies and a few of you got minds, We'd like to use them but we never get the time'. But lines like 'Think of your children' and 'They'll never listen to your cries, They'll keep on talking and wasting precious time', were a tad preachy, and the absurd reference 'They'll send us packing on a dreadlock holiday' cheapened the lyric.

But again, the musical side worked – the semi-funk-meets-prog-pop scenario providing a depth all but absent from the opener 'One-Two-Five'. But there must've been a level of frustration for Fenn and Mackay, finding themselves applying their original material to a successful band whose remaining founders were losing interest in the operation. Maybe that's why this track worked on a listening level, as it gave Gouldman and Stewart a chance to step outside themselves while remaining within the framework of 10cc, just like the presence of Godley and Creme had once done.

### 'How'm I Ever Gonna Say Goodbye' (Rick Fenn, Graham Gouldman)
This safe semi-reggae ballad represented all that the contemporary 1980 pop climate was moving on from – that is, the middle-of-the-road, and unfortunately, craftsmanship. In itself, the song worked. The simple story of a guy who can't find a way to tell his lover he's leaving, had some depth with lines like 'Got de devil sittin' on me shoulder' and 'Got my ticket, Made my reservation/Want my name address and occupation/So I go and change my mind'. Whether it was meant for 10cc is another thing. It could've worked for gulf-western exponent, Jimmy Buffett. Apparently it didn't work for Eric Stewart who on this track was credited with being 'Out to lunch'.

### 'Don't Send We Back' (Rick Fenn)
Gouldman and Stewart were willingly accepting the political material brought forward by new band members. Rick Fenn and Duncan Mackay's dynamic 'Welcome to the World' had taken a prime *Look Hear?* position. Though debatable whether it suited 10cc, Fenn's 'Don't Send We Back' – a song expressing the plight of the Vietnamese boat people – somehow made the cut. Its manic energy seemed sprightly for the subject matter, but it did reflect the panic involved. Plus its finely-metricised lyric caused it to be easily singable, if not exactly a party piece.

**'I Took You Home'** (Eric Stewart)
Side one's closer is an emotive and clear ballad telling of the night Eric and Gloria met at a Mindbenders show in 1964. It can't be about anything else. The details are there according to how Eric has told the story since – the love at first sight, the staying up talking all night, the grumpy father the next morning etc. It was possibly dangerous territory if you were looking for pop credibility in 1980, but I doubt musicians of 10cc's pedigree cared, and why should they have? Stewart was just doing his thing and it was honest. As it goes, the love lyric was objectively put across and didn't lose itself in the syrup that so many similar songs did, can and do. Remove the designation 'baby' and it would be perfect.

**'It Doesn't Matter At All'** (Graham Gouldman, Eric Stewart)
Released as a single A-side, 23 May 1980 (UK and EU), b/w 'From Rochdale To Ocho Rios'.
Released as a single A-side, May 1980 (US), b/w 'Strange Lover'.

Another love song, but it lacked the power and appeal of 'I Took You Home'. Comparatively it was also a downer, but, despite that, was chosen as the second single. The highlight was the instrumental middle section with its dramatic guitar harmonies moving to yet another teasing exposition of the 'I'm Mandy Fly Me' 'spinning ball' chord pair. Not that it was an uncommon pattern, but somehow whenever 10cc did it, it sucked you right back into their *How Dare You!* heyday and gave you hope.

**'Dressed To Kill'** (Graham Gouldman, Eric Stewart)
An almost Doobie-Brothers-style syncopated drum rhythm sets up an expectation that is never fulfilled. It's another let's-go-out-and-make-a-killing-at-the-club lyric that seems to have become either a fallback position in lieu of inspiration, or a record label preference in hopes of scoring a hit. But as expected, performance high-points prevail including multi-layered guitar harmonies recalling the Allman Brothers, and Eric's wailing slide guitar solo – every bit as urgent as that in 'Blackmail' on *The Original Soundtrack*.

**'Lover's Anonymous'** (Graham Gouldman, Eric Stewart)
On the surface another love song, this lyric is saved by an interesting twist. The character is calling a helpline looking for relationship advice. Not breakup advice, but advice at the front end to help him avoid falling in any deeper. The mood is upbeat and happy but with a dark underside that comes through in the mostly instrumental and dramatic central section. But the dream is broken as the song abruptly stumbles back into the chorus. The song deserved more work, the whole idea seeming bigger than a five-minute pop song could contain.

## 'I Hate To Eat Alone' (Graham Gouldman)
Released as a single B-side, 22 May 1981 (UK), b/w 'Les Nouveaux Riches'.

Eric Stewart has claimed that the breakup lyrics that poured from Graham Gouldman's pen were part of this album's downfall. It can be an issue if your writing partner is in a different space, and sure, this down ballad could've been passed over. But it didn't change the fact that the song worked. The subject choice must be viewed objectively after all. Beyond such judgment, the track is completely listenable and enlivened by Duncan Mackay's sterling synthesizer solo and the rhythmic vocoder accents of the last verse. In the period, if a song lacked vigour, you could always beef it up with synthesizers, which by 1980 were sounding extremely good and were more reliable to operate. In fact, considering all the fuss made over electronic music since the '80s, the fundamental tones were never really improved upon past the digital algorithms of the Yamaha DX7 – still to appear at the recording of *Look Hear?*. But that clean digital beast would've worked hard to replicate the analogue warmth exhaled by the Yamaha CS-80 heard on this track.

## 'Strange Lover' (Graham Gouldman, Eric Stewart)
Released as a single B-side, May 1980 (US), b/w 'It Doesn't Matter At All'.

At this stage of 10cc, any material with a dark harmonic overtone usually stood up the strongest. A pattern of creating adventurous middle sections had definitely formed. 'Strange Lover', along with 'Lovers Anonymous', rivalled the more dramatic moments of *Bloody Tourists,* following in the footsteps of 'For You and I', 'Shock On the Tube', 'Tokyo' and 'Everything You Wanted To Know About!!!'.

It's easy to think that a copy of Pink Floyd's new offering *The Wall* was within shouting distance of the *Look Hear?* sessions if the melody of 'Strange Lover' is anything to go by. The line, 'I see the magic in your eyes and I can't move', finds its full flowering towards the end as 'I want to look away, But I can't look away, I'm in your power and I'm lost' – the melody strangely resembling Pink Floyd's 'Goodbye Blue Sky' line, 'Did you ever wonder why we had to run for shelter when the promise of a brave new world unfurled beneath a clear blue sky'. It's not identical, but it's unmistakably there. No one would've stolen that then, considering the absolute blanket coverage *The Wall* was receiving at the time, so I'd guess the similarity was completely unconscious.

But the line leads into an endless circular chord movement in the style of The Beatles 'I Am the Walrus' ending, fading the track out, replete with subtle pig noises, which tells me that *that* reference *was* a conscious one.

## 'L.A. Inflatable' (Graham Gouldman, Eric Stewart)
*Look Hear?* reached its climax with a straight rock and roll paean, not only to Los Angeles immigrants, but more specifically those denizens of the '60s and

'70s rock scene, groupies. It was a party song on the surface, but the lyric dug deeper to uncover rewards for those that cared to look, seeing beneath the inane Hollywood shell to find people of substance. 'Her words had me thinkin' too deeply, The meaning belying her face'.

There were L.A. references galore. Some were completely obvious, but others required more investigation, like the clever double entendre completing the below stanza.

> L.A. smiles to hide the frown
> L.A. promises to follow you down
> L.A. teeth and L.A. hair
> L.A. curves that shouldn't be there

Was that a reference to Dead Man's Curve, newly-acquired bodily curves or both? It was still good to have some 10cc lyrics that made you think.

Like some rides approaching the above-mentioned Sunset Blvd curve, *Look Hear?* comes to a potentially messy end via frantic traded solos between guitarist Rick Fenn and keyboardist Duncan Mackay, as if attempting to outdo each other in the speed stakes. They eventually fade into the distance, not a wreck in sight.

## Contemporary Tracks

### 'Only Child' (Graham Gouldman, Eric Stewart)
Released as a single B-side, 29 February 1980 (UK), b/w 'One-Two-Five'.
Released as a single B-side, 31 January 1980 (EU and NZ), b/w 'One-Two-Five'.
Released as a single B-side, April 1980 (AU), b/w 'One-Two-Five'.

This only child moves in a mysterious Mixolydian way. That is, it has the blues, not helped at all by Eric Stewart's searing slide guitar solo. These, of course, are positive statements, with the exception of the narrator's fear of being alone. I thought the blues was the most popular companion for the lonely. The Beatles certainly liked it – their presence very close to the surface here with a near-outright quote of their 'I Feel Fine' guitar riff in the verses. This B-side's bluish hue would've certainly felt fine added to *Look Hear?*, perhaps in the place of 'Don't Send We Back' or 'Dressed to Kill'.

# Ismism (1981) – Godley & Creme
UK Release date: September 1981 US Release date: October 1981.
Personnel:
Lol Creme: Vocals, Keyboards, Guitar, Bass
Kevin Godley: Vocals, Drums, Percussion, Drum machine
Bimbo Acock: Saxophone
Recorded April and May 1980 at Godley and Creme's Lymehouse Studios, Leatherhead, Surrey, UK
Producers: Lol Creme, Kevin Godley
Engineer: Lol Creme
Chart placings: UK: 29, US: -, NL: 28

1981 was a busy year for Godley & Creme, now in demand as music-video makers after successes with the Visage singles 'Fade to Grey' and 'Mind of a Toy'. They also built a small studio in Lol's house to record the new album, wrote a book – *The Fun Starts Here (Out-Takes from a Rock Memoir)*, made the famous video for Duran Duran's third single, 'Girls On Film', and followed that with the release of *Ismism*. Life was hectic.

Kevin slipped a disc during the studio installation, complicating things and relinquishing him to the couch for the duration of *Ismism*'s making. He took advantage of the situation by focusing on lyrics, churning them out in screeds for songs like 'Snack Attack', 'The Problem' and 'The Party'. Music and technology were changing fast, and with playing the drums not an option, Kevin and Lol moved further into the world of programmable drum machines and synths.

Designer, Ben Kelly, soon to be famous for his interior design of Manchester nightclub, The Hacienda, constructed the minimalist *Ismism* cover art. German illustrator, Lou Beach, was responsible for the wacky American cover, the album there re-titled to *Snack Attack*. But only the Netherlands and the UK bit, both taking *Ismism* to the top 30.

### 'Snack Attack' (Lol Creme, Kevin Godley)
Released as a 7' single A-side, 22 February 1982 (UK), 21 June 1982 (AU), b/w 'Strange Apparatus (An Englishman in New York)'.
Released as a 12' single A-side, 22 February 1982 (UK), b/w 'Strange Apparatus (An Englishman in New York) (Extended version)' and 'Wide Boy'.
Released as a 7' single A-side, 1982 (FR), b/w 'Under Your Thumb'.

Confined to the couch due to slipping a disc during the studio installation, Kevin Godley used *Ismism* as a chance to stretch out lyrically. Out of necessity, the third single, 'Snack Attack', was sung lying down. Chewing solids made eating painful, so the lyric came as a sheer outpouring of food cravings and generous wordplay.

The restless backing track of drum unit, sax, synth organ, guitar and appropriately stylish unfunky funk bass was built on a two-chord repetition.

The mix was sparse enough to allow the barrage of virtually rapped verses to come through clearly.

> I feel like Kojak sitting in a Cadillac
> I gotta eat, I gotta eat a flapjack
> A stack, a rack, a six-pack Jack
> Just call me Jack Kerouac
>
> Cold turkey's what I'm going through
> Cold turkey's what I need
> But they hung a sign on my appetite
> Saying 'Danger do not feed'

But the public might've been expecting something a little more substantial from Godley & Creme. Unlike the *Ismism* UK hit singles 'Under Your Thumb' and 'Wedding Bells', 'Snack Attack' was appropriately starved of chart action, despite a 1987 reissue as a remix.

### 'Under Your Thumb' (Lol Creme, Kevin Godley)
Released as a single A-side, 21 August1981 (UK), 4 September 1981 (EU, AU and NZ), b/w 'Power Behind the Throne'. UK: 3. IE: 7. BE: 32. NL: 13. AU: 94. Released as a single B-side, 1982 (FR), b/w 'Snack Attack'.

By 1981, the great tradition of novelty death songs had peaked. But following on a line of past UK successes like Ray Peterson's 'Tell Laura I Love Her', The Shangri-Las' 'Leader of the Pack', and Terry Jacks' 'Seasons in the Sun', Godley & Creme's surprise hit proved the death song wasn't about to cark it just yet. Taking it a step further, they added the twist of a predominant paranormal streak. A train passenger sees and hears the apparition of a screaming woman who had committed suicide by jumping from the train. Oddly, a newspaper happens to be lying there open to that very story. A pretty convenient song plot, but they weren't attempting a Poe re-write.

The song's creation had been painless. Kevin arrived at the studio one morning, heard the frantic synthesizer track Lol had made the night before and immediately began singing along. Galvanised by the rolling rhythm, the eerie story and undeniable chorus hook came quickly. They spent a couple of days perfecting the lyric and vocal, and there it stood.

Cut to Saturday 12 September 1981 on a disused airfield where Godley & Creme were busy towing a makeshift Roman chariot containing pop singer, Toyah, for her video of 'Thunder in the Mountains'. They were there informed that 'Under Your Thumb' had entered the UK singles chart at number 64 – their first chart hit at home. Peaking at number three on 17 October, the single would be their biggest ever UK hit.

**'Joey's Camel'** (Lol Creme, Kevin Godley)
Lightening things up a bit, Joey and Beau are two British characters on an Egyptian safari that takes a sour turn. Joey lays out the whole sorry tale in a letter to his mother, including his discovery of stone tablets inscribed with the ten commandments.

But more fascinating was the backing track – the 'Snack Attack' instrumental slowed down six keys lower in pitch. The saxophone was removed, replaced by new guitar, synth organ and percussion.

**'The Problem'** (Lol Creme, Kevin Godley)

> If a man who weighs 11 stone
> Leaves from his home at 8:30 in the morning
> In a car whose consumption is 16.25 mpg
> At an average speed of 40 m.p.h
> To his office which is 12 miles away......

And it goes from there becoming increasingly more ridiculous – but of course entertaining – by the word. At 3m:41s we arrive at the closing question; 'How long would it take to fill the bath?'. As we know, Mr Blint's bath took eleven minutes to fill but correctly calculating *'The Problem'*'s problem might be beyond even the finest mathematician.

As in 'Snack Attack', the mix makes way for clearer narration, two voices speaking simultaneously over a blend of drum unit, synth bass, synth and guitar. In a distinctly innovative move at 3m:44s, 'The Problem' bassline changes to that of the following song, 'Ready for Ralph', which shares a similar rhythm on the same tempo. But at this point it's still 'The Problem' we're hearing. The track then fades out, 'Ready for Ralph' coming in on the beat as a continuation. 'Ready for Ralph' was ready for the listener before anything in the lyric was ready for him.

**'Ready For Ralph'** (Lol Creme, Kevin Godley)
The *Ismism* pattern was now established – spoken word against unobtrusive minimalist backing. Now that 'The Problem' had introduced us, 'Ready for Ralph' was ready. Saxophonist, Bimbo Acock, was more than ready, decorating the track with harmony layers and virtuosic soloing throughout.

As always, the unexpected made an appearance, the luscious stereo synth bass suddenly switching to mono at 0m:29s, unfortunately rendering the track's remainder less sonically interesting. But you wouldn't notice it unless you were listening in headphones, and there was always a reason for these things. It didn't matter much with the track being at the cutting edge of post-punk avant-garde anyway. With *Ismism*, Godley and Creme were even giving electronic pioneers like Switzerland's Yello a run for their money, and they or anyone would've been working hard to keep up, at least lyrically.

The comedic and experimental lyric asked whether the room was ready for Ralph. Suddenly Ralph wasn't there and the questions were asked; is the room ready for Rose, Barry, Roy or Rod? The answer was always no; it's ready for Ralph.

### 'Wedding Bells' (Lol Creme, Kevin Godley)
Released as a single A-side, 13 November 1981 (UK), 1981 (EU), 22 February 1982 (AU and NZ), b/w 'Babies'. UK: 7. IE: 13. AU: 44. BE: 23. NL: 44.
Released as a single A-side, 1981 (CA), 1982 (US and FR), b/w 'Sale of the Century'.
Re-released as a single A-side, November 1985 (US), b/w 'Lonnie'.

Two soul pastiches broke up the otherwise modernist *Ismism* – 'Sale of the Century' and the second single, 'Wedding Bells'. The Temptations' influence sat proudly on the surface, inevitably finding its way into the video featuring the silver-suited Godley & Creme flanked by two additional dancers in a faux choreography.

> Oh I'd do it but the pleasure isn't worth the pain
> We'd run out of track before we got on the train
> Can't you hear the sound of heartstrings snappin' under the strain
> Of those wedding bells

The message was clear, reflected in the video by Lol Creme searching his pockets for rings, instead finding a pair of miniature handcuffs. But the proposed marriage seemed to be on a positive trajectory for a while at least if the upward key change after the bridge was anything to go by. But even that was reversed with an appropriately awkward-sounding key change and audio edit back down for the final verse at 2m:32s.

In spite of the big day not arriving, the UK public's collective schadenfreude walked 'Wedding Bells' down to the top ten, hot on the heels of 'Under Your Thumb' – both singles present in the chart of 21 November 1981.

### 'Lonnie' (Lol Creme, Kevin Godley)
Released as a single B-side, November 1985 (US), b/w 'Wedding Bells'.

The slow but bustling drum unit and the piano-led backing track take a back seat to the story, narrated in a noir detective style. Photographer Lonnie Garamond is sleepless during the early hours of 22 November 1963, the date of President John F. Kennedy's assassination. At 12:30 pm, with his camera set up on the scene opposite the Texas School Book Depository, Lonnie calmly squeezes off three shots, places the camera back in its case and melts into the panic.

### 'Sale of the Century' (Lol Creme, Kevin Godley)
Released as a single B-side, 1981 (CA), 1982 (US and FR), b/w 'Wedding Bells'.

The slow shuffle of The Platters' 1955 hit, 'The Great Pretender', appeared to be an influence here. But did 'Sale of the Century' measure up to Buck Ram's R&B standard? There were enough ideas for two solid songs here, but the focus was blurry. The *Sale of the Century* analogy was strong but didn't reflect in the chorus with its obvious hook suggesting an alternative title might've been 'I've Gone Yvonne'.

Anything to help keep the song on as positive a note as possible might've helped. The inexplicably low key was raised for the second chorus and could've stayed there. But after a final verse, it was dropped again for the final chorus. Downward key changes, though not unheard of, were rare, especially for a pop song chorus. But it probably helped reflect the story's trajectory. The guy was leaving after all, and there was always a market for breakup songs.

An option for this song might've been to identify it as a medley – 'Sale of the Century/I've Gone Yvonne' – with the shift to the second song being the first chorus, never to return to the 'Sale of the Century' verse. It feels like the track was unfinished and done quickly. Kevin Godley's vocal, however, was convincing and believable.

### 'The Party' (Lol Creme, Kevin Godley)

The longest track here sticks rigidly to the *Ismism* repetition pattern. The musical document outlines guest arrivals and conversations at a Godley house party, the two-bars of broken-down funk with a synthesizer twist acting as background music.

The first conversation passes judgment on the host himself, as does a later commentary from someone showing how badly researched they are.

> Damn it I know you're in a bit of a spot
> And you're used to the Merc and the Moet and the yacht
> And it must be a blow to the ego, what!
> But forget about this video rot
> And write yourselves a hit or three
> Like 'I'm Not in Paris' or 'The Dean and Me'

'The Party' is typically self-deprecating, and any accusation of pretension within it would have, like the party-goers, no legs. Kevin and Lol didn't even pretend it might be single material. But 'I hope the whole world comes to my birthday party' was a substantial enough hook that, with some judicious editing, it could've made a good novelty hit.

## Contemporary Tracks

### 'Power Behind the Throne' (Lol Creme, Kevin Godley)

Released as a single B-side, 21 August 1981 (UK), 4 September 1981 (EU, AU and NZ), b/w 'Under Your Thumb'.

This poor bloke's other half treats him like a doormat. But at least now he can use the instrumental single, 'Submarine', as a platform to vent his frustrations from. The instrumental mix is identical to the former single but 28 seconds shorter.

### **'Babies'** (Lol Creme, Kevin Godley)
Released as a single B-side, 13 November 1981 (UK), 1981 (EU), 22 February 1982 (AU and NZ), b/w 'Wedding Bells'.

This character, who just wants to make babies all night, is clearly not the same character from the A-side, 'Wedding Bells'. Unless he's talking to someone else, here. At least, stylistically, this entire melange of drum unit, reverberated synths, simplistic bass, percussion and spoken word could've talked itself into the brains of the then-forming Pet Shop Boys. It's easy to imagine Neil Tennant and Chris Lowe bonding over this B-side and branding a template for their entire career – a career I might add that earned them the Outstanding Contribution to Music Lifetime Achievement Award at the 2009 Brit Awards. No specific thank-yous were offered, but it might've been appropriate for the two blank head shapes on the screen behind their performance to have shown Godley and Creme's faces, even for a moment.

# Ten Out Of 10 (1981) – 10cc

UK Release date: 27 November 1981. US Release date: June 1982.
Personnel:
Graham Gouldman: Vocals, Bass, Double bass, Guitar, Sitar, Percussion
Eric Stewart: Vocals, Guitar, Bass, Piano, Synthesizer, Percussion
Keith Bessey: Maracas
Paul Burgess: Drums
Lenni Crookes: Saxophone
Vic Emerson: Synthesizer, Synclavier, Piano, Bass
Rick Fenn: Guitar, Fretless bass, Backing vocals
Andrew Gold: Piano, Synthesizer, Guitar, Bass, Vocoder, Percussion, Backing vocals
Mark Jordan: Organ, Piano, Backing vocals
Simon Phillips: Drums
Recorded 1981-1982 at Strawberry Studios South, Dorking, UK, and Strawberry Studios North, Stockport, UK
Producers: Eric Stewart, Graham Gouldman and Andrew Gold
Engineers: Eric Stewart, Keith Bessey, Martin Lawrence and Chris Nagle
Chart placings: UK: -, US: 209, CA: 31, NL: 49, NO: 17, SE: 24

Manchester's Joy Division recorded their seminal single 'Love Will Tear Us Apart' at Strawberry North in March 1980, right before 10cc departed on a European tour to promote *Look Hear?*. Times and music were changing at breakneck speed. By 1981, you had, on one hand, bleak moptop and slacks brigades nationwide, dividing joy and being joke buzz-kills like there was no tomorrow and, on the other, richly-rouged frowning porcelain popsters – all a league of humans intent on obliterating the musical past. If 10cc wanted to stand their ground and survive this whirlwind guard-change, they needed new blood. But rather than find some young hotshot producer with his eye on the right colour hair dye to propel them into the present, they merely did what they did best – write pure pop songs with an intellectual edge, performed with an agility borne of decades honing their craft.

Who could ask for anything more? Warner Brothers, that's who – specifically Lenny Waronker, head of A&R. He thought it would benefit the album to have a few cuts tailored for the American market, so he invited California-based singer/songwriter, Andrew Gold, aboard. It was exactly Waronker's request to bring in an American influence that helped *Ten Out of 10* sound so accomplished. Not that the initial UK version wasn't sturdy and consistent. Where *Look Hear?* might've been perceived as the band floundering, *Ten Out of 10* was fresher, more relaxed and comfortable in its skin. Who needed to keep up with trends anyway?

Work had been ongoing to this point. With Duncan Mackay, Eric had written and recorded what amounted to his first solo album, *Girls*, a soundtrack to the French movie of the same name, to which all 10cc members contributed. In April 1981, Warners offshoot, Sire Records, hired

Graham Gouldman to up-sticks to New York to produce the Ramones album, *Pleasant Dreams*. Basic tracks were cut in the big apple, Joey Ramone then flown to the UK where his vocals were diced at the small strawberry back in Stockport.

Strawberry North was also used for parts of *Ten Out of 10*, including 'Don't Ask' and 'Action Man in Motown Suit', the former which enlisted Sad Cafe keyboardist, Vic Emerson, now a 10cc band member and Duncan Mackay's replacement. The two songs also featured Nashville organist, Mark Jordan – not the Canadian singer/songwriter Marc Jordan mistakenly listed on internet discographies. But the bulk of recording occurred down at Strawberry South, including contributions from British session drummer, Simon Phillips.
After the UK album release in November 1981, Andrew Gold came in to produce new tracks intended for the American issue. Spending three weeks in the UK, he, Stewart and Gouldman hit it off extremely well. They cut three tracks at Strawberry South – 'The Power of Love', 'We've Heard It All Before' and 'Run Away'. Gold mixed them with Jim Isaacson back at Sunset Sound in Los Angeles. Included on the US release was the 10cc-produced 'Tomorrow's World Today', while 'Action Man in Motown Suit', 'Listen with Your Eyes', 'Lying Here With You' and 'Survivor' were omitted.

Incredibly, *Ten Out of 10* failed to chart in the UK or USA but reached the top 40 in Canada and Sweden, peaking at 17 in Norway. Chart stats aside, the album was a musical success, spawning material as substantial as the best work on *Bloody Tourists* and stronger even than some of the lesser tracks on *How Dare You!*. Plus the relationship with Andrew Gold led to his being invited aboard as a 10cc member proper. He declined in favour of continuing his solo career in the USA, but was later to regret the decision. Ultimately the relationship would find it's flowering several years later in his teaming up with Graham Gouldman as the duo Wax. *Ten Out of 10* was 10cc's last album with Warner Brothers in America.

### 'Don't Ask' (Graham Gouldman)
Regardless of Eric Stewart's thoughts on the Graham Gouldman breakup songs dotted over *Look Hear?*, there's no denying this one worked. Its sheer up semi-reggae energy deemed it the most suitable album-opener too. Although, the Andrew-Gold-produced attention-getter 'We've Heard It All Before' sure would've made a killer opening for the American release. As an invitation to listen, that song title would've brought back the old 10cc self-deprecation that had been mostly absent since *How Dare You!*.

'Don't Ask' was impressive for other reasons. Early on, Vic Emerson's rich-sounding Synclavier was hard to miss. Its four-voice digital synthesis made for some lavishly programmed sounds as evidenced by the chord-swell leading into the first bridge and the backwards attacks throughout it. The Synclavier was cutting-edge at the time, and though it was used here with subtlety, its presence was undeniable.

One fun occurrence was the outright melodic and lyrical quote from Little Richard's 1957 hit, 'Keep A-Knockin'', sung in the bridge section as backing vocals – varied the first time and verbatim the second.

But the piece de resistance was surely Rick Fenn's sophisticated guitar solo starting at 1m:53s and ending stunningly 16 bars later – certainly the slickest guitar solo on a 10cc record to this point. 'Don't Ask' was one of only two tracks Fenn would contribute to on this album.

The track possessed a high energy level for a breakup song where the protagonist got the raw end of the deal. His resignation was admirable and his predicament positively infectious, if that's even possible.

**'Overdraft In Overdrive'** (Graham Gouldman, Eric Stewart)
Released as a single B-side, 8 October 1982 (UK), b/w 'We've Heard it All Before'.
Released as a single B-side, 1982 (NL and PH), b/w 'Memories'.

There are no misunderstandings here. This money lyric in the tradition of 'The Wall Street Shuffle' and 'Art For Art's Sake' sees the main character living close to the edge, sometimes falling over. 'I started with nothing and worked my way down'. Verse 2 drops a fun pun – 'I got a letter from my broker, He say he broker then me' – and the bridge explains.

> It's a strange way of living
> But I like playing with fire
> I'm always walking the wire

Like 'Don't Ask', it's a dramatic and sobering situation set to a playful soundtrack, this time by a concise trio of Eric, Graham and drummer, Paul Burgess. The palpably positive ska rhythm acts as an emotional bankruptcy safety net. To leave the guy struggling in mystery would've worked, but instead, he inherits a fortune, tying the story up in a bow to finish. Where's the drama in *that?*

**'Don't Turn Me Away'** (Eric Stewart)
Released as a single A-side, 6 November 1981 (UK), 27 November 1981 (NZ), January 1982 (US, CA, AU), b/w 'Tomorrow's World Today'. CA: 38. AU: 94. NL: 49.

The second single was a lacklustre but uptempo breakup song, made dryly conventional by the addition of two unimaginative sax solos built on cliches. The instrumentation overall was a tad creamy for the angular sounds that were tearing through 1981, causing 'Don't Turn Me Away' to sound pickled in an insipid 1977 pop brine. But not as insipid as the mimed promo video where the only guy appearing to have any fun was keyboardist, Vic Emerson, twiddling with his Sequential Circuits Prophet-5 synthesizer, playing some energetic and completely inaudible part. The track was, however, the album's most successful single.

**'Memories'** (Graham Gouldman, Eric Stewart)
Released as a single A-side, 1981 (NL and PH), b/w 'Overdraft in Overdrive'.

'Memories' can be summed up as a hankering for the carefree bygone '60s, a future its youth didn't want to know about, and an over-riding acceptance of that future reality now come about. These philosophical ingredients made the song everything that the current 1981 crop of dissenting delinquents didn't want to know about. It was too grown-up. Too mature.

> We dream in the night of mythical days
> And nights in white satin
> But when the child wakes
> The fantasy breaks

The mellow verses contrasted with the jolly chorus reggae. Where 'Overdraft In Overdrive' and 'Don't Turn Me Away' were self-concerned, 'Memories', like 'Don't Ask', was more resigned, attempting to break through the clouds. But it didn't change the fact that so far *Ten Out Of 10* was a collection of lyrically sombre songs. Where was that sparkling hit the album was crying out for?

The track was remixed for the American issue, made more palatable for teenage taste buds by an electronic synth pulse added to the introduction and other drumless sections. But with that version a single only in Holland and the Philippines, 'Memories' was quickly forgotten.

**'Notell Hotel'** (Graham Gouldman, Eric Stewart)
Here's a potential single right here. It was certainly novel and accessible. Why was it overlooked? Too slow? Possibly, but no slower than 'Hotel California' a few years before. That might've been part of the problem – the creeping surreal hotel mystery anthem had been done, and much more elaborately. It's a shame. A deft lyrical swerve into less-recycled subject matter could've shed 'Notell Hotel' of its *Cluedo* overtones and been the making of the moody and tasteful ballad.

As it stands, it completes a triad of songs that began with Al Kooper's 'Hollywood Vampire', which almost certainly fed into Eagles' 'Hotel California', the existence of which cut 'Notell Hotel' off at the pass. The song was a sterling effort at a micro-genre all but ruined by the above-mentioned giant peering over its shoulder.

**'Les Nouveaux Riches'** (Eric Stewart)
Released as a single A-side, 22 May 1981 (UK), b/w 'I Hate to Eat Alone'.

A most cerebral corner, the enticing first single is like a thinking man's more manic 'Dreadlock Holiday' with a less snappy chorus. Don't get me wrong, the fine chorus has oodles of energy but over-intellectualises itself, stopping short as a potential hit but completely succeeding as a composition. It's the spiteful yarn of a young independently wealthy tourist who ruins her tropical vacation by getting burnt to a crisp before even hitting the water. The chorus blatantly lambasts her type, in the eyes of the fictional narrator.

> Les nouveaux riches
> When they tres fatigue
> They fly off to the sunshine
> They hot-foot away
> They don't get a kick
> They don't get a buzz, man
> They talk in circles
> They must be thick
> A say tick dem
> A tick tick tick-a

The single, issued six months ahead of the UK album, was a slightly shorter mix with less backing vocals, making the choruses easier to understand but not much easier to interpret. But the affected language was there for a reason, the narrator obviously one of the locals that can't be fooled.

A bit smart for a single perhaps, the song didn't chart. But the finely-wrought track took risks and covered ground untrod by 10CC since *How Dare You!*.

**'Action Man in Motown Suit'** (Graham Gouldman, Eric Stewart)
Released as a single B-side, May 1982 (US), b/w 'The Power of Love'.
Released as a single B-side, 23 July 1982 (UK), September 1982 (AU), 19 July 1982 (NZ) b/w 'Run Away'.

There's no real clue as to what musician was the specific lyrical target here, presuming the lyric is non fiction. It was an accessible, dynamic track with a rock chorus sounding the part completely. But ambiguous lyrics meant album-cut status was assured. It's dark stuff really, but there are fine vocal harmonies and guitar line pairings that alone make the track worth a listen.

**'Listen With Your Eyes'** (Graham Gouldman, Eric Stewart)
Side two, the home of the lyric nitty-gritty, now brought the third song in a row semi-critical of a lifestyle choice. The search for a religious guru was a conceptual pop bubble first floated in the late '60s. By 1981, though no longer predominantly mainstream, the idea persisted depending on where you looked. But this lyric also referred generally to those that look to the outside

for fulfilment. The point of 'Listen With Your Eyes' was to advise against such folly and get on with living your life.

The track was stylistically eclectic, with a touch of Indian drone on the hook lines, 'I don't like sitar, It don't touch guitar', shifting to the middle section's almost Stray-Cats-style '50s rockabilly. An authentic-sounding Pink Floyd – or more specifically Roger Waters – moment then occurred at the words 'Mr Blue', with their continued echo delay panning from side to side beneath a Gilmour-esque guitar solo. Quite a mix of influence was felt considering the song made its point quickly and was over and out at just over three minutes.

**'Lying Here With You'** (Graham Gouldman)
Where 'Memories' was Eric's vehicle to express feelings via the past, this heartfelt piano love ballad was firmly focused in the present. Though written by Graham Gouldman, clearly it was decided that Eric's voice would again be appropriate to deliver such sentiments. Graham would've done a fine job too, but the fact that they were still effectively auditioning each other's voices, instead of simply singing their own songs, was a good sign that collaboration was still strong and meaningful.

The melancholy approach might've suggested 'Lying Here With You' to be a breakup song, but it was, in fact, the most powerfully positive lyric on the album. It kept you guessing. At verse two's end, pianist, Vic Emerson, gave a touch of the bittersweet for balance, which stopped either side of the see-saw from dropping like a stone.

**'Survivor'** (Graham Gouldman, Eric Stewart)
A harmonically rich picked guitar introduction begins the closing rock ballad on the original UK album edition. It sets up the story of a relationship end. She longs to be free and he wants to stay. Pretty straightforward. But it becomes more complex in the faster progressive-rock-styled middle section where the guy is arrogantly confident she'll be back after he uses skilful damage control to make her forget. What? We don't know.

> Listen, I know what she's like
> She's just a dreamer
> But I'll win in the end, I'm a schemer
>
> So I'd better get my story together
> Got to make it good, she's no fool

It's a complex piece. The lyric regularly swaps perspective from narrator to character and back again. But there's a lot to like. The multi-section track takes the album's UK edition out with a long guitar solo from Eric in true 'Feel the Benefit' fashion, drummer Simon Phillips packing a wallop throughout.

**'The Power of Love'** (Andrew Gold, Graham Gouldman, Eric Stewart)
Released as a single A-side, 5 March 1982 (UK), 24 March 1982 (NZ) b/w 'You're Coming Home Again'.
Released as a single A-side, May 1982 (US), b/w 'Action Man in Motown Suit'.

The first new track on the US edition and first US single was co-written and produced by Graham's future Wax partner, Andrew Gold. A synthesizer riff sounding typical for its time, waved the track in, repeating as a short refrain later. It took an atmospheric cue from UK pop singer Kim Wilde's single, 'Cambodia' – a hit in the UK at the time, but not in America. It's easy to imagine Gold arriving in England, hearing the song and being influenced by it.
The now-signature reggae mode carried the track and octave vocal lines punctuated – Graham Gouldman's baritone clearly audible. Gold's presence was obvious from the first pre-chorus with its slick L.A. piano touch. This was technically Wax with Eric Stewart as a member and drummer Paul Burgess as a session player. You could call it 10cc if you wanted, but it's fair to say that now the goalposts had moved and the primary aim was to accomplish hit records.

Whether the last two albums had prolonged the 10cc tradition as faithfully as *Deceptive Bends* did was a matter of opinion. But the US edition of *Ten Out of 10*, as good as it was, forced you to squint to see any remaining semblance of the 10cc idea. Purist fans might've baulked, but as a pure pop record, 'The Power of Love' was fine work, even if the lyric was a cliché.

**'We've Heard It All Before'** (Andrew Gold, Graham Gouldman, Eric Stewart)
Released as a single A-side, 8 October 1982 (UK), b/w 'Overdraft in Overdrive'.

A glorious return to form reeled 10cc's quirky and humourous side back in. Suddenly it all came together – the musicality, the nuttiness and the exuberance – returning for one final splurge.

The '80s synthpop verse spoke of the difficulty of pop songwriting. Einstein 'Took his whole life explaining his theory, Try squeezing your life into three-minute songs'. The pre-chorus then took a left-field dive into a tango and an old-time vocal, purposefully declaring love in the corniest fashion. A key-change then interrupted with the chorus complaining 'We've heard it all before, Don't want to hear it anymore' in a state-of-the-art pop presentation. Leading back to the verse, if you can imagine the 1969 Beach Boys colliding with the UK's 'Oi' punk sub-genre, you've got it.

A bed of electro-pop updated the second old-time vocal section, the bridge bringing lyrical self-deprecation, suggesting video was killing the radio star again.

> You plug us in and we regurgitate the hits
> Bombard your senses with the sound of microchips

Program it digitally into the top five
Brainwash your ears
Is it tape or is it live?

Andrew Gold's production pretty much nailed the spirit of the original 10cc. The song itself could've worked on *How Dare You!*, though it wasn't necessarily recognisable as 10cc at all. If you didn't know, you wouldn't guess it was them. Maybe that was the point – to sneak under the radar into that digitally programmed top five. If so, it didn't work. But the line 'Mozart would freak at the crap on the radio' might've played a part.

**'Tomorrow's World Today'** (Graham Gouldman)
Released as a single B-side, 6 November 1981 (UK),27 November 1981 (NZ), January 1982 (US, CA, AU), b/w 'Don't Turn Me Away'.

Considering the song title, this track sounded pretty dated even for 1981. Other than listing newish technological items (some laughable even then like 'sci-fi flicks' and 'CB hams'), there was nothing futuristic about the track at all. In fact, it was sufficiently old-fashioned and conventional in a rock sense that it could've worked better for someone like Bob Seger.

Graham Gouldman helmed the recording early in the album sessions with keyboardist, Vic Emerson and drummer, Simon Phillips. Eric didn't contribute. It was left off the UK album, and that might've been advisable for the US one too, with either 'Action Man in Motown Suit' or 'Listen With Your Eyes' taking its place. Its positive attitude is likely what resurrected it from its B-side obscurity.

**'Run Away'** (Andrew Gold, Graham Gouldman, Eric Stewart)
Released as a single A-side, 23 July 1982 (UK), September 1982 (AU), 19 July 1982 (NZ) b/w 'Action Man in Motown Suit'.UK: 50.

'Run Away', the album's only single to get any UK traction, was brazen middle-of-the-road fare compared to the new romantic breed of Visage, Japan and Yazoo dominating the charts. Even Cliff Richard's 'The Only Way Out' sounded provocative against it. But with safe pop like Bananarama, Bucks Fizz and Hot Chocolate's startlingly drab 'It Started With a Kiss' in the chart's upper reaches, 'Run Away' was fair game. Who knows what the public wanted – the week of its UK release, Lynyrd Skynyrd's 1973 country-rock hit 'Free Bird' was actually at 23 on its third issue. Anything went in those days.

Not that 'Run Away' was weak for its field. It was a finely-wrought soft love song, coated in a layer of intermingling Beach-Boys-style backing vocals courtesy of Angeleno, Andrew Gold. Soft rock boasting '70s traits was still applicable in 1982, if on its last legs.

## Contemporary Tracks

### 'You're Coming Home Again' (Eric Stewart)
Released as a single B-side, 5 March 1982 (UK), 24 March 1982 (NZ) b/w 'The Power of Love'.

Stewart and Gouldman did this kind of thing in their sleep. But the writing wasn't up to Eric's usual standard and the performances sounded totally uninterested. No time was taken to even get a reasonable guitar tone to bring the solo to life. The focus was clearly on stronger material.

# Birds of Prey (1983) – Godley & Creme
UK Release date: April 1983. US Release date: 1983.
Personnel:
Lol Creme: Vocals, Guitar, Keyboards, Bass
Kevin Godley: Vocals, Percussion
Guy Barker: Trumpet
Recorded 1982-1983 at Lymehouse Studios, Leatherhead, Surrey, UK
Producers: Lol Creme and Kevin Godley
Engineer: Lol Creme
Chart placings: UK: -, US: -.

By the time *Birds of Prey* was recorded, Kevin Godley, still suffering from back problems, could at least stand at the microphone. There was little choice but to be active, with the requests to make rock videos coming thick and fast. 1982 alone had seen two videos for British artist Joan Armatrading and two for progressive rock act Asia's global hits, 'Heat of the Moment' and 'Only Time Will Tell'. The highly-prized Police video for 'Every Breath You Take' was also in the can at the release of *Birds of Prey*.

The work pressure distracted Godley & Creme in the album's making. Nevertheless, they produced a pure slice of 1983 that used cutting-edge instrument technology, more as an aid than a feature, giving the songs room to breathe. Minimalism was an aspect, certainly in the case of 'Worm and the Rattlesnake' with its lack of a defined bass part, beating Prince's 'When Doves Cry' to the punch by a year. Other innovation came in the form of experimental vocals.

Neither the two singles nor the album charted. But there was much more to the trajectory of a record promotion campaign when fired through the machinations of the bonkers '80s music biz circus. *Birds of Prey* was a solid body of work regardless. Themes of obsession, incarceration and escape prevailed through tales of some sizably crazed individuals. The songs certainly leaned towards the darker end of Kevin and Lol's oeuvre, but an often joyous instrumentation that took itself lightly, provided balance.

## 'My Body the Car' (Lol Creme, Kevin Godley)
Released as a 7' and 12' single B-side, May 1984 (UK), b/w 'Golden Boy'.
Released as a 7' and 12' single B-side, 1985 (DE) b/w 'Golden Boy (Remix)'.

Using a motor car wear-and-tear analogy for that on the human body was clever and entertaining enough. But going a step further, all vocal and percussive sounds came from the human voice. All-vocal recordings were nothing new, but imitating percussion was rare. American jazz vocalist extraordinaire, Bobby McFerrin, had done so on his 1982 track 'All Feets Can Dance', but included a real kick drum. R&B vocalist, Al Jarreau's 1976 a-cappella 'Hold On Me' was an obvious precursor, but even that included a real shaker.

'My Body the Car' was completely unique in its impression of current technology, with the Simmons electronic drums vocal fill at 0m:45s being astonishingly authentic. As an opener, it was a fine colour-splash that could've also functioned well as a closer.

**'Worm and the Rattlesnake'** (Lol Creme, Kevin Godley)
A year before American musician, Prince, accidentally discovered the spatial joys of no bass guitar while mixing 'When Doves Cry', Godley & Creme put the bass aside, allowing pounding tribal rhythms to fill much of the low sonic space in 'Worm and the Rattlesnake'. A bass was present, but soloing in a high register, acted more like a guitar. Also absent were cymbals, a technique catching on after Peter Gabriel and Kate Bush forerunners.

The lyric was a non-specific picture of youth in local fairgrounds, the Quiff Street mentioned, fictional. The protagonist remembered longing to be a rebel in his youth to compete for a girl who was wrong for him. He was recalling a time of teenage angst, wondering if she was married with five kids by now.

If she wasn't yet spliced, the song ending certainly was – the closing three 'oh yeah' refrains edited in as a repeat to accommodate the fade.

**'Cats Eyes'** (Lol Creme, Kevin Godley)
A Temptations-style soul atmosphere dominated here, squeezed through a Prince-like Linn Drum prism. The '60s met the '80s in Joe's garage, the workplace of a grease monkey, Johnny. It could even be the same Joe's garage and same Johnny featured in the 1972 10cc track, 'Johnny Don't Do It'. Except here he's fallen for the boss's wife. But Johnny is angry. 'Johnny thought it was love, but she was only slumming'. He wants to tell her, 'Going after your love is like following cat's eyes' – a lyric as smooth as a Wolfman Jack line.

Also smoothly integrated were the bridge backing vocals behind the line 'He's making a fool of himself', recalling the 1967 Aretha Franklin standard, 'Chain of Fools'. It was even in the same key and an unmistakable reference – the first of its kind to turn up on *Birds of Prey*.

**'Samson'** (Lol Creme, Kevin Godley)
Released as a single A-side, March 1983 (UK), b/w 'Samson (Dance mix)'.

A bizarre choice for a single, 'Samson' joined the ranks of the great racehorse songs alongside the British folk song 'Stewball', Spike Jones & his City Slickers' 'William Tell Overture' (Otherwise known as 'Beetlebom'), and perhaps the most finely-crafted of its kind, Dan Fogelberg's soft-rock waltz, 'Run for the Roses'.

Racehorse songs were not exactly standardised, 'Samson' being rugged in a reggae cover with lashings of cheesy organ and, oddly, eastern-sounding synthesizer. Whether that related to the biblical figure Samson's eastern folk hero lineage is difficult to determine from the lyric alone, but the biblical reference was certain in light of the dying racehorse's pregnant partner, Delila without an h.

The single B-side was a virtually instrumental dance mix of same, showered with dub echoes and clearly whipped off quickly after the main song was mixed. With little to differentiate it from the original, it has not been given a unique entry here.

### 'Save a Mountain for Me' (Lol Creme, Kevin Godley)
Released as a single A-side, 1 October 1982 (UK), February 1983 (AU), b/w 'Welcome To Breakfast Television'.

The first *Birds of Prey* single was an obvious contender for the 'Wedding Bells' soul crown. Where that song put a potentially happy situation in a negative light, 'Save a Mountain for Me' skewed the dire situation of imprisonment to express a positive ideal. The two lyrics shared a theme of escape – the former from the chains of betrothal, the latter from the chain gang as reflected by the vocal melody divided among octaves.

The lyric's prisoner longs to be in nature again and delivers his plea to the court in a pure piece of musical theatre. To the strains of British jazz trumpeter, Guy Barker, a guilty verdict is brought down. The prisoner must return to his cell and the sound of distant midnight trains – a sound heard in sample form throughout the song verses.

### 'Madame Guillotine' (Lol Creme, Kevin Godley)
Following on the incarceration theme was the surreal story of a guy whose date stands him up. Seeing her with someone else, he shoots her. In jail, he asks the priest to pray for heaven for him because he can 'hear them singing in hell'. An intense snare drum roll slowly built the instrumental sections to a tastefully understated guillotine sound effect. More could've been made of it, but it wouldn't be Godley & Creme if they didn't stop short of gimmick.

The Roland TR-808 drum unit often sounded like a gimmick. But in 1983 it was, along with the Linn LM-1, at the forefront of that technology. Godley & Creme chose whichever unit worked best to serve a given song. Considering the sheer amount of electronic equipment then exploding onto the market, instrument technology was kept complimentary on this album and the song was the thing – and even then was limited to its essentials. The uptempo but controlled 'Madame Guillotine' played out over virtually one chord except for two others alternating in the short instrumental sections, some of which contained the 'Why are we waiting' cliché used in the 'Jump' section of 1978's 'This Sporting Life'.

### 'Woodwork' (Lol Creme, Kevin Godley)
The 'Orchestra Hit' sample was first heard in the original 1979 Fairlight CMI as ORCH5. By 1983, various orchestra hits and stabs were heard everywhere.

'Woodwork' used a fairly subtle strings-dominated one used for the verse bass line. Bowed string samples took over in the choruses, though the middle section added bass guitar which vied for sonic attention.

Otherwise, rhythm guitar and oddball synth noises carried the lively track beneath the character's complaints of a romantic bounce-back.

> When you cut the thing that held us together
> You were pulling the wings off a fly
> Now you're back from the dead
> Pushing a double bed
> And I want to know why

Those few lines said it all. Not intended as a happy story in the first place, the clearly negative hook line 'You came crawling out of the woodwork' probably disqualified the song for single-release consideration.

### 'Twisted Nerve' (Lol Creme, Kevin Godley)

The obvious attention-getter is the remarkable first-verse rhyme 'racehorse/gale force'. This describes the movement of a woman obsessed with her husband who is extremely bad for her, and she knows it. At the beginning, he was like a religion, but now her eyes 'shiver, shift and curve'. The static but frenetic one-note synth bass part never falters for a moment, but constantly resonates up and down through a higher frequency band as if searching for a way out. The chords also attempt to escape, but the singular bass note stops them short of an exit, just as the husband does in averting his wife's departure. Twisted stuff alright, on an album where Godley & Creme contorted their usual playful spirit into concepts dark and in some cases, hopeless.

### 'Out in the Cold' (Lol Creme, Kevin Godley)

The luxurious closer began with the unmistakable pump of a LinnDrum kick on a medium-tempo pattern. All vocals were through a vocoder, which in 1983 was still novel enough to make a track single-worthy. At that very time, Dutch pop singer, Taco, was in the flush of his global hit cover of the Irving Berlin standard, 'Puttin' On the Ritz'. Like 'Out in the Cold', it featured vocoder and combined a saxophone section with other electronic sonorities, producing the air of a synthetic cabaret.

It's doubtful whether 'Out in the Cold' was superior in composition to the Berlin marvel – not helped by Taco's dazzling synthesizer arrangement which outshone virtually everything similar on the chart at the time. But Godley & Creme's brooding futurist spectacle bared its own rewards. The verse melody, reminiscent of the Leon Russell standard 'This Masquerade', twisted up that cliché, adding intrigue through descending chromatic swaps and a creepy minor sixth quality. The hook line 'The night you left me out in the cold' was a particularly luscious low point.

An overcast gloom descended on the 1983 singles charts. If so issued, 'Out in the Cold' would've been right at home surrounded by other swooning black atmospheres like The Fixx's 'Saved By Zero', Genesis' 'Mama' and Robert Plant's 'Big Log'. But as if in a self-fulfilling prophecy, it was left out altogether, finding its end appropriately on the chord landing on the word 'cold', abandoned to dwell and fade out.

## Contemporary Tracks

### 'Welcome To Breakfast Television' (Lol Creme, Kevin Godley)
Released as a single B-side, 1 October 1982 (UK), February 1983 (AU), b/w 'Save a Mountain For Me'.

As album-worthy as could be, this fabulous satirical dig at morning television could've broken up *Birds of Prey* quite nicely, as a kind of commercial break. Its electronic backing resonated with the generic TV music of the time.

> With news and views and world opinion
> To stimulate your mind
> With music by the deaf
> Directed by the blind
>
> Welcome to breakfast television
> Live from Smithfield Market
> Where we'll show you how to pluck a chicken
> While cleaning vomit off the carpet

The sarcastic hook 'We'll send you on your way to work, In a happy frame of mind' set you up for the below sublime narcissistic slice.

> Welcome to breakfast television
> Welcome to BTV
> We'll interrupt your morning sex
> With lots of lovely me

# Windows in the Jungle (1983) – 10cc

UK Release date: September 1983. US Release date: September1983.
Personnel:
Graham Gouldman: Vocals, Bass, Guitar, Percussion
Eric Stewart: Vocals, Guitar, Keyboards, Percussion
Mel Collins: Saxophone
Vic Emerson: Keyboards
Rick Fenn: Vocals, Guitar
Steve Gadd: Drums, Percussion
Simon Phillips: Drums
Mike Timoney: Keyboards
Stuart Tosh: Vocals, Drums, Marimba, Percussion
Recorded in 1983 at Strawberry Studios North, Stockport, UK
Producers: Eric Stewart and Graham Gouldman
Engineers: Eric Stewart, Martin Lawrence and Chris (CJ) Jones
Chart placings: UK: 70, CA: 97,NL: 7

In 1982, Eric Stewart recorded his second solo album, *Frooty Rooties,* at Strawberry South. But with the studio booked out when it came time to record *Windows in the Jungle*, sessions took place back at Strawberry North. The first full 10cc album to be recorded there since 1975's *How Dare You!*, it would also be the last. Sadly, Strawberry South went into liquidation in 1983. Eric and Gloria, severally liable with Graham Gouldman for the studio mortgage, sold their home to cover the debts. Peter Tattersal continued to run Strawberry North, selling it in 1987.

Eric's original idea for *Windows in the Jungle* as a concept album, chronicling the ups and downs of the human race over a 24-hour period, was quickly consumed by the pressure to produce hit singles. He longed to make larger statements like 'Une Nuit a Paris' or 'Feel the Benefit', but it had become impossible. All that remained of the concept were the two songs book-ending the album – '24 Hours' and 'Taxi! Taxi!. Increasingly uninspired commercial attempts filled the abyss in-between. Eric later regretted not pursuing the concept.

The album still gets a bad rap in some quarters for its so-called '80s production – a sweeping criticism not based in reality. Its techniques were barely reflective of contemporary trends. The mix was superlative and the drum sounds alone were world-class. Session players featured, including first-call drummers Steve Gadd and Simon Phillips, and saxophonist, Mel Collins, augmenting the core band of Eric, Graham, Vic Emerson, Rick Fenn and Stuart Tosh.

The real issue with *Windows in the Jungle* was the songwriting, which reeked of record label pressure to make hits. The two remaining concept elements were a good frame, but the view through them was less than picturesque. The first three songs were solid. But the following four, balancing precariously between commercial fodder and attempts at social and semi-political comment, fell flat. The worst offenders were the axiomatic shopping list, 'Americana Panorama', and the clumsy 'Working Girls'.

All was not lost with the album and two singles, 'Feel the Love' and 'Food For Thought', becoming minor hits in Europe. Godley & Creme's tennis-slanted music video gave levity to the former, while the latter was coupled with the album-worthy B-side, 'The Secret Life of Henry'.

But it wasn't enough. Eric felt the time was right to end 10cc once and for all, which happened with little discussion or fanfare. Thankfully it would be temporary and two substantial albums would appear in the '90s. The first, ...*Meanwhile*, would be a partial reconciliation with Godley & Creme.

## '24 Hours' (Graham Gouldman, Eric Stewart)
Released as a 7' single A-side, April 1983 (UK), b/w 'Dreadlock Holiday (Live)'. UK: 78.
Released as a 10' single Maxi A-side, April 1983 (UK), b/w 'Dreadlock Holiday (Live)' and 'I'm Not In Love (Live)'.

It was immediately obvious that *Windows in the Jungle* had high production values. The drums alone had a sonic richness, the backing vocals possessed that classic 10cc liquidity and Rick Fenn's elegant guitar solo on the opening track, a soaring highlight.

This all made '24 Hours' a superior-sounding recording as opposed to a song. Being the morning portion of a 24-hour period, it worked in with Eric's initial album concept and worked as a lengthy album cut. As a single, it was a different story. There was no obvious vocal hook, and with virtually half the track jettisoned in the edit, it lacked the full version's substance. There must've been some logic to releasing it five months in advance of the album. Any high hopes for the single were ultimately dashed. But it didn't change the fact that '24 Hours', was and is a worthwhile listen – especially if you let the lavish album version wash over you.

## 'Feel the Love (Oomachasaooma)' (Graham Gouldman, Eric Stewart)
Released as a single A-side, 17 June 1983 (EU), b/w 'She Gives Me Pain'. BE: 13. NL: 7.
Released as a single A-side, 29 August 1983 (AU and NZ), b/w 'She Gives Me Pain'. AU: 76.
Released as a single A-side, September 1983 (UK), b/w 'She Gives Me Pain'. UK: 87.

'Oomachasaooma' was a nonsense word that Eric's two-year-old son used to sing in the car, so Eric took it for an extra chorus hook. The lyric, another along the lines of *Look Hear!*'s 'I Took You Home', recalled the glorious early and ongoing days of a relationship.

The video stood as a reconciliation of sorts of the four original 10cc members. Directed by Godley & Creme, it applied their lateral visual approach to lyrics. Eric and Graham were two of a group of otherwise half-naked men watching a tennis game from behind glass. The pair sang and the others accompanied with choreographed head movements. For the guitar solo, all but Stewart and Gouldman mimed to it in air guitar, the tennis players with their racquets.

More successful than '24 Hours', the single reached the top 20 in parts of Europe. The promo single for radio omitted the vocal bridge, cutting straight to the guitar solo. Drummer Steve Gadd claimed the song to be unique as the first reggae track he'd ever cut. He said he'd always wanted to do one, but must've forgotten recording the Grover Washington Jnr. cover of the Bob Marley classic 'Jamming' in 1981.

### 'Yes I Am' (Graham Gouldman, Eric Stewart)
Eric Stewart has since expressed frustration with the pressure on 10cc to come up with singles in the '80s. 'Yes I Am' comes across as the offspring of such pressure. Another love song, it messed with the cliché, as if in protest, by giving the impression the character involved was settling for less than he wanted.

The American-sounding smooth sax solo would certainly have been a bone of contention for 10cc purists, despite Mel Collins' flawless performance. To be fair, as with this entire album, all the playing was slick and the sound rich and satisfying. But minus a strong hook, the track lacked single potential.

### 'Americana Panorama' (Graham Gouldman, Eric Stewart)
Was this a 10cc record? From the corny component of having a B.B. King styled guitar lick after his name is sung, to the clumsy line, 'Doctor Winston, J.F.K., You had a dream but they blew you away', you could've been forgiven for thinking it wasn't. Touching on America's dangerous aspects, political history and growing military capability, this protest concept was expressed with little real flare. A mere shopping list of American things, it could've been so much more. 'Yes I Am' was sounding pretty good about now.

### 'City Lights' (Graham Gouldman, Eric Stewart)
10cc mark two would often play a funky disco rhythm and make it obvious by saying so. Lines like 'Truck down the street feeling kinda funky' and 'No way to stop when the music's in your body' seemed so flippant it was hard to tell if it was mockery or approval. Maybe it was ironic. But the only irony was the gaping abyss between what 10cc once were and in part still wanted to be, and what they had become as exemplified by 'City Lights'. Enough said. Having single potential, it could've been some measure of a hit were it 1977.

### 'Food For Thought' (Graham Gouldman, Eric Stewart)
Released as a single A-side, October 1983 (BE and NL), b/w 'The Secret Life of Henry'. BE: 25. NL: 18.

By song six of eight, we were running out of time for this album to make a positive impression. Lyrics like 'Your lips are milk and honey' and 'Your body's soft and dreamy' betrayed the song, showing it for exactly what it was – the result of record company pressure. In fairness, it was a reasonable pop outing, and moderately successful when issued as a single in Belgium and the Netherlands.

Plus the central 'Starve without your love' vocal section was a pleasing high point.

**'Working Girls'** (Graham Gouldman, Eric Stewart)
A completely different lyric might've saved this for me. It could've at least lived up to the title's implication, which might've given it some street cred at least. Sadly it delivered little more than a faux pas. The details of dodgy typing pool Romeos were laid out non-judgmentally. But ultimately the lyric's opinion was ambiguous, its title analogy applied to average office workers who failed to escape the same judgment levelled at the assortment of surrounding leches. The ambiguity was the issue, not the topic.

Don't get me wrong. Any topic is up for grabs in a song. With sensitive subject matter, it's all about how it's handled. Pink Floyd's Syd Barrett handled the risque 'Arnold Layne' quite tastefully in 1967. Furthermore, Randy Newman's 1977 deep cut, 'In Germany Before the War', leaves you most unbelievably close to sympathy with a serial killer's self-justification. These things *can* be done with words. It's just a matter of whether you're capable, which Gouldman and Stewart were – and whether you want to get it right, which is a matter of opinion in this case.

**'Taxi! Taxi!'** (Graham Gouldman, Eric Stewart)
The lengthy closing track was as worthy as the album opener, '24 Hours'. But the damage was done and the pair of songs didn't justify the remaining tracks. 'Taxi! Taxi!', yet another love song and representing the end of the day, was more finely woven than most of *Windows in the Jungle*. But some melody snatches seemed borrowed from outside. At 4m:30s the intro chords from '24 Hours' *were* tastefully incorporated in a slight rhythmic variation – the only remaining semblance of Eric's original concept.

The three closing minutes of instrumental were a treat, the focus being the understated percussive intricacy of drummer, Simon Phillips. A classy touch to close what would be 10cc's last album for nine years.

## Contemporary Tracks

**'She Gives Me Pain'** (Graham Gouldman, Eric Stewart)
Released as a single B-side, 17 June 1983 (EU), b/w 'Feel the Love'.
Released as a single B-side, 29 August 1983 (AU and NZ), b/w 'Feel the Love'.
Released as a single B-side, September 1983 (UK), b/w 'Feel the Love'.

Things that sounded a bit like disco were still being made in 1983 and this was one. An instrumental, it appeared to give a nod to the Alan Parsons Project, and the melody was strong enough to deserve a lyric. As it stood, it functioned as short sharp B-side filler.

**'The Secret Life of Henry'** (Graham Gouldman, Eric Stewart)
Released as a single B-side, October 1983 (BE and NL), b/w 'Food For Thought'.

The central character here, Henry, is described at first as an angel. He kisses his wife goodbye each morning and steps onto the train a devil. After ten years in the same job, he plans to steal a computer, take the information and make a killing in the city. It's a worthy concept and the frantic track could've worked well on *Windows in the Jungle*, adding some vitality into the bargain. But it was fated to be a European B-side.

## The History Mix Volume 1 (1985) – Godley & Creme

UK Release date: June 1985. US Release date: 1985
Personnel:
Lol Creme: Vocals, Guitar, Keyboards, Percussion
Kevin Godley: Vocals, Drums, Percussion
Graham Gouldman: Vocals, Bass, Guitar
Eric Stewart: Vocals, Guitar, Keyboards
Uncredited: Backing vocals
Recorded 1972-1985 at Strawberry Studios, Stockport, UK, Surrey Sound Studios, Leatherhead, Surrey, UK, and Sarm East Studios, London, UK.
Producers: Kevin Godley, Lol Creme, 10cc, Nigel Gray, Trevor Horn and J. J. Jeczalik
Engineers: Lol Creme, Eric Stewart, Nigel Gray, J. J. Jeczalik
Chart placings: UK: -, US: 37, CA: 50.

MTV and other networks were now exploding with Godley-&-Creme-directed rock videos. The pair were consumed with the work, and music had taken a back seat. 1984 had seen only one Godley & Creme release, the single 'Golden Boy', which scraped the Belgium top 40 only.

In New York that year, editing the Police' *Synchronicity Concert* video, Godley and Creme struck up a camaraderie with UK record producer, Trevor Horn, when staying at the same hotel. After meeting in the bar at midnight, they went back to the studio and had a blast fooling around with music until 7 am. They made plans to meet up again six months later at Horn's Sarm East Studios in London's East End, where they would ultimately record their biggest global hit, 'Cry'.

An album was due, but Kevin and Lol had no new songs and no desire to write any. They concluded that some kind of audio celebration of their 25th year working together might be appropriate. Creating a pile of audio samples culled from their entire career, they pulled in Sarm engineer and Art of Noise band member, J.J. Jeczalik, to make some musical sense of them. It was his baby really. Godley & Creme were mere ingredients (as were Stewart and Gouldman), popping in occasionally to check progress and make suggestions.

The initial UK vinyl release consisted only of 'Cry' and the two sample constructions 'Wet Rubber Soup' and 'Expanding the Business'. Some international vinyl issues omitted the latter. CD, cassette and vinyl track listings differed for some territories but basically consisted of the above with some added combination of the single 'Golden Boy', its B-side 'Light Me Up', the *Birds of Prey* single, 'Save a Mountain for Me', 'Englishman in New York' and the 'Cry' 7' version.

**'Wet Rubber Soup'** (Lol Creme, Kevin Godley, Graham Gouldman, Eric Stewart)
Released as an edited single B-side, June 1987 (UK), b/w 'Snack Attack (Remix)'.

Art of Noise band member and Sarm East engineer J.J. Jeczalik constructed this 12m:26s beast, consisting of samples from early 10cc and Godley & Creme music. Supported by a drum machine pattern, the only other newly-created feature was Kevin Godley's 20-second rap at 2m:31s.

The ability to pitch-adjust samples without affecting their speed (in order to match an existing tempo) was generally not yet available in 1985, despite Godley & Creme finding a gadget that essentially performed that very task on 1979's 'I Pity Inanimate Objects'. So some 'Wet Rubber Soup' samples (Such as the 'Life is a Minestrone' vocals) would lag or speed up as they progressed, only coming back in time when re-struck. Only the attacks were lockable in time with quantize-capability. (Quantization being the ability to lock the attack of a sound on an exact mathematical beat division.)

'Wet Rubber Soup' includes samples from the below songs, but this is not intended to be an exhaustive list:

Begins with part of Peter Cook's spoken introduction to 'Blint's Tune' from Consequences.
Vocals: 'Rubber Bullets', 'Business is Business', 'Life is a Minestrone', 'Wedding Bells', 'I'm Not In Love' and 'Cry'.
Instrumental details or sound effects: 'Rubber Bullets',' Life is a Minestrone', 'Sand In My Face' and 'Light Me Up'.
Actual sections: 'The Flood', 'Life is a Minestrone', 'Light Me Up' and 'I'm Not In Love'.

## **'Cry'** (Lol Creme, Kevin Godley)
Released as a 7' single A-side, March 1985 (UK), July 1985 (US), 1985 (CA), May 1985 (AU), 1985 (NZ)b/w 'Love Bombs'. UK: 19. IE: 27. US: 16. CA: 7. AT: 12. BE: 34. DE: 8. NL: 13. AU: 43. NZ: 16.
Released as a 12' single Extended Version A-side, March 1985 (UK) b/w 'Love Bombs'.
Released as a 12' single Extended Remix A-side, 1985 (UK, AU and NZ) b/w 'Love Bombs'. UK: 66.
Released as a 7' single Remix A-side, 1985 (US) b/w 'Love Bombs'.
Released as a 12' single Extended Remix A-side, 1985 (US) b/w 'Cry (Single version)' and 'Cry (Extended version).
Released as a 12' single Extended Remix A-side, 1986 (CA) b/w 'Love Bombs' and 'Cry' (12' Club version).
Released as a CD single B-side, 1988 (UK and EU), b/w '10'000 Angels', 'Hidden Heartbeat' and 'Can't Sleep'.

After having met in New York and vowed to work together, Godley, Creme and producer, Trevor Horn, reconvened at Sarm East Studios at 9 Osborn Street in London's East End in late 1984. Initial work on a song titled 'Hit the Box' went nowhere fast, so they hauled out a two-line song fragment known as 'You Don't Know', which had existed since circa 1970. The lines were so strong that Kevin and Lol had always felt it their duty to make the rest even stronger. Over the years, they'd made many attempts to finish it, always coming up short. Taking an instant liking to it, Horn with fellow Art of Noise member J.J. Jeczalik at the Synclavier, began a backing track. Kevin sang the two vocal lines and he and Lol disappeared, leaving them to it.

Returning later, they didn't need to add many lyrics for the song to be coaxed from the germ of the first two lines. Kevin sung, vocal lines were judiciously placed with digital editing, and the song came to life, appearing before them from less effort than they'd thought it might require.

Lol's impressive liquid chord introduction (the verse melody a $5^{th}$ higher) was a way to grab the listener's attention. But Trevor Horn's configuration of the very few lyric and melodic fragments that made up 'Cry', was the key. Horn's work here was a masterclass in pacing and song construction. On a macro level, small pieces were placed like blocks, building to a crescendo, while smaller pieces were moved around and used as gateways to line repeats.

It would be no exaggeration to say Horn treated 'Cry' as a space wormhole, bending it back on itself, creating shortcuts to disparate moments in time. For example, the lone statement of the phrase 'You don't know' at 0m:50s in the single version, acted as a hook that linked back to a new verse. But that verse was only three bars long before leading to the full 'Cry' hook. After several instrumental bars, a new verse began, half as long again as the first. But a new hook, 'You don't even know how to say goodbye', interrupted at 2m:17s, cleverly delayed until two-thirds of the way through. Its arrival elevated the entire track, and the hook was applied three times in a row. It was so effective it was able to be stretched over an entire 50 seconds without sounding overstated. Horn had judiciously placed minimal ingredients, with landmarks along the way ensuring a satisfying journey, leading to that unforgettable ending.

The duo had a global hit on their hands, their first and only to hit the American top 40. The innovative video was a huge aid in the song's success. Originally, 1984 Winter Olympics gold-medal-winners Torvill and Dean were asked to ice-skate to the song, but synchronising schedules proved impossible. So Godley & Creme fell back on the simple idea of many crossfading faces. (Not morphing as some seem to think.)

The 7' single was the definitive version of 'Cry'. The 6m:32s album mix took liberties with the song form, adding little value, though that length likely existed first with the single edited down from it. The long introduction included the whispered 'Don't cry' sample from 'I'm Not In Love', giving a connection to the preceding 'Wet Rubber Soup'.

The 7m:14s 12' extended remix began with a verse of solo voice followed by a minimalist mix. But some snatches of vocal within it were nonsensically placed – a gimmick customary to many '80s 12' single mixes. Even worse, leading to the lead vocal entrance was a big ol' train wreck of an audio edit at 3m:33s, cut one beat too late. From there it was more or less the single form with additional percussion, vocal samples, and a longer ending lead-out.

Every audio gimmick has a definitive recorded moment. The ending of 'Cry' was the historical home of the keyboard-pitched vocal sample – that is, Kevin singing the word 'cry'. With it risking a possible level of mockery, the dramatic Synclavier chord base rendered it appreciable one time. That ending is still a spine-tingler and is likely the only sped-up voice in recorded history that you take seriously, due to the sheer instrumental expanse beneath it.

**'Expanding the Business/The 'Dare You' Man/Hum Drum Boys in Paris/Mountain Tension'** (Lol Creme, Kevin Godley, Graham Gouldman, Eric Stewart)
J.J. Jeczalik's second sample construction ran for a full 17m:04s. It consisted largely of samples from the below with newly added drum patterns.

> Begins with an a-cappella mix of backing vocals from 'Golden Boy'.
> Vocals: 'Business is Business', 'I'm Not In Love', 'Une Nuit a Paris', 'The Dean and I', 'How Dare You', 'Sand In My Face', 'This Sporting Life', 'Donna' and 'Umbopo'.
> Instrumental details or sound effects: 'Business is Business', 'How Dare You', 'Art For Art's Sake', 'Wind'.
> Actual sections: 'Business is Business', 'Neanderthal Man', 'Une Nuit a Paris' and 'Sand In My Face'.

**'Light Me Up'** (Lol Creme, Kevin Godley)
Released as a 7' and 12' single B-side, September 1985 (UK),1986 (CA) b/w 'Golden Boy (Remix)'.

Considering great chunks of it were inserted into 'Wet Rubber Soup', this blue-eyed soul number had the air of the digital sample constructions. Placements of the group vocals, and key ambiguity thanks to a roving bass line, made it sound messed with. But it was originally constructed this way. It was issued on the album's CD edition.

**'Golden Boy'** (Lol Creme, Kevin Godley)
Released as a 7' and 12' single A-side, May 1984 (UK and EU), b/w 'My Body the Car'.
Released as a 7' and 12' single A-side remix, September 1985 (UK), b/w 'Light Me Up'.
Released as a 7' and 12' single A-side remix, September 1985 (EU), b/w 'My Body the Car'. BE: 35.
Released as a 7' single A-side remix, 1986 (CA) b/w 'Light Me Up'.

The lone Godley & Creme release for 1984 was a Motown-inspired soul song. Only the remix got some action, scaling the lower reaches of the Belgium top 40. Despite the lack of success, the song was strong and could've worked well for Culture Club.

The remix sounded superior to the initial release. The vocals were clearer, and previously unheard female vocal lines added a pleasing melodic element to the second chorus.

### 'Love Bombs' (Lol Creme, Kevin Godley)
Released as a 7' single B-side, March 1985 (UK),July 1985 (US), 1985 (CA), May 1985 (AU), 1985 (NZ)b/w 'Cry'.
Released as a 12' single B-side, March 1985 (UK) b/w 'Cry (Extended version)'.
Released as a 12' single B-side, 1985 (UK) b/w 'Cry (Extended remix)'.
Released as a 7' single B-side, 1985 (US) b/w 'Cry (Remix)'.

A purely abstract piece of manic textural percussion, minus any chordal accompaniment. A brief vocal describes love as an explosion going off in your head and guitar effects develop into distorted lines towards the end.

Vocal echo delays gave the track the feel of a dub mix – possibly one of the last of its kind. By 1985, dub mixes, which were pretty easy to generate (All you had to do was throw some delays on a few things and mute the vocal randomly), were largely superseded by more elaborate mix techniques thanks to the proliferation of new technology and the ease of digital editing.

### 'Snack Attack (Remix)' (Lol Creme, Kevin Godley)
Released as a single A-side, June 1987 (UK) b/w 'Wet Rubber Soup (Edit)'.
Released as a 12' single Extended A-side, 1987 (UK) b/w 'Wet Rubber Soup (Edit)' and 'Jack Attack Dub'.
Released as a 12' single Extended A-side, 1987 (CA) b/w 'Wet Rubber Soup (Edit)', 'Snack Attack (7' Remix)' and 'Jack Attack Dub'.

The 'Snack Attack' remix (included on the 1987 greatest hits compilation *Changing Faces – The Very Best of 10cc and Godley & Creme*), and it's B-side 'Jack Attack Dub' were more predominantly representative of re-mixer Phil Harding's work. With unnecessary newly-programmed drums and keyboards, the remixes sounded more like an advertisement for the current new jack swing craze than an interesting development on pre-existing material. Tasteless audio gimmicks prevailed, most disconcertingly the introduction vocal sample aping Deep Purple's 'Smoke on the Water' guitar riff. And this was the same Phil Harding responsible that year for the sparkling mixes of *Time and Tide*, the debut solo album from Matt Bianco vocalist, Basia.

To remix 'Snack Attack' was clearly a business decision. Like Harding's work for British production team, Stock, Aitken and Waterman, it felt like just another item rolled off a production line.

# Goodbye Blue Sky (1988) – Godley & Creme

UK Release date: February 1988. US Release date: 1988.
Personnel:
Lol Creme: Vocals, Guitar, Bass, Keyboards
Kevin Godley: Vocals, Drums, Percussion
Jimmy Chambers: Backing vocals
George Chandler: Backing vocals
Mark Feltham: Harmonica
Mitt Gamon: Harmonica
Jimmy Helms: Backing vocals
Recorded in 1987 at Lymehouse Studios.
Producers: Godley & Creme
Engineer: Martin Heyes
Chart placings: UK: -, US: -.

The previous couple of albums had been recorded to fulfil a contract. The technology had been convenient and the method reliable. But details like designing the perfect song rhythms, or what Godley called 'The perfect mediocrity', had become tiring. So the Synclavier was cast out, and Godley and Creme took it upon themselves to relearn their instruments.

To help make the album unique, two harmonica players were brought in; Mitt Gamon and Nine Below Zero vocalist and session player, Mark Feltham. Adding to the recipe were three future vocalists from UK pop/dance group, Londonbeat. The usual level of musical experimentation was diverted into more of an exercise in overall concision. An interesting and original aesthetic was found and stuck with for the entire record.

Godley later described a slow sense of impending apocalypse seeping into the songs, due to the dire possibility being in the minds of he and the other co-founders of ARK – an organisation devoted to bringing environmental issues to the public's attention.

Recording took place again at Lol's home studio, Lymehouse, in the summer of 1987. Despite the often serious subject matter, the album was a joy to make. The more organic feel agreed with them, as they were going against electronica to an extent. Real drums returned, the pair finding a way to squeeze a kit into Lol's limited studio space. The reality was a compromise between organic and electronic, with drums, guitars and harmonicas on one side, and synthesizers and sampled double bass on the other. The amalgam worked.

Despite significant sales only for the first single 'A Little Piece of Heaven', *Goodbye Blue Sky* was a solid swansong, housing some of Godley & Creme's grandest lyrical statements.

## 'H.E.A.V.E.N./A Little Piece of Heaven' (Lol Creme, Kevin Godley)
Released as a 7' single A-side ('A Little Piece of Heaven'), January 1988 (UK), 1988 (US), April 1988 (AU) b/w 'Bits of Blue Sky'. DE: 26. NL: 17.

Released as a 12' single Extended A-side ('A Little Piece of Heaven'), 1988 (UK) b/w 'Bits of Blue Sky' and 'Rhino Rhino'.
Released as a CD single A-side (A Little Piece of Heaven (Extended mix)), 1988 (UK and EU) b/w 'Bits of Blue Sky', 'Rhino Rhino' and 'A Little Piece of Heaven (7' version)'.

The three future Londonbeat singers, Jimmy Chambers, George Chandler and Jimmy Helms, here took a cue from the African mbube a-cappella vocal style. The short eight-line stanza effectively developed the 'Save a Mountain For Me' ecology-meets-ideal concept into a more all-encompassing philosophy, as if that song's captive had mulled it all over for quite some time. In the process, the idea progressed from self-centred wish to humane ideology – the perfect preface to the coming apocalyptic themes. Either that or Godley & Creme had just unleashed their most meaningful eight lines ever, whatever was behind their creation.

The companion song, 'A Little Piece of Heaven', took influence from country, folk, blues and traditional Mexican music. But the single's failure to register in an age of massive hits drawing on world music – like Paul Simon's *Graceland* and Los Lobos' hit version of the Mexican folk song, 'La Bamba' – was possibly due to a level of lyric ambiguity. But that was part of the beauty – not everything needed to be spelt out.

**'Don't Set Fire** (To the One I Love)' (Lol Creme, Kevin Godley)
With all abandon, *Goodbye Blue Sky* unleashed its first apocalyptic vision in the form of an earthquake. Verse two addressed trying to enter heaven when they 'turn out the light', entertaining the possibility that it might be closed. 'But the other place is open'. It was all set to a pounding '60s Motown rhythm and a melody closely resembling parts of 'Golden Boy'.

**'Golden Rings'** (Lol Creme, Kevin Godley)
It was again time for a happy Godley & Creme story to turn sour. The narrator told of his marriage ending, his wife re-marrying and again divorcing, but still wearing only his ring. A well-trodden path, all the more dramatic thanks to superlative vocal group interjections – the bass voice supplying the bass line in places – which elevated *Goodbye Blue Sky* wherever they appeared. 12-string acoustic guitars were the bulk of chordal accompaniment with the support of bass and brushed drums.

**'Crime & Punishment'** (Lol Creme, Kevin Godley)
The themes of faith and redemption that poured from the introductory 'H.E.A.V.E.N.' cast a shadow over the entire album, and never more than on this slice of political intrigue. Politics were brought unashamedly front-and-centre in support of justice.

> You're charged with doing the devil's work
> Using God's name
> He may forget and he may forgive
> But he can see through the walls of the house
> Where the guilty live

The harmonica lifted the track from its digital synth mechanics, giving an old-time Dust Bowl preacher feel – the solos doubled an octave below, suggesting the Devil had a hand in it. But in opposition, the Latin phrase of the holy trinity, 'In nomine patris, Et filii et spiritus sancti' was repeatedly sung as background under the verses and closing section.

### 'The Big Bang' (Lol Creme, Kevin Godley)

Religion and politics combine here. God sits on his throne looking for something to do. Then 'Big bang went the thing that created you and me'! In a twist, 'The devil was given the job of looking after man'. Everything goes downhill from there. In the end, 'The church was empty, They were praying to a gun, They were making big bangs of their own'. It's all over in a flash – an energetic ball of breakneck roots-rock fire, with some burning harmonica to boot.

### '10,000 Angels' (Lol Creme, Kevin Godley)

Released as a single A-side, March 1988 (UK), b/w 'Hidden Heartbeat'. Released as a CD single A-side, 1988 (UK and EU), b/w 'Hidden Heartbeat', 'Can't Sleep' and 'Cry'.

The Stan Jones standard 'Ghost Riders in the Sky' and its theme of redemption appeared to be the prevailing influence on the second single.

> As the riders loped on by him he heard one call his name
> If you want to save your soul from hell a-riding on our range
> Then cowboy change your ways today or with us, you will ride
> Trying to catch the Devil's herd
> Across these endless skies

'10,000 Angels' communicated a more general idea.

> 10,000 angels runnin' after you
> 10,000 devils close behind
> 10,000 reasons for doing what is true
> Possess your body and your mind

The track contained the closest sonic thing *Goodbye Blue Sky* had to the Godley & Creme of old. At 3m:05s as the mix layers subsided momentarily, a fast sequenced synthesizer pattern joined the frantic drum unit, instantly transporting the listener back to the electronic experiments of *Freeze Frame* and *Ismism* – most notably the manic 'Under Your Thumb'. The pattern continued along for the ride, largely hidden but for one re-emergence at 3m:53s.

Towards the end, the lines, '10,000 angels playing gold guitars' and 'I saw them, They used to be stars', flirted with a development on the ageing musicians concept of the 1974 10cc song, 'Old Wild Men'. In that song, they were alive and well. In the confines of '10,000 Angels', they'd passed.

### 'Sweet Memory' (Lol Creme, Kevin Godley)

This plainly tangible concept with a melancholy twist cried out to be a single. The fictional story slowly unfolded from the memory of a woman, to the memory of a woman who died, leading to the surprise line, 'She smoked too many cigarettes'.

The conventional smooth '80s treatment was a compliment – the bonus bass harmonica grunts a familiar hook that hadn't snagged some of us since The Beach Boys' *Pet Sounds*. The superlative soul drum-fill leading into verse one proved Kevin Godley was undoubtedly match-fit, and the central instrumental section was darkly beautiful. Amongst all the experimentation it was easy to forget that Godley & Creme could easily write pure pop if they chose. They *had* written 'Donna' and 'Cry' after all. The worthy 'Sweet Memory', the hit that should've been, stood up there in merit alongside those successes.

### 'Airforce One' (Lol Creme, Kevin Godley)

In a similar theme to 10cc's 'Clockwork Creep', an aeroplane has a bomb on board, but this time it's Air Force One. The warning comes from a radio call, unlike the older song where most information was revealed by the bomb and plane as characters. The revelation that there is nowhere to land adds further tension. In spite of that, a touch of military snare drum keeps the instrumentation stoic.

The constant vocal group answers are probably over the top in this case. They feel forced. One singular lead vocal delivering the sobering message could've been more effective. It also feels like they intended to replace the synthesizer bass (due to it actually being an electric piano timbre with the bottom end cranked up) but never got around to it. That combined with the generic synth organ patch gives the unpolished feel of a demo. Traditionally, demos carried an excitement formed from initial inspiration sparks. But in the '80s, keyboards often came with bland factory preset sounds that demanded editing if they were to be taken seriously. If left unaltered, they lay as lifeless victims of electronic algorithms, resulting in many a cold clinical and soulless demo.

'Airforce One' felt somewhat abandoned. But the idea was solid and the guitar breathed some life into it.

**'The Last Page of History'** (Lol Creme, Kevin Godley)
Apocalypse has arrived, confirmed for the narrator as he burns rubber down the highway with the sight of a mushroom cloud in his rear-view mirror. Like 'Don't Set Fire (To the One I Love), the mood is kept high, this time in a joyous Tex-Mex swing jam, despite the song being inspired by a general desperation for the state of our species.

The song incorporated fragments from outside pieces of music. The chorus began with a melodic quote from the French National Anthem, 'La Marseillaise', on the line 'We're rolling down the road again' – the same melody The Beatles borrowed for the introduction of 'All You Need is Love'. Approaching the end, came a melody and lyric quote from the Roy Rogers/Dale Evans standard, 'Happy Trails'; 'Happy trails to you, Until we meet again'.

**'Desperate Times'** (Lol Creme, Kevin Godley)
The statement 'Desperate times are what we live in' is as meaningful now as it was in 1988, if not more. The backing vocal group, in full flight above the gospel piano base, made way for Kevin Godley's fine lead vocal, complimenting it perfectly. The harmonica solo was a powerful final feature, making 'Desperate Times' a fine close, not only to the underrated *Goodbye Blue Sky* but to the Godley & Creme album discography.

**Contemporary Tracks**

**'Bits of Blue Sky'** (Lol Creme, Kevin Godley)
Released as a single B-side, January 1988 (UK), 1988 (US), April 1988 (AU) b/w 'A Little Piece of Heaven'.
Released as a 12' single B-side, 1988 (UK)b/w 'a Little Piece of Heaven' and 'Rhino Rhino'.

An edit of pieces of every song from *Goodbye Blue Sky* except for 'A Little Piece of Heaven'. Some are hard-cut together and others fade out into long reverberation.

**'Hidden Heartbeat'** (Lol Creme, Kevin Godley)
Released as a single B-side, March 1988 (UK), b/w '10,000 Angels'.
Released as a CD single B-side, 1988 (UK and EU), b/w '10,000 Angels', 'Can't Sleep' and 'Cry'.

Kevin Godley in full soul flight sounded in places like a ringer for soul singer, Sam Cooke. The track though was overly electronic, especially on the unison drum and brass sample accents. But the surprising chordal rock guitar instrumental was a real breath of fresh air.

### 'Rhino Rhino' (Lol Creme, Kevin Godley)
Released as a 12' single B-side, 1988 (UK) b/w 'A Little Piece of Heaven' and 'Bits of Blue Sky'.

This outtake from the *Goodbye Blue Sky* sessions is about a rhinoceros that 'Broke out of a zoo on the east side, When the keeper committed rhinocide'. Sadly, while taking his 'revenge on America', the rhino gets shot in a hail of bullets on live TV. Like some of the darker material on the album, the musical mood is kept light, rendering the song as almost a novelty.

### 'Can't Sleep' (Lol Creme, Kevin Godley)
Released as a CD single B-side, 1988 (UK and EU), b/w '10'000 Angels', 'Hidden Heartbeat' and 'Cry'.

Another *Goodbye Blue Sky* outtake, not without its appeal. The harmonicas added to the fast rock mood, but the lyric about a guy losing sleep, because he can't make up his mind about anything, lacked vitality.

### 'Love Is Dead' (Lol Creme, Kevin Godley)
This was a single that charted in the UK on 16 January 1988 for three weeks, reaching number 84. It's listed as having no record label. I can find no other reference to it and Kevin Godley denies its existence. It's a total mystery.

The following year, Kevin and Lol called it a day. Their individual tastes were changing. Kevin had started working on music videos alone, which didn't go down well. He wanted the freedom to make decisions without needing the approval of another party. He felt he and Lol had worked together so long that it had become as confining as being in 10cc. The pair were like two brains that had outgrown one body.

Lol Creme has viewed the parting philosophically, grateful that people were interested for so long in whatever he and Kevin chose to record. He felt neither of them should have any complaints from their time working together.

> How many people ever get the chance to be in that position?. We were the luckiest bastards on the planet.

# ...Meanwhile (1992) – 10cc

UK Release date: 11 May 1992. US Release date: 1992.
Personnel:
Graham Gouldman: Vocals, Guitar
Eric Stewart: Vocals, Guitar, Piano, Electric piano, Synthesizer
Lol Creme: Backing vocals
Kevin Godley: Vocals
Gordon Gaines: Guitar
Andrew Gold: 12-string guitar
Paul Griffin: Synthesizer
Dr John: Grand piano
Bashiri Johnson: Percussion
Michael Landau: Guitar
David Paich: Organ, Synthesizer
Jeff Porcaro: Drums, Percussion
Freddie Washington: Bass
Horn section: Gary Grant (Trumpet), Jerry Hey (Trumpet), Dan Higgins (Saxophone), Kim Hutchcroften (Saxophone), Bill Reichenbach Jr. (Trombone)
Backing vocals: Tawatha Agee, Frank Floyd, Curtis King, Vaneese Thomas, Fonzi Thornton
Recorded 1990-1991 at Bearsville Studios, Woodstock, NY, Bill Schnee Studio, LA, The Hit Factory, NY, River Sound Studios, NY, Village Recorders, LA
Producers: Gary Katz and 10cc
Engineers: David Michael Dill, Robert Hart, Chris Laidlaw, Jim Lauber, Jay Ryan, Brian Sperber, Wayne Yurgelun
Arranger: Jerry Hey
Chart placings: NL: 39, JP: 84

In the intervening years, Eric Stewart had produced Abba's Agnetha Faltskog and shared lead vocals on the 1990 Alan Parsons Project album *Freudiana*. He also co-wrote half of Paul McCartney's 1986 album *Press To Play*. Those writing sessions yielded 'Don't Break the Promises', resurrected for *Meanwhile* with an added Graham Gouldman credit. Graham in the meantime had teamed up with Andrew Gold and recorded three albums as the duo Wax, having several hits, most notably 1987's 'Bridge To Your Heart'.

Due to ongoing sight problems and operations as a result of the 1979 car accident, Eric's left eye was removed in 1989, he and Gloria moving to France that year. By the time *Meanwhile* rolled around, they were living in Barbados.

In light of the success of the 1987 compilation *Changing Faces – The Very Best of 10cc and Godley & Creme*, Polydor Records requested a reformation of the original four-piece for a new album. 10cc now felt the time was right. But it soon became obvious that the old working patterns were not to return.

All songs were written by Stewart/Gouldman and recorded in New York under producer, Gary Katz, who assembled an entourage of session players.

Graham was prepared to make it work, but Eric was unhappy with the need for outside musicians, despite the fact that they were among the best in the world and he enjoyed working with them.

Godley & Creme were not involved in the songwriting and weren't even together at the sessions. Spirits were high, but with the rhythm tracks pre-recorded, Kevin and Lol were mere backing singers – Creme on six songs and Godley on two, except for his lead vocal on 'The Stars Didn't Show'. This meant the four original members were together on only three songs. Godley spent only two days at the studio and has since recalled an awkward atmosphere where everything seemed perfect, but some vital element was absent. Except for Creme providing the album title, that was the extent of their involvement.

Basic tracks were recorded at Bearsville in Woodstock, NY, and overdubs partially at the Gary Katz and Donald Fagen-owned River Sound in Manhattan. Founder Steely Dan member, Fagen, dropped into the sessions more than once, but Eric and Graham barely got a chance to talk to him.

*Meanwhile* charted only in the Netherlands and Japan, the single 'Woman in Love' only in the former. The recording also signalled the beginning of Eric and Graham's separation. Later that year, Polydor, who had signed 10cc to a five-album deal, failed to take up their option.

Those that accused *Windows in the Jungle* of suffering from an overly '80s-sounding production would've been better to point that bony finger at *Meanwhile*, with the modification from the '80s to '90s. The former album had in reality done a tasteful job of keeping its era's sonic signatures as unobtrusive. *Meanwhile*, on the other hand, was awash with the newly freeze-dried pad-like synthesizer sounds of its era such as the Roland D-50, the Korg M1 and others. What was now passing for an electric piano sound was really a synth sound with added harmonics designed to replicate the striking of a hammer on a reed or a tine. It made little difference what keyboards were used on *Meanwhile*. You could take your pick, as these machines lacked such personality as to be virtually indistinguishable from each other anyway, giving much musical product of the time a soulless feel. Having said that, *Meanwhile* was certainly as polished as the prior album, with the unfortunate detail of it being mixed with the snare drum over-resonating at around 235hz virtually all the way through.

*Meanwhile* was dedicated in memory of Graham Gouldman's father Hyme 'The Rhyme' Gouldman (1908-1991). The album's drummer Jeff Porcaro also passed just three months after its release.

**'Woman in Love'** (Graham Gouldman, Eric Stewart)
Released as a single A-side, 13 April 1992 (UK and EU)b/w 'Man With a Mission'. NL: 55.
Released as a CD Maxi single, 1992 (UK)b/w 'Wonderland', 'Welcome to Paradise' and 'The Stars Didn't Show.

Similar to the *Windows in the Jungle* opener '24 Hours', this introduction was too long, and combined with the clumsy spoken phrase leading to the drum rhythm, made too big a deal of itself for the style. At six minutes, the medium-tempo track was overly lengthy. At least the radio issue (but not the single) was an edit.

Where '24 Hours' was a substantial concept, 'Woman in Love' had a standard love song signature, albeit articulated more generally. Lyric cliches overflowed, from 'Look at her eyes, See the glow in her cheeks' to 'Look at her face, She's a picture' – not helped by nonsense lines like 'These mixed emo's make your senses to reel'. In the track's defence, it contained Eric Stewart's fine slide guitar-playing.

### 'Wonderland' (Graham Gouldman, Eric Stewart)
Released as a CD Maxi single, 1992 (UK) b/w 'Woman in Love', 'Welcome to Paradise' and 'The Stars Didn't Show'.

A step up from the opening song, the brisk and sonically airy 'Wonderland' was a slightly tense window into the thoughts and surroundings of a star in ascendancy. He even seemed a little arrogant, which added depth. But the lyric could've been more conversational. Isolated statements like 'The power of communication', 'A simple trade in real affection' and 'I'd like to introduce you to a special substance, Good for you', felt awkwardly crammed in. In an otherwise clear lyric, there seemed little reason to be abstruse.

Nevertheless, 'Wonderland' was a signal to expect further quality material. There was also the bonus of Graham Gouldman and Lol Creme singing together on the chorus, the first time we'd heard this since *How Dare You!*.

### 'Fill Her Up' (Graham Gouldman, Eric Stewart)
You'd never know that New Orleans musician, Dr John, was playing the piano on this semi-country-rock piece. More guitars than were necessary clouded the instrument. The lyric preached, critical of people's diet and exercise choices. This was fine if a character expressed it, but the technical faux pas sounded more like it came from the songwriters' mouths. The words inspired no empathy for whoever was speaking them. Best moved on from.

### 'Something Special' (Graham Gouldman, Eric Stewart)
Everywhere 'Fill Her Up' failed, 'Something Special' succeeded. The New Orleans-styled track was the catalyst for Dr John's presence. Eric Stewart had told producer Gary Katz he was going for a Dr John piano vibe. Katz responded by calling up the pianist himself and getting him down to play. This time the piano was crystal clear and the star of the show.

The lyric made its unapologetic point – the character forced to steal money and luxuries in order to keep his lover. Lol Creme's chorus backing vocals teased with the old 10cc lushness. 'Something Special' was a satisfying cut, but the ante was about to be upped.

**'Welcome to Paradise'** (Graham Gouldman, Eric Stewart)
Released as a single A-side, June 1992 (UK and EU)b/w 'Don't'.
Released as a CD single, June 1992 (UK and EU)b/w 'Don't' and 'Lost in Love'.
Released as a CD Maxi single, 1992 (UK)b/w 'Woman in Love', 'Wonderland' and 'The Stars Didn't Show'.

This second single synchronised a satisfying hook with substantial subject matter. The lyric's protagonist leaves his family to live in another country. But with a coup coming on, the place is dangerous. He takes refuge in the music but has to watch his back. In the end, he realises he should never have come, but now he can't leave. It was deep stuff for a single, but the chorus hook was hard to resist, and the elegant chic of Michael Landau's lead guitar added extra class.

Also noteworthy were Godley & Creme's backing vocals, making 'Welcome to Paradise' the album's first reformation of the original four-piece 10cc, albeit flanked by a raft of session players.

**'The Stars Didn't Show'** (Graham Gouldman, Eric Stewart)
Released as a CD Maxi single, 1992 (UK)b/w 'Woman in Love', 'Wonderland', and 'Welcome to Paradise'.

Kevin Godley's lone lead vocal on *Meanwhile* was a heartfelt tribute to singer Roy Orbison, who had passed in December 1988. The medium-tempo ballad stood out in the context as the finest-crafted piece present. Even so, lines like 'You cast a magic spell' and 'You played the part so well' could've been more descriptive and meaningful had Godley contributed to the songwriting. An interesting comparison would be Jimmy Webb's 1993 Elvis Presley tribute, 'Elvis and Me'. That outstanding lyric virtually breathed life back into the icon – a quality lacking from 'The Stars Didn't Show'.

Elsewhere, the track benefited from Michael Landau's precise if conventional guitar solo, and of course, Lol Creme's backing vocals which made the track the second here featuring the four original 10cc members.

**'Green-Eyed Monster'** (Graham Gouldman, Eric Stewart)
When Gouldman and Stewart's lyric love partners were in critical mode, it worked better on a slow and more serious track like this. The minor key, combined with arranger Jerry Hey's pinch of brass dissonance, took the heat off overdone cliches like 'Who's that creeping out of my back door' and 'My fire is burning but you're as cold as ice'. I thought they'd crossed the taste line with 'Someone else's lotion on my side of the mattress' until it was cleverly matched with 'Green-eyed monster's got me by the Niagaras'.

An interesting aside is the title being placed in the verses, which are all otherwise different. So too are the 'Don't think I'm mad' sections, which kind of act like a chorus. This means when the actual bridge arrives, it seems like too much. But I'm quibbling. It certainly moves back to the verse key beautifully. It's a more adventurous track than it appears on the surface. Taste-versus-accessibility met a fine balance here.

### 'Charity Begins at Home' (Graham Gouldman, Eric Stewart)
When it comes to lyrics, preaching is the last refuge of those with writer's block. That's if you believe in writer's block.

> Everywhere that we turn there are mouths to be fed
> How can we sleep
> The battle goes on while we're safe in our beds
> So don't turn away

Clunker alert! I thought charity began at home? Suddenly in the middle of the song, we were forced to feel guilty? Still, they had just done a whole verse extolling the joys of having fame, money and hit songs under your belt.

By this stage of the album, the snare drum fatigue sets in. Almost every song's snare over-resonates at around 235hz. Such a thing becomes tiring after a while. Steve Macmillan and Robin Barclay mixed *Meanwhile* at Sarm West in London, except for this track helmed by Eric Stewart. This suggests that the 235hz resonance crept in at the mastering stage. At least there was Gordon Gaines' adventurous guitar solo to admire.

### 'Shine a Light in the Dark' (Graham Gouldman, Eric Stewart)
In the structuring of any album sequence, the least interesting track usually comes second to last. 'Fill Her Up' might've suited this position more. 'Shine a Light in the Dark' was similarly inspiring except for two pleasantly surprising chords which really hit the sweet spot in the middle and end of the bridge. Nevertheless, this uptempo plea to God for help when things get tough, fit alongside 'Fill Her Up' and 'Charity Begins at Home' as album filler. The slower songs were winning the race.

### 'Don't Break the Promises' (Graham Gouldman, Paul McCartney, Eric Stewart)
Paul McCartney and Eric Stewart wrote this ballad during sessions for McCartney's 1986 *Press to Play* album. Not used for that record, it made sense to resurrect it for *Meanwhile*. The song had that indisputable McCartney quality of saying something universal with a twist. The concept was as old as time, but 'Don't break the promises' wasn't particularly a phrase you'd say to someone, making it original.

It was an important track for the album, not least of all for the fact that McCartney played bass on it. Though it worked well as a closer, it deserved prominence. It could've worked as track three, and simply replacing 'Fill Her Up' to the end of the album would've been acceptable.

McCartney included his solo version of the song as part of a 1997 B-side titled 'Oobu Joobu (Part 4)'. Re-titled to 'Don't Break the Promise', the lyrics were largely different and laid against a lively reggae lilt.

## Contemporary Tracks

### 'Don't' (Graham Gouldman, Eric Stewart)
Released as a single B-side, June 1992 (UK and EU)b/w 'Welcome to Paradise'. Released as a CD single B-side, June 1992 (UK and EU)b/w 'Welcome to Paradise' and 'Lost in Love'.

The mind boggles why a song this good wasn't included on *Meanwhile*. It would've been a quality Graham Gouldman vocal to include and could've replaced 'Charity Begins at Home', making that a B-side instead.

The intro had that classic tropical 10cc feel, its two minor chords fooling you into thinking you were about to hear an alternative version of 'Dreadlock Holiday'. The lyric's recommendation to not give everything away at the dawn of a relationship was as accessible as could be. So too the melodic hooks strewn everywhere, as strong and as vital as those contained in classics like Gouldman's 'Bus Stop' or 'No Milk Today'. This song was a total earworm.

### 'Lost In Love' (Graham Gouldman, Eric Stewart)
Released as a CD single B-side, June 1992 (UK and EU) b/w 'Welcome to Paradise' and 'Lost in Love'.

There are enough ideas here to fill two songs. The verses are a lyrically abstract take on the inevitable, building to a chorus that doesn't quite fit them. The two sections could easily be seeded out for separate compositions. But it still works, unified by that slick slow funk rhythm section. 10cc mark two had a thing for referring to being onstage, which can make a message like this come across to the outsider as if being performed in a void.

### 'Man With a Mission' (Graham Gouldman, Eric Stewart)
This feels like a lyric that was abandoned as a first draft, with perspective changes that needed ironing out. It starts in the third person, warning of a man at the top pulling the strings. Suddenly with the chorus, it becomes 'I'm a man with a mission and I'm breaking the arm of the law'. With verse two, it's back to the third person. A deft change to 'He's a man with a mission' would've avoided the unnecessary confusion. If the character is admitting he's really the culprit, why would he offer the assistance of 'The evidence is there in black and white, Your number's up for grabs if you don't fight' and 'Open your eyes to the lies while you've still got a chance'? Even the listener wasn't beyond criticism with the line 'How long will it take you to see the light?'.

Add to this some pitchy singing in places and you get a real picture of where 10cc were at. They cared enough to get this far, but the motivation to polish had all but disappeared. The race to the finish line via a serviceable but irrelevant blues harp blow over the lengthy ending said it all.

It was frustrating when brilliant moments shone through the dark – the bridge's sudden psychedelic mode for example. But in general, 'Man With a Mission' sounded like a 10cc that had had enough.

# Mirror Mirror (1995) – 10cc

UK Release date: June 1995. US Release date: 28 March 1995.
Personnel:
Graham Gouldman: Vocals, Bass, Guitar, Mandolin, Percussion
Eric Stewart: Vocals, Guitar, Keyboards, Percussion
Lise Aferiat: Violin
Gary Barnacle: Saxophone
Nicola Burton: Violin
Rick Fenn: Lead guitar
Andrew Gold: Vocals
Chris Goldscheider: Viola
Andrew Hines: Cello
Patrick Jones: Cello
Adrian Lee: Bass, Keyboards, Acoustic guitar, Vibraphone, Accordion, Percussion, Backing vocals
Paul McCartney: Guitar, Piano, Keyboards, Percussion, Frogs, Crickets
Steve Pigott: Keyboards, Drum programming
Ian Thomas: Drums
Peter Thoms: Trombone
Gary Wallis: Drums, Percussion
Recorded at Strawberry Studios, UK, Living Code Studios, London, Lyndale Studios, Metropolis Studios, London, Templar Studios, France
Producers: 10cc, Adrian Lee and Rod Gammons
Engineers: Jonathan Cook, Noel Harris, Kevin Jacobs, Sheridan Tongue
Chart placings: JP: 46.

Thanks to a healthy Japanese following, local company, Avex, commissioned a new 10cc album in 1994. With Eric living in France and Graham in the UK, the plan was to record separately and come together later to contribute to each other's tracks. But the collaboration didn't eventuate. Mike + the Mechanics member, Adrian Lee, co-produced the two principal members' songs, also programming and performing himself.

Included was a semi-acoustic recording, 'I'm Not in Love (Acoustic session '95)', performed while filming a TV special at the BBC in Maida Vale, London. Issued as an advance single, it became 10cc's final UK hit, reaching number 29. But effectively, *Mirror Mirror* was an album of Eric and Graham solo tracks.

Eric wrote some new songs and recorded two Paul McCartney co-writes, 'Yvonne's the One' and 'Code of Silence'. Though McCartney performed on the latter, his original computerised performances were rearranged to an extent. Graham supplied co-writes with British theatre lyricist, Tim Rice, fellow Wax member Andrew Gold, and 10cc live band member, Steve Pigott, who'd played on the 1993 *Meanwhile* tour. 10cc's final single 'Ready to Go Home' was sung by Andrew Gold, making it their only single sung by a non-band member.

The US edition of *Mirror Mirror* omitted five tracks; 'Yvonne's the One', 'Blue Bird', 'Margo Wants the Mustard', 'Now You're Gone' and 'I'm Not in Love (Acoustic session '95). The last was replaced with a live version of the song known as 'Rework of Art Mix' which opened the album, the remaining tracks re-sequenced.

After the promotional tour for *Mirror Mirror*, Eric Stewart called it a day once and for all. The cover image seemed to reflect the dissolution, its shattered fragments all but separated.

**'Yvonne's the One'** (Paul McCartney, Eric Stewart)
Working with Paul McCartney on his *Press to Play* album in 1985, Eric received a postcard from Pink Floyd drummer Nick Mason. On the front was a picture of a girl with volcanoes erupting behind her. Eric showed it to Paul, who asked what it said. Eric said 'When I first saw Yvonne, volcanoes erupted'. Paul responded by singing the line right back at him with the melody fully-formed. From there they wrote the song. Not suitable for *Press to Play*, Eric resurrected it for *Mirror Mirror*.

The opening bars suggested a possible return to form. But despite the real guitar (rhythm part by McCartney), the backings were programmed. There was certainly no lack of skill in them. Regardless of the bad rap computerised tracks could get, you couldn't be a slug. You still had to know what you were doing; the computers didn't play themselves – they were as good as what you gave them. The issue was the stultifying effect they were capable of inducing in a listener over a short time.

Though it was a carefree atmosphere drawing on the tropical 10cc signature, 'Yvonne's the One' was not of the ilk of Stewart and McCartney's *Meanwhile* track, 'Don't Break the Promises'. By the end, the stultifying effect had kicked in, creating a kind of digital numbness that didn't bode well for whatever was coming next. The track was left off the album's US edition.

**'Code of Silence'** (Eric Stewart)
'Code of Silence' began life one afternoon after Paul McCartney visited Eric's for lunch. McCartney came up with the chords, layered some synth sounds over a simple bass part and left it with Eric to finish. That original track, which Eric wrote the song against, was more rhythmically abstract and choppy-sounding. For *Mirror Mirror*, the key was raised, which was easy to do with computer sequencers after the fact, provided no live performances had been added yet. Paul's keyboard parts were embellished, and the chords floating around above the constant bass part gave a smoother, more liquid result.

The 5m:40s track could've used further editing, even after being cut down from the 6m:30s demo. Either length was a long time to be lectured about the dangers of holding pain inside. What the track lacked was a strong hook to enliven it and make it memorable.

### 'Blue Bird' (Graham Gouldman)
Released as a single B-side, 6 March 1995 (UK and EU) b/w 'I'm Not In Love (Acoustic Session '95)' and 'I'm Not In Love (Rework of Art Mix)'.

The jump in songwriting quality here was obvious. The highly-crafted and folky 'Blue Bird' had a hint of Crosby, Stills & Nash about it, and verse two's 'bluebird' word repeats surely referred to McCartney and Wings' 'Bluebird' from *Band On the Run*. What can you say? Gouldman had a songwriting pedigree to die for, and clearly he wasn't losing his touch. Why the song was left off the album's US edition is a mystery.

### 'Age of Consent' (Eric Stewart)
Released as a single B-side, 20 June 1995 (UK and EU) b/w 'Ready To Go Home'.

An embracing of modern times and developing sexual mores pervaded this lyric. But as was often the case when Stewart went near these subjects, a line or two screamed with ambiguity.

> I'm not holding you back
> Heaven's sake
> Have you got to jump out of the cake
> I don't want your endeavours to fail
> But that pouch has got a sting in the tail

What the track didn't scream was Eric's claimed Steely Dan influence on it. If you contort your eardrums, I guess you can hear a kind of style hybrid of their songs 'Sign in Stranger' and 'FM (No Static At All)', but it's kept well in check.

### 'Take This Woman' (Graham Gouldman, Eric Stewart)
A classic lyric twist takes place here. The character, who thinks his woman is too much to handle, suddenly marries her at the end. Producer Adrian Lee's backing vocals steer the sound away from being recognisably 10cc, but the beautifully liquid bridge reels it back, cross-fading in as a surreal surprise. It's here that the character sees the error of his ways. But the section seems overly-substantial for a song that half cares to be popular but is usurped by an awkward lyric.

### 'The Monkey and the Onion' (Graham Gouldman, Tim Rice)
Once you were used to the idea that *Mirror Mirror* was effectively dual Gouldman and Stewart solo tracks, it was easier to drop expectations and accept things as they were. This acoustic piece was a real insight into Graham Gouldman's melodic skill, which was in top form. The words were relinquished to the eloquent lyricist, Tim Rice (*Jesus Christ Superstar, Evita*).

The idea of a monkey peeling an onion and not understanding why there are tears acted as an analogy for human need and lack of contentment with what we have. 'Too much investigation, You know the rest'. When Tim Rice was present, you could always expect a killer lyric payoff too, and 'The Monkey and the Onion' was no exception.

> Oh that we could be contented
> With the good things that we've gained
> But in the end we're empty-handed
> Just because we need the world explained

### 'Everything Is Not Enough' (Eric Stewart)
None of these songs were going to come out unscathed following the sheer craftsmanship of 'The Monkey and the Onion', except perhaps for the fine 'Blue Bird' which would've followed it strongly.

The contrast with the prior song couldn't have been greater. We were moved from clever but understandable wordplay against inventive melody, to over-wordy proselytising over a slow semi-blues chord-monotone. Meaningful lines and melodic hooks failed to appear. But in its favour, the lead guitar was slick. The playing sounded like Rick Fenn, though he was not credited. But Eric was capable of flitting between styles with ease, so it's really a fine showcase for his playing. This track would've benefited from using a real band.

### 'Ready To Go Home' (Andrew Gold, Graham Gouldman)
Released as a single A-side, 20 June 1995 (UK and EU)b/w 'Age of Consent'.

This fine tribute to the passing of Graham Gouldman's father, Hymie, had a lead vocal by co-writer Andrew Gold. It could pass as a Wax recording, but Gold's performance was limited to the vocal, producer Adrian Lee stepping in on programming duties. Real drums appeared here for the first time on *Mirror Mirror* thanks to London session drummer, Ian Thomas.

Gouldman re-recorded the song for his 2000 solo album *And Another Thing*..... But on *Mirror Mirror,* the raw emotion was captured and the song was allowed to breathe.

### 'Grow Old With Me' (Graham Gouldman)
In assessing a song's worth, it's not just the what, but also the when. A simple love song like this would've been more well-received in, say...1965, when the popular way of doing things was still developing to an extent. By 1995 there were so many songs like this in existence that 'Grow Old With Me' simply seemed like just another one. That, of course, had no bearing on the skill at hand. The ballad was tight, made its point easily and was difficult to criticise. It wasn't Gouldman's greatest work, nor was it his worst. It was timeless in a

way, despite Andrew Gold's closing backing vocal counterpoint placing the track squarely in a dreamy post-Pet-Sounds Beach Boys late-'60s. The track brought things full circle, fading out to reveal the closing chord anyway, just like Hotlegs' 'Run Baby Run' had done 24 years prior.

**'Margo Wants the Mustard'** (Eric Stewart)
This doo-wop progression was painted as typically tropical 10cc fare. But its lack of lyrical flair sat uncomfortably next to the undeniable 'Blue Bird' and 'The Monkey and the Onion'. Like in 'Take This Woman', the lyric blundered. Best left as a B-side, or just left out, as was the case for the US release of *Mirror Mirror*.

**'Peace In Our Time'** (Graham Gouldman, Steve Pigott)
The drum feel here sat right in the pocket with mid-'90s R&B hits like Des'ree's 'You Gotta Be'. But the lyric's preaching aspects branded it as bland. Another unnecessary inclusion on an album that would've been better issued in one defined edition.

**'Why Did I Break Your Heart?'** (Graham Gouldman, Eric Stewart)
With a strong ballad like 'Ready To Go Home' present, it's difficult to fathom this inclusion. The lyrical self-pity might be hard work for any listener, let alone the one that might be asking the title's question. Songs certainly don't have to be happy all the time, but surely there has to be *some* hope.

**'Now You're Gone'** (Graham Gouldman)
This semi-country breakup song worked fine with just acoustic guitar and was for all intents and purposes, a demo. It was left off the album's US edition. The final verse was appropriate for the song's status as the final ever released new 10cc composition. Here is the deliciously ambiguous stanza.

> Now I'm sittin' in the dark place
> I got murder on my mind
> Say goodbye to the rat race
> No more setting sun
> 'Cause soon I'll be gone

**'I'm Not In Love (Acoustic Session '95)'** (Graham Gouldman, Eric Stewart)
Released as a single A-side, 6 March 1995 (UK and EU) b/w 'I'm Not In Love (Rework of Art Mix)' and 'Blue Bird'. UK: 29.

10cc's final UK hit was an unplanned live acoustic version of 'I'm Not In Love', recorded by Gouldman and Stewart in the process of filming a TV special.

## Contemporary Tracks

**'I'm Not In Love (Rework of Art Mix)'** (Graham Gouldman, Eric Stewart)
Released as a single B-side, 6 March 1995 (UK and EU) b/w 'I'm Not In Love (Acoustic Session '95)' and 'Blue Bird'.

As was the case for most 10cc concerts, this live version used the instrumental backing track from the original recording. It was used to open the US edition of *Mirror Mirror*, which omitted the 'Acoustic Session '95'.

# The Last Page of History

Many music historians, and probably all 10cc fans, would agree that the band no longer receive appropriate recognition for their achievements. 'I'm Not in Love', of course, still gets multiple plays on classic pop stations and has been used in a plethora of TV shows and movies.

Acts that had more of a visual aspect have traditionally been served a larger slice of retrospective reverence. We're often reminded of David Bowie's theatrical esoterica or Elton John's once outlandish costumery and glamourous piano-pounding. When it comes to bands, the attention goes to those that had extrovert frontmen, like Led Zeppelin's Robert Plant or the guv'nor of all things grand on and off the stage, Queen's Freddie Mercury. But what of equally commendable acts that made a similar mark in the same time period, like Deep Purple's Ian Gillan or Bad Company's Paul Rodgers (arguably one of the most technically gifted rock singers of all)?

And what of 10cc? Do they and all of the above not deserve recognition based on more than their level of visual impact or indeed regardless of it? After all, like many of their contemporaries, 10cc devoted themselves to delivering the finest audio artefacts they could muster. The four original members between them consisted of two recording engineers, three guitar players, two keyboard players, four bass players and four vocalists – not to mention individual abilities that stretched to orchestral and exotic instruments. As for Godley & Creme's art and video work, this book has barely even scratched that surface.

Musical skill was the primary ingredient in the 20th century when a recording artist required at least a moderate level of it to get a foot in the door if it even opened at all. Today, visual and showy entertainment aspects are valued more than the cerebral, which is why the more ostentatious past artists, musically or otherwise, are more predominantly remembered.

Kevin Godley put it most eloquently in 2012 when he told *The Guardian*, 'We only had 50% of what's required for a successful cultural moment. We had the noise, not the look.' Times change. But I guess that's just the way the croissant crumbles after all.

In 2004, Stewart, Gouldman and Creme attended a Performing Rights Society dinner where all four original 10cc members were presented with Ivor Novello awards for Outstanding Song Collection. Vindication!

Like the screenplay in 'The Film of My Love', a 10cc reformation would be 'A blessing from heaven'. But those that would wish for it must face the fact that the lush and cinematic audio experience that was the music of 10cc and Godley & Creme is, in their words, gone with the wind on the Orient Express, to join The Magnificent Seven.

> I'm getting better thanks to Luxembourg
> But I didn't stop to thank the radio
> Today when I was downstairs eating
> Its Eveready heart stopped beating

Also from Sonicbond Publishing

# On Track series
**Queen** – Andrew Wild 978-1-78952-003-3
**Emerson Lake and Palmer** – Mike Goode 978-1-78952-000-2
**Deep Purple and Rainbow 1968-79** – Steve Pilkington 978-1-78952-002-6
**Yes** – Stephen Lambe 978-1-78952-001-9
**Blue Oyster Cult** – Jacob Holm-Lupo 978-1-78952-007-1
**The Beatles** – Andrew Wild 978-1-78952-009-5
**Roy Wood and the Move** – James R Turner 978-1-78952-008-8
**Genesis** – Stuart MacFarlane 978-1-78952-005-7
**JethroTull** – Jordan Blum 978-1-78952-016-3
**The Rolling Stones 1963-80** – Steve Pilkington 978-1-78952-017-0
**Judas Priest** – John Tucker 978-1-78952-018-7
**Toto** – Jacob Holm-Lupo 978-1-78952-019-4
**Van Der Graaf Generator** – Dan Coffey 978-1-78952-031-6
**Frank Zappa 1966 to 1979** – Eric Benac 978-1-78952-033-0
**Elton John in the 1970s** – Peter Kearns 978-1-78952-034-7
**The Moody Blues** – Geoffrey Feakes 978-1-78952-042-2
**The Beatles Solo 1969-1980** – Andrew Wild 978-1-78952-030-9
**Steely Dan** – Jez Rowden 978-1-78952-043-9
**Hawkwind** – Duncan Harris 978-1-78952-052-1
**Fairport Convention** – Kevan Furbank 978-1-78952-051-4
**Iron Maiden** – Steve Pilkington 978-1-78952-061-3
**Dream Theater** – Jordan Blum 978-1-78952-050-7
**10CC** – Peter Kearns 978-1-78952-054-5
**Gentle Giant** – Gary Steel 978-1-78952-058-3
**Kansas** – Kevin Cummings 978-1-78952-057-6
**Mike Oldfield** – Ryan Yard 978-1-78952-060-6
**The Who** – Geoffrey Feakes 978-1-78952-076-7

# On Screen series
**Carry On...** – Stephen Lambe 978-1-78952-004-0
**Powell and Pressburger** – Sam Proctor 978-1-78952-013-2
**Seinfeld Seasons 1 to 5** – Stephen Lambe 978-1-78952-012-5
**Francis Ford Coppola** – Cam Cobb and Stephen Lambe 978-1-78952-022-4
**Monty Python** – Steve Pilkington 978-1-78952-047-7
**Doctor Who: The David Tennant Years** – Jamie Hailstone 978-1-78952-066-8
**James Bond** – Andrew Wild 978-1-78952-010-1

# Other Books
**Not As Good As The Book** – Andy Tillison 978-1-78952-021-7
**The Voice. Frank Sinatra in the 1940s** – Stephen Lambe 978-1-78952-032-3
**Maximum Darkness** – Deke Leonard 978-1-78952-048-4
**The Twang Dynasty** – Deke Leonard 978-1-78952-049-1
**Maybe I Should've Stayed In Bed** – Deke Leonard 978-1-78952-053-8
**Tommy Bolin: In and Out of Deep Purple** – Laura Shenton 978-1-78952-070-5
**Jon Anderson and the Warriors - the road to Yes** – David Watkinson 978-1-78952-059-0

*and many more to come!*

**Would you like to write for Sonicbond Publishing?**

At Sonicbond Publishing we are always on the look-out for authors, particularly for our two main series:

On Track. Mixing fact with in depth analysis, the On Track series examines the work of a particular musical artist or group. All genres are considered from easy listening and jazz to 60s soul to 90s pop, via rock and metal.

On Screen. This series looks at the world of film and television. Subjects considered include directors, actors and writers, as well as entire television and film series. As with the On Track series, we balance fact with analysis.

While professional writing experience would, of course, be an advantage the most important qualification is to have real enthusiasm and knowledge of your subject. First-time authors are welcomed, but the ability to write well in English is essential.

Sonicbond Publishing has distribution throughout Europe and North America, and all books are also published in E-book form. Authors will be paid a royalty based on sales of their book.

Further details are available from www.sonicbondpublishing.co.uk. To contact us, complete the contact form there or email info@sonicbondpublishing.co.uk

www.ingramcontent.com/pod-product-compliance
Lightning Source LLC
Chambersburg PA
CBHW020907080526
44589CB00011B/485